Legends & Lore
of
Texas Wildflowers

Number Twenty-Four:
The Louise Lindsey Merrick Natural Environment Series

Legends & Lore OF Texas Wildflowers

Elizabeth Silverthorne

Texas A&M University Press
College Station

The paper used in this book meets the minimum requirements
of the American National Standard for Permanence
of Paper for Printed Library Materials, Z39.48-1984.
Binding materials have been chosen for durability.

Library of Congress Cataloging-in-Publication Data

Silverthorne, Elizabeth.
　　Legends and lore of Texas wildflowers / by Elizabeth
Silverthorne. — 1st ed.
　　　　　p.　cm. — (The Louise Lindsey Merrick natural
environment series ; no. 24)
　　Includes bibliographical references (p.　) and index.
　　ISBN 0-89096-702-4
　　1. Wild flowers—Texas. 2. Wild flowers—Utilization—
Texas. 3. Wild flowers—Texas—Folklore. 4. Plants, Useful—
Texas. 5. Medicinal plants—Texas. 6. Materia medica,
Vegetable—Texas. 7. Folklore—Texas. I. Title. II. Series.
QK188.S535　1996　　　　　　　　　　95-45245
582.13'09764—dc20　　　　　　　　　　CIP

To Polly Miller,

whose love of nature and whose friendship

have inspired and enriched my life

And he is happier who has power

To gather wisdom from a flower.

—William Wordsworth

Contents

Preface

To begin, a caveat: There are a number of excellent field guides and identification books for Texas wildflowers, including regional guides, and this book is not intended to be either. I am neither a botanist nor a certified naturalist but have always had a large bump of curiosity and a deep interest in flowers and mythology, folklore and history. Writing this book has given me the opportunity to combine these interests and to satisfy to some extent my curiosity.

Having grown up in South Texas in my grandmother's house, I find my memory filled with her flowers—narcissus borders, sweet peas on fences, rose hedges, violets under trees, blue and pink hydrangeas on the north side of the house, altheas by the living room windows, fruit trees in bloom in the back garden and a huge poinsettia bush by the side door. Although in our area we took for granted hedges of Cherokee roses, shrubs and fences covered with bright trumpet vine and fields and vacant lots enameled with coreopsis, Indian blanket and black-eyed Susan, the national flower of Texas, the bluebonnet, didn't quite reach our coastal county. But it wasn't far on Sunday drives to where enormous patches of our state flower stretched so far and wide the sky and earth seemed to meet. I don't remember where I first heard the legend of the little Indian girl who sacrificed her favorite doll and created the bluebonnets from the ashes, but it was probably at the weekly storytelling sessions in our one-room community library.

I do remember making endless clover chains and telling fortunes with dandelions and buttercups (as we called evening primroses), tasting sourgrass and peppergrass and sucking drops of nectar from honeysuckle blossoms. We learned to admire the pretty blooms on prickly pear cactus, and prickly poppies from a distance, and we knew where to find the curly dock weed whose leaves we crushed and rubbed on rashes caused by brushing against stinging nettles. On frequent trips to the nearby beach at the Gulf of Mexico, we made bouquets of beach morning glories, beach daisies, and yellow beach evening primroses. At Christmas time we decorated with branches of yaupon and mistletoe and with poinsettias after singeing the stems to keep the milky sap from running out.

After I left home to live in cities—Houston, Miami, and New York—and flowers were confined to yards or pots or bought from vendors, they were even more valued. In working on the biographies of Marjorie Kinnan Rawlings and Sarah Orne Jewett, I was delighted to find that though they had such different personalities, each had a passion for flowers, and just as Marjorie recorded the lives and habits of Florida's wildflowers Sarah did the same for the flowers of Maine. Realizing that as much as I had always loved Texas' wildflowers, I knew little about them other than what I had learned by observation over the years, I began to collect information, at first haphazardly and eventually with more organization. The more I learned about the habits, myths and folklore connected with these plants and the more I understood how important they have always been to humans and other animals and the more I realized their potential for even more significant contributions, the more fascinated I became. Eventually the urge to put it altogether to share with other wildflower enthusiasts became irresistible.

Searching for the material for this project has truly been the most enjoyable research I have ever done. Not only have I acquired a deeper understanding and appreciation of wildflowers, but also I have met many people with a kindred passion. Talking wildflowers with experts like Barton Warnock or Dorothy Matizza or Flo Oxley is truly an enlightening experience, and so are discussions with wildflower buffs who have simply loved them and studied them over many years. Wildflower expeditions have taken me from Central Texas, where I live, north, south, east, and west from the Panhandle to the Valley and from the Big Thicket to the Big Bend.

I am particularly indebted to Flo Oxley, resource botanist, at the National Wildflower Research Center in Austin, for her expert assistance and for the help of other members of the staff at the Center. Bill Carr, botanist for the Texas Natural Heritage Program for the Texas Parks and Wildlife Department, has helped with information on endangered species. Stan Reinke, range conservationist for the United States Department of Agriculture, gave me good advice and a practical bibliography. And Ronald R. Switzer, superintendent of the Big Thicket National Preserve, has provided me with useful information in his area. University libraries and research centers around the state and public libraries in many towns and cities have been helpful in supplying material.

Polly Miller gave me her choice collection of books and literature collected over many years on Texas plants and flowers, and it has been of invaluable help to me. Other friends who have kindly lent me material or directed me to information on Texas flora include Joan Blum, Barbara and Martha Harper, B. J. and Bob McConnell, Betty Wilds, Holly Greenwood and Mary Hill. Thelma Fletcher as always generously supplied me with material and gave me her enthusiastic support. Doug Blockley culled rare books in England for information on the history and uses of wildflowers there. Dorothy Mattiza sent me helpful material and gave me valuable leads and encouragement. My sisters, Patricia Merrill and Geneva Fulgham, have helped me with my research in many ways and have accompanied me on a number of wildflower forays.

It has been difficult to call a halt to the amassing of material, and although I had to do this in order to bring the book into being, I know that I shall go on, as Joseph Campbell advised, "following my bliss," and learning about wildflowers as long as I live.

In addition to their natural history, I have included political and social history in which various wildflowers have been involved. And in addition to descriptions of various family members and their habitats, I have included their name origins as well as references to them in literature, folklore, and various mythologies. There are also many mentions of the uses that have been made of different wildflowers over the years; however, these are not to be considered recommendations for the use of any of these plants as medicine or food.

Introduction

Texas has more than five thousand species of wildflowers. Because its vast size encompasses dramatically different geographical areas with extremes in temperature and rainfall, the state is usually divided into about ten vegetation zones. Even before settlers began to push back geographic frontiers, the area attracted scientists, both professional and amateur, who came to study its diverse flora and fauna. The first botanical collector of record is Dr. Edwin James, surgeon and naturalist with Major S. H. Long's first expedition to the Rocky Mountains in 1820. In the summer of that year, James came down the Canadian River into what is now the Panhandle and collected numerous plants for study.

Eight years later a Swiss botanist, Jean Louis Berlandier, came to Texas with a Mexican Boundary Commission to make collections of plants. After 1830 many well-trained German intellectuals settled in Texas. Among them was Ferdinand Lindheimer, who reached the area in 1836 intending to help in the fight for independence from Mexico but arrived at San Jacinto one day after the decisive battle.

Lindheimer stayed in Texas and arranged to collect sets of plants to send to Asa Gray, professor of natural history at Harvard and the leading authority of his time on plant life in the United States. For months at a time Lindheimer trudged across uncharted land exploring the Brazos, Colorado, and Guadalupe River valleys with only a two-wheeled horse cart, two hunting dogs, a supply of flour, coffee, salt, and the precious pressing paper for his plants. His dedication and ability earned him the title "Father of Botany in Texas." In 1845–47, when the great German geologist Karl Ferdinand Roemer spent eighteen months in Texas, he made collecting excursions with Lindheimer, whom he came to admire.

Another plant collector for Asa Gray was Charles Wright, a Connecticut yankee, who discovered many hundreds of new species of plants in Texas during the years 1844–52.

The intrepid Scotsman Thomas Drummond worked in Texas from 1833 to 1834 making extensive collections of animal and plant material to send to Sir William Hooker, professor of Botany at the University of Glasgow and later keeper of the Royal Botanical Gardens at Kew. In their letters and journals, these courageous pioneers detailed the hardships they endured: freezing northers, burning heat, floods, maddening flies and mosquitoes, cholera, dysentery, malaria, saline water, skimpy rations, hostile Indians, rattlesnakes, mountain lions, and harrowing traveling conditions by foot, horse, or wagon.

Many other men and two women, both named Young, followed these early explorers in making important contributions to early Texas botany. Maude Jeannie Fuller Young, who taught botany in Houston, wrote the first book devoted entirely to the flora of Texas and one of the first textbooks written by a Texan. Published in 1873, *Familiar Lessons in Botany* contained more than six hundred pages and was used in schools for a number of years. Maude Young held the official position of State Botanist for several years.

Dr. Marie Sophie Young, instructor in botany at the University of Texas and director of the university's herbarium, was an expert on plants in the Austin area and in the Trans-Pecos. Traveling with a young student and a stubborn burro, she collected specimens in the rough terrain around the mountains of the Trans-Pecos in areas where she reported that every bush reached out its "claws" to catch clothing and tear skin. She died of cancer in 1919, but in her nine short years of botanizing in Texas, she made a significant addition to the existing knowledge of the state's plants.

In 1928 Ellen D. Schulz (Mrs. Roy W. Quillin), supervisor of Nature Study and Science and director of the Witte Museum at San Antonio, published *Texas Wild Flowers*. Written in everyday language, the book described the unique characteristics of common Texas wildflowers, along with their economic value and usefulness and many of the traditions connected with them. It was a valuable reference book for schools and libraries as well as for the "great flower-loving public" for which it was written.

Since a *Manual of the Vascular Plants of Texas* by Donovan Stewart Correll and Marshall Conring Johnston was published in 1970, it has been the standard reference for information on all the native and naturalized flowering plants and ferns known to occur in the state. Others who have made enormous contributions to our wildflower data include the late Carroll Abbott, who published a newsletter devoted to wildflowers; Barton Warnock, who has devoted most of his life to studying the flora of the Davis and Guadalupe Mountains and Big Bend area; Geyata Ajilvsgi, who has made an intensive study of the plants in the Big Thicket; and Benny Simpson, who uses his botanical expertise in a constant search for trees, shrubs, and flowers that will survive in North Texas despite growing problems with water shortages. In the bibliography will be found the names of dozens of other devotees of Texas wildflowers who have shared their insights and who continue to enlarge our understanding of these complex plants.

It may be helpful to say a word about the names of wildflowers. Before Carolus Linnaeus, the renowned Swedish naturalist of the eighteenth century, all was chaos in the language of botany, with long Latin names and numerous synonyms making it difficult for people to converse about flowers and know just which plant they were talking about. After Linnaeus established the binomial system of nomenclature by which each living thing was distinguished by two Latin names—and only two—it was easy even for people who spoke different languages to exchange information about specific plants. In this system each plant has a genus name (a last name like Jones or Smith) and a specific name (a first name like John or Mary); conventionally the last name comes first and is capitalized, and the first name, not capitalized, follows. Like human nicknames, the common names of flowers are often colorful and descriptive and sometimes amusing or poetic, but as Barton Warnock says, "Common names can give you a headache." This, of course, is because so many flowers have the same common names; for example, Texas star can apply to at least five different wildflowers; sweet William can be either a phlox or a verbena; Texas mountain laurel is not the same as mountain laurel east of the Mississippi—and the same wildflower can have a dozen different common names.

The Latinized scientific names become more interesting when we understand their origins. Many come from characteristics of the plant: Thus a plant that is called *noctiflorus* blooms at night; a *compactus* plant stays small but a *columnaris* plant grows vertically; a *cardinalis* flower is red; a *contortus* one is twisted; and since *foetidus* indicates "bad smelling," we can assume that whoever named *Iris foetidissima* (stinking iris) didn't care for its aroma. Some wildflower names honor the pioneers who discovered them back in the 1800s: Thus we have *Berlandiera pumila*, (soft green eyes), a dwarfish or low-growing plant discovered by Jean Louis Berlandier; *Phlox drummondii*, named for Thomas Drummond; *Opuntia lindheimeri* (prickly pear) for Ferdinand Lindheimer; *Verbena wrightii* for Charles Wright; and *Salvia roemeriana* (cedar sage) for Ferdinand Roemer.

In 1819 a little book, *Le Langage des fleurs*, crossed the channel from France to England. The idea of expressing feelings through flowers immediately caught on with the Victorians, who adopted the language of flowers and greatly expanded its vocabulary, assigning meanings not only to individual flowers but also to the way they were arranged and presented. Many poets and writers, such as Kate Greenaway, published their own lists of the meanings of various flowers, and it became the fashion to communicate through the language of flowers.

All medicines were once herbal, and during the Renaissance and for many years after, the doctrine of signatures was a popular concept in Europe. According to this belief each plant displays a sign (a signature) that reveals the purpose for which it is intended. Thus, plants with liver-shaped leaves or of liver color were meant to be used to treat problems of the liver; bladder-shaped parts indicated the plants were meant to treat urinary problems; heart-shaped leaves indicated they were meant to treat heart problems; hairy plants supposedly made hair grow; plants with "eyes" were intended to treat eye ailments; and reddish colored plants were used to treat blood disorders and yellowish colored ones to treat jaundice.

We know that plants are the key to life on earth. They existed before us, and as long as we have been here we have used and sometimes abused wildflowers as food, medicine, in making clothing, as building material, as fuel, in dyes, in cosmetics, to obtain oils and waxes and other manufacturing materials, and as decorations. Many species, like many species of birds and other wildlife, are gone forever. Today many of our medicines are derived from wildflowers, and the field of herbal medicine is expanding at an astonishing rate. Experiments to find cures for cancers, AIDS, and other diseases include numerous wildflowers. Recently we have become aware of the potential importance of using native plants to prevent soil erosion and in xeriscapic gardening to conserve our natural resources. If we are to continue to inhabit this planet, it is of the utmost importance that we study our plant life in order to preserve it and use it wisely. It is my hope that these brief wildflower profiles will contribute to a deeper understanding and appreciation of these remarkable plants—and above all to a greater enjoyment of them.

Legends & Lore
of
Texas Wildflowers

Agarita

Barberry Family (*Berberidaceae*)

*Common names: Agarito, Algerita, Chaparral Berry,
Wild Currant, Texas Barberry, Desert Holly*

Of the four species of barberry in Texas, the best known is the one called agarita or agarito, a seemingly unfriendly but actually very useful shrub. Quail, rabbits, and other small birds and animals use these evergreen bushes as cover, and in February and March the clusters of small, fragrant, roselike yellow flowers that appear on the branches are an important early browse for bees, which make a welcome spring honey from the nectar. Like other members of the barberry family, the agarita has a simple but effective pollination scheme. The stamens inside the petals are hair-trigger sensitive, and when they are touched by a visiting insect searching for nectar, they flail the visitor's head, showering it with pollen that, with luck, will be deposited on the pistils of the next flower the insect visits.

Early Texas pioneers found that the gray stem of the agarita contained yellow wood, which, along with the root of the plant, made a good yellow dye for their homespun. Craft workers in Europe used the yellow wood to create small beads and other jewelry as well as fine marquetry. Seventeenth-century herbalist Nicholas Culpeper noted that hair washed in lye made of barberry ashes mixed with water would turn yellow; there have been barberry blondes ever since.[1]

Across the caliche hills of Central Texas in late spring, bright red berries amid stiff gray-green leaves with sharp, spiny edges give agarita the look of holly. Mexicans call the plant *agrito* (little sour) because of the tartness of the pea-sized red berries. Birds love the berries and scatter the seeds in thickets and along roadsides and fences in their droppings. Some people enjoy eating a few of the sharp-tasting berries raw, but most prefer them in tasty jellies, tarts, pies, and cobblers or made into wine. The trick is to gather the fruit without being jabbed by the needle-sharp leaf tips, and nobody seems to have found a better method than that suggested by the late wildflower expert Carroll Abbott, editor of the *Texas Wildflower Newsletter:* "Wrap an old sheet out flat underneath a laden bush and whale the daylights out of it. Then let the insects run off the sheet and scrape away the dead leaves."[2]

Barberries have been used medicinally in many ways. Culpeper, who was as much an astrologer as an herbalist, claimed that Mars had given the shrub to men to purge their bodies of "choleric humours" and recommended drinking a half-cup of barberry tonic (made by boiling the inner bark of the plant with white wine) every morning.[3] In accordance with the doctrine of signatures (which held that a plant's appearance indicated the type of ailment it was intended to cure), barberry plants, with their yellow flowers and yellow wood, were once used to treat patients who were jaundiced. Some nineteenth-century American physicians, in addition to prescribing barberry for jaundice, also used it to treat dysentery, cholera, fevers, eye infections, and syphilis. Ancient Egyptians made a syrup containing barberry juice to use against plague, and modern researchers confirm that the plant does have antibacterial properties. Today berberine salts derived from the plant are used in eyedrops and eyewashes.[4]

Mayapple (*Podophyllum peltatum*), another member of the barberry family, grows abundantly in damp woods in East Texas, where it tends to form large colonies. The genus name from the Greek *podos* (foot) and the common name "duck's foot" refer to the shape of the leaves, which hang like twin umbrellas over the single waxy white flower that grows out of their axil. Most of the other common names refer to the large, egg-shaped yellow fruit; these include wild lemon, Indian apple, raccoon berry, and hog apple. Although the plant is also called American mandrake, it is not related to the infamous European mandrake, but it does have its own potential danger. All parts, except the pulp of the lemonlike fruit, are poisonous if ingested to excess. Native Americans used the plant for its powerful purgative effect, as a cure for warts, and even as an insec-

ticide. They recognized its toxicity and sometimes ate the roots and shoots in order to commit suicide. Mayapple has been listed in *The Pharmacopoeia of the United States of America,* and a derivative from a substance in the rhizomes is used to treat human cancer.[5]

Mayapple fruit was described by early explorers as tasting like lemons or figs, and nineteenth-century botanist Asa Gray called it "somewhat mawkish, beloved of pigs, raccoons and small boys." Euell Gibbons liked to make mayapple marmalade, which he called "ambrosia."[6]

Agarita is close kin to the barberries used as ornamental plants and hedges in the northern and eastern United States. But some species of barberry have been outlawed in wheat-growing states because they are hosts in the life cycle of the destructive parasitic wheat-rust fungus.[7] The San Antonio Botanical Center recommends the Texas barberry (*Berberis swaseyi*), which is similar to agarita (*Berberis trifoliolata*), as a good landscape hedge plant. An endemic species of the Edwards Plateau, it is resistant to both cold and drought, and the fruits are considered to be superior to those of agarita for making wines, jellies, and jams. Because it hybridizes freely with agarita, intermediate forms between the two are common.[8]

Agave/ Century Plant

Agave Family (*Agavaceae*)
Common Names: Maguey, Mescal, Amole, Lechuguilla, Yucca

*A*gave is a relatively new family designation, and until recently members of this family were distributed between the lily and the amaryllis families. It is appropriate that the Greek root for agave is *agavos*, literally "admirable" or "illustrious," for in the plant world the agave or century plant is hard to match for drama. It spends its whole life of fifteen to twenty years preparing for one grand performance, and then, exhausted, it dies.

While the agave matures, it exists as a rosette of thick, fleshy blue-green leaves from one and a half to two and a half feet long, each edged with sharp thorns. Finally, one spring when there is enough nourishment stored in the leaves, a stout shoot emerges from the cluster of leaves and begins to grow at the astonishing rate of about a foot a day to a height of twelve to twenty feet. This giant flower stalk branches until it resembles a tall candelabra holding clusters of upturned tubular yellowish flowers. After giving up their store of food and water to sustain the flowering stalk, the leaves die. The stalk too dies after it has set seed, but the dried flower stalks with their armlike branches remain an impressive sight for many weeks.

Many creatures, including humans, make good use of the plant. Birds, butterflies, ants, and other insects feast on the flower clusters and seeds. Early desert dwellers depended on the century plant for survival to provide them with food, beverages, fiber, medicine, shelter, and lances for rattlesnake bites. In some species the thorn at the end of each leaf blade can be broken off so that two long fibers peel off with it, providing needle and thread together. The strong fibers of the leaves are used in making rope, twine, baskets, mats, brushes, cloth, and paper. The leaves have been used as shingles, and for centuries Native Americans and Mexicans have used the saponin found in agaves as soap. In folk medicine the sap in the leaves has been used to treat cuts, burns, and skin abrasions and made into a tonic to treat stomach problems, and the roots have been used to make a tea to treat arthritis and jaundice.[1]

In areas where potable water is scarce, the agave provides a valuable nutritious beverage. After the large leaf bud is cut out of a living plant, a basin is formed where the sap (*aquamiel* or honey water) pools and can be drawn off twice daily. This sweet juice contains calcium, phosphorus, vitamins, and amino acids.[2] Fermented agave juice becomes pulque, a beerlike intoxicant used in religious rituals by the Aztecs and still enjoyed in Mexico and along the Texas border. After the Spanish introduced the indigenous people of the Southwest to the process of distillation, mescal and tequila, highly intoxicating agave beverages, were developed.[3] Today the production of tequila is an important industry, and large haciendas in Mexico grow *Agave americana*, commonly called maguey, for the distilleries.

A common Spanish name for the century plant is mescal, and both the fiery drink and the food made from the century plant are called mescal. Spaniards, observing that the Apaches depended heavily on mescal for food, drink, and fiber, named the Mescalero Apaches for the plant. The Apaches roasted and ate both the flower stalks and the hearts of the agave. They combined religious rites with preparation of mescal, levering the whole heart or crown of the agave with a stout branch from its fierce cradle of protective leaves and then baking it in rock-lined pits for up to two days, depending on the size of the crown. Today baked agave, which is rich in nutritious sugars, can still be found in some Mexican markets.

The juice of the agave is used in Mexico in a number of medicines and is valued especially for its diuretic and antisyphilitic properties.[4]

Among the many other medicines compounded from the plant are cough syrups and poultices; cortisone and steroids also have been synthesized from the saponins in a number of agave species.[5]

Lechuguilla (lay-chu-GHEE-yah), a common century plant in Texas, was a formidable obstacle for early explorers of the Southwest. The spiky banana-shaped leaves often lamed horses and might impale a rider falling on them. Today small lechuguilla are a hazard to off-road vehicles. Sheep ranchers are not fond of them, but deer and javelinas relish the offshoots by which the plant reproduces. The stalk of the lechuguilla, which grows up to fifteen feet tall, does not branch like other agave. Its yellowish or purplish flowers grow in a solid mass at the upper part of the tall stalk, which bends in a graceful arc under their weight. A single plant may have a thousand flowers, an important source for delicious honey. Because they contain toxic compounds, lechuguilla hearts are not edible, but Native Americans found the toxic juice good for arrow poison and the leaf fibers useful for bowstrings. They also discovered that the roots of the amole, as they called the plant, produce soaplike suds when mixed with water, and today amole soap is produced commercially and considered beneficial for the skin. Barton Warnock suggests that the lechuguilla has steroids that might be used in birth control or for fattening cattle.[6]

At least ten species of agave are found in Texas. Harvard agave, a spectacular century plant with palmlike sprays of greenish yellow flowers, is endemic to the grasslands around the Chisos Mountains, while parry agave, which has reddish flower buds, has a wider range. Yucca, an important member of the agave family, is discussed in a separate chapter.

Like southern gardeners in the United States, nineteenth-century Europeans cultivated the attractive agave plants as ornamentals. After returning from a delayed honeymoon in Italy, Tennyson wrote the poem "Daisy" to his wife, recalling their boat trip to Lake Como and the sights they had enjoyed together. Among his memories was:

> *The moonlight touching o'er a terrace*
> *One tall Agave above the lake.*

Anemone

Buttercup or Crowfoot Family
(*Ranunculaceae*)

*Common Names: Windflower, Pasque Flower,
Prairie Smoke, Prairie Crocus*

The anemone, which means "expectation" in flower symbolism, is one of the first signs of spring in Texas. As early as late January, residents of South Texas come upon these delicate-looking blossoms blowing on slender stalks in meadows and prairies. Throughout the state they bloom in shades of white, pink, and bluish hues ranging from lavender to violet to purple from February until April. In Europe, the Middle East, and other regions, scarlet anemones are common. Although they appear fragile, anemones can adapt to a variety of habitats and are found on creek banks, on open hillsides, at the edges of woods, and in limestone pockets as well as in fields and meadows.

Anemones are also known as windflowers, from the Greek *anemos,* meaning wind. In 1653 Nicholas Culpeper wrote: "[T]hey say the flowers never open but when the wind bloweth. Pliny is my author, if it be not so, blame him." Native Americans, seeing the flower nod and bow in the spring breezes, called it "the flower of the wind."[1] A classical myth connects the creation of the flower with the west wind: Anemone, a beautiful nymph, lived at the court of Flora, the goddess of flowers, and her husband Zephyr, the west wind. Realizing that Zephyr and the nymph were in love, jealous Flora banished Anemone from the court. When the broken-hearted nymph pined away and died, Zephyr persuaded Venus to change Anemone's body into a flower that would always come to life with the return of spring. Soon, however, fickle Zephyr lost interest in Anemone and abandoned her to Boreas, the rude north wind. After Boreas found he could not gain Anemone's affection, he roughly opened her blossoms and then quickly caused them to fade.[2] This myth probably accounts for sentiments attached to the anemone in nineteenth-century catalogs of the language of flowers, such as "forsaken," "Go Away!" and "Refusal and Abandonment."

In mythology the anemone was dedicated to Aphrodite or Venus, and an even more famous legend connects the anemone with the love story of Aphrodite and Adonis. When Aphrodite, the goddess of love, saw Adonis at his birth, she determined to keep him for herself. Unwisely she chose Persephone, Queen of the Underworld, as his guardian. When Aphrodite went down to the Underworld to claim the handsome youth, Persephone refused to give him up. Zeus, called upon to mediate, issued a Solomon-like decree: Adonis would spend six months with each goddess. While he was underground with Persephone, the world was bleak and winterish, but when he returned to the upper world, all nature smiled and bloomed. As a young man Adonis became a brave and bold hunter who loved chasing dangerous wild game. Aphrodite begged him to abandon this risky sport and stay with her, but he laughed and ran away to join his hunter friends. One day he rashly attacked a huge wild boar and wounded it with his spear. Maddened, the beast rushed at Adonis and buried its tusk in his side. Aphrodite flew to her beloved in her swan-drawn chariot, but all her tears could not save him. He died in her arms, and through her magic his blood became the blood-red anemones of Greece. In other versions of the myth, as Aphrodite wandered about the fields and woods, her tears became the pale anemones. The English poet and translator John Addington Symonds combines these ideas: "Scarlet and white anemones are there, / Some born of Adonis' blood and some of Aphrodite's tears."[3]

There are some 120 species of anemones worldwide, and some of the folklore that grew up around the flower is negative. Although Romans hunted the anemone in early spring and wore the first one they found to bring them good luck, Persians adopted windflowers as the emblem of illness. Egyptians thought the plant tainted the air and caused illness; early Europeans ran past fields of them, holding their breath because of a superstition that the wind that blew across anemones became poisoned. In

China, where the anemone is used in funeral rites, it is called the death flower.

Religious floral symbolism cites the anemone as one of the flowers that turned red with the blood that trickled down from the cross at Christ's crucifixion. Anemones grow abundantly in the Holy Land, and many authorities believe they are the "lilies of the field" referred to in the New Testament.

In his *Herball* John Gerard recorded that although he had twelve different kinds of anemones in his garden, he had heard of "divers more," and he concluded that the variety of this flower was "without number."[4] The various kinds of anemone have amassed many credits in medical lore. Pliny relates that in his day magicians gathered windflowers and tied them around the neck or arm of a patient as a remedy or charm to cure diseases. Apparently the same idea existed in Britain, for an old English ballad says: "The first spring-blown anemone she in his doublet wove / To keep him safe from pestilence wherever he should rove."[5] Pliny recommended the plant for curing toothache, headache, and eye ailments among other problems. Culpeper goes even further and says that when the body is bathed in "a concoction" of the leaves of the plant, it may be cured of leprosy.

Ancient Romans made a tea from anemone leaves to prevent fever. In America various native peoples esteemed the plant and used it to make poultices for treating burns and wounds, as a tea for consumption, headaches, and dizziness, and as a wash for eye ailments. They also made lozenges from it to clear the throat so that they could sing well.[6] We now know that the leaves and roots of anemones contain proto-anemonin, an irritant that can cause contact dermatitis and if taken internally may affect the nervous system and cause convulsions. The plants are also toxic to cattle, which usually avoid them because of their burning acrid taste.

Texans who live in the northwest corner of the state are fortunate to be able to see the beautiful silky pasqueflower (*Anemone patens*), one of the most interesting members of the anemone tribe. Its cup-shaped blooms are usually a bluish shade, and after the fruits ripen they produce long silky plumes that create the illusion of smoke or haze when seen in large patches, giving rise to its common name of prairiesmoke. In Europe this plant was originally called passe flower or paschal flower because it bloomed at Passover time, and it came to be considered a symbol of Easter. In the thirteenth century it was used to produce a bright green dye to decorate Easter eggs. The household accounts of Edward I of England show that four hundred eggs were dyed and gilded for the Easter court festival and that the pasqueflower was among the plants used to make the dye.[7] Dakota Sioux revered the pasqueflower as a symbol of spring and used it in ceremonial rites. They called it twinflower because it usually produces two flower stems. In 1903 South Dakota adopted it as the state flower. Vita Sackville-West, who grew pasqueflowers in her famous garden, described them in *The Garden:* "Lavender petals sheathed in silver floss / Soft as the suffle of a kitten's fur."

Botanists explain that the anemone is one of the natural barometer plants affected by dampness, and this accounts for its habit of folding early in the evening or in cloudy weather. But romantics may prefer to believe the fairylore that ascribes the folding of the petals to the actions of the fairies who curl up in the heart of the blossoms and pull the leaves over themselves when a shower threatens.

In Texas, where the appearance of windflowers is one of our earliest and loveliest promises of spring, we may remember the myth of the beautiful nymph Anemone and agree with the poet Rapin who wrote in "The Anemone":

> *She, though transformed, as charming as before,*
> *The fairest maid is now the fairest flower.*

Aster

Sunflower Family (*Asteraceae*)

Common Names: Starflower, Heath Aster,
Farewell-to-Summer, Annual Aster, Fall Aster

The name aster comes from the Greek and Latin words for star, and according to Greek myth, Astraea (star maiden) was a goddess representing innocence and purity who lived on the earth in the Golden Age. When people became cruel and greedy and violent, the gods abandoned the earth, one by one. The last to leave was Astrea, who became the constellation Virgo (the Virgin). In her compassion for humanity, she wept, and her tears falling to earth as star dust became the starflowers.[1]

Of the 650 species of asters throughout the world, perhaps some forty-five grow in Texas. Both in the wild and in cultivation, asters hybridize freely with each other with no respect for the scientists who struggle to classify them. "Never was there so rascally a genus," cried American botanist Asa Grey, who brought some order into its chaos. "They reduce me to despair."[2] Even experts like Donovan Correll and Marshall Johnston admit that the lines are blurred by hybridization and back-crossing and call asters "one of our more difficult genera."[3] The multiplicity of common names given these daisylike plants reflects efforts to pigeonhole them by color, size, or some other feature (broad-leaved, small-leaved, narrow-leaved, smooth, baby, dwarf white, dwarf blue, amethyst, golden) and by location (roadside and river).

The most abundant variety in Texas is *Aster subulatus,* commonly

called annual aster, baby's breath aster, or blackweed (because its foliage turns a dark purple in its old age). The Spanish nickname is uncomplimentary: *hierba del marrano* (pig's herb or dirty person's herb), but the bunches of white or lavender heads of these common asters are a pretty sight along roadsides in the fall. Not all lawn owners are pleased to find that the more they cut the slender stems the more the plants branch and spread. Others, like landscape designer Sally Wasowski, bow to the (almost) inevitable and enjoy having their lawns studded with the tiny white and lavender starflowers.

An attractive variety that grows throughout most of Texas is the heath aster (*Aster ericoides*), which often forms colonies. The abundance of tiny white florets on fresh plants have a not unpleasant tarlike odor. Because of its late blooming habit, it is also called fall aster and frost aster. Delena

Tull suggests that the heath aster has potential as a source of polyphenol adhesives.[4]

Texas beekeepers value the annual aster as a source of delicious honey. Ancient Romans also associated asters with honey, and Virgil recommended putting aster leaves that had been boiled in wine near a beehive to improve the taste of honey. The Romans placed wreaths of aster blossoms on the altars of their gods to keep away evil spirits, and the Greeks burned the leaves of the plants to drive away evil spirits and strewed them on their floors to keep serpents away. The Chinese made aster wine from fermented leaves and stems of their native aster plants, and Geraldine Nicholson relates that inhabitants of the Li district of China, who reportedly lived fabulously long lives (120 years or more), credited their longevity to the aster-flavored water that flowed from the surrounding hills.[5] Native Americans who boiled and ate the young leaves of numerous species of asters made a tea from dried stems to drink as a blood tonic and used a wash made by soaking the stems and flowers to ease rheumatic aches.[6] Aster plants have also been used to treat bites from rabid animals and snake bites. Cosmetically, they have been used to improve complexions and to deter balding.

Like many common objects, American asters were not truly appreciated until they were taken up by strangers. When asters from the New World were imported to England some three hundred years ago, the English welcomed them to their gardens enthusiastically and worked at selecting and hybridizing them into a large number of new varieties. They called them Michaelmas daisies as they usually were in full bloom by St. Michaelmas Day (a church festival on September 29 honoring the archangel Michael). Belatedly Americans, too, came to recognize the potential of asters as attractive garden plants. Another member of the *Asteraceae* family, the tansy aster (*Machaeranthera tanacetifolia*), became one of the most popular garden annuals in this country. It is now widely sold under the name Tahoka daisy, so the same Texas gardeners who strive to eradicate the lowly annual aster from their lawns often display showy masses of purple blooms of tansy asters in their flower beds.

In astrology the aster is a herb of Venus and therefore connected with romantic love. In *Flora's Dictionary* they represent "cheerfulness in old age," and in various lists of the language of flowers they symbolize variety, elegance, and daintiness. One of their most evocative common names is farewell-to-summer, and for many they are welcome harbingers of the coming coolness of fall.

William Quayle captures their charm in his description in *God's Calendar:* "They are stars fetched from the night skies and planted on the fields of day."[7]

Bluebell

Gentian Family (*Gentianaceae*)

Common Names: Prairie Gentian, Centaury, Mountain Pink, Meadow Pink, Catchfly, Bottle Gentian

Many flowers are called bluebells, and there is a bluebell family. The common Texas bluebell (*Eustoma grandiflorum*), however, is not a member of this family but belongs to the gentian tribe. Its bell-shaped violet-blue blossoms are especially welcome as they appear in summer after many earlier wildflowers are only memories. Texas bluebells thrive in Central Texas near Brenham, where the makers of the famous Blue Bell ice cream have adopted their name. Once bluebells were common in moist, sunny habitats throughout most of the state, but their beauty and durability as a cut flower have almost led to their undoing through indiscriminate collecting.

Eustoma, which means "open mouth," refers to the large throat of the flower. The variety called catchfly (*Eustoma exaltatum*) has lighter blue flowers and is found in salty areas, particularly around alkali-encrusted streams. Unfortunately, the closed or bottle gentian, with its deep blue flowers that barely open, is near extinction in the Big Thicket area because of destruction of its habitat.

Other attractive members of the gentian family in Texas are the centaurys, named after the mythical centaur. Mountain pinks (*Centaurium beyrichii*) have small, pink, star-shaped flowers that grow in natural bouquets out of sunbaked limestone. Early settlers, who learned from the Indians to make a tea from this plant to use as a fever remedy, called it quinine plant. Meadow pink, which is similar to mountain pink, prefers moist, sandy soil and has larger flowers of a deeper rose-pink color with distinctive star-shaped yellow markings in the center of the flower. A similar plant is Lady Bird's centaury (*Centaurium texense*), which is named for Mrs. Lyndon B. Johnson's interest in this attractive plant and her efforts to collect seeds and grow the plant on the Johnson Ranch in the Hill Country.

Gentian is named after Gentius (180–167 B.C.), king of the ancient country of Illyria on the Balkan peninsula. Like many ancient rulers he was interested in botany, and according to Pliny he discovered the medicinal virtues of gentians and used them to cure a mysterious fever that had stricken his army. He was not, however, the first to explore the healing properties of the plant. There are records on papyrus showing that over a thousand years earlier Egyptians had used them in medicinal prescriptions.[1]

A family characteristic of gentians is the clear, bitter juice that has long been considered one of the purest and best tonic bitters in the pharmacopoeia. The effectiveness of this tonic has led to extravagant claims for the gentians' powers. Seventeenth-century English herbalist Nicholas Culpeper called it a miraculous healer and claimed it was under the domination of Mars: "one of the principal herbs he is ruler of . . . a more sure remedy cannot be found to prevent the pestilence than it is . . . when kine [cows] are bitten in the udder by any venomous beast, do but stroke the place with the decoction of any of these and it will instantly heal them." He also maintained that decoctions of gentian aided digestion, killed intestinal worms, and prevented fainting.[2]

In China, where the gall bladder was considered the seat of courage and resolution, *Gentiana scabra* was called "Dragon's gall," and its root was used to improve the energy (*chi*) of the liver and gall bladder and to arrest fear. Taken over a long period of time, it was said to "improve wisdom, lessen forgetfulness and lighten the body." Recently Chinese physicians have prescribed it for arthritis because studies there have shown it has strong anti-inflammatory properties.[3] European colonists learned from Native Americans many uses for native gentians, including treatments for general debility, digestive problems, backache, colic, and malaria. However, they brought along their own methods for administering the herb. Blossoming plants were collected, dried, and soaked in brandy. This mix-

ture was given to the patient three times daily, and whether or not it cured the illness, it must have made the patient feel more cheerful.

According to Hungarian legend, when Hungary was devastated by a terrible plague in the eleventh century, King Ladislas took his bow and arrow and went out into a field, where he shot it, praying it would be directed to a plant that would save his people. The arrow flew straight to the heart of a gentian; the plants were gathered and wondrous cures effected.[4]

Gentian was listed in *The Pharmacopoeia of the United States of America* from 1820 to 1955 as a digestive stimulant. It is still considered effective by American and European herbalists as a bitter tonic for increasing the appetite and improving general debility.

Before hops, gentian root was used in brewing beer. In Europe an extract of the roots of the yellow gentian is fermented and distilled to make Gentian brandy, and the roots are a favored ingredient of aromatic bitters for use in liqueurs and vermouths.

The slang term "moxie" (courage with a dash of cunning) comes from the name of a bitter soft drink made with gentian root. First introduced in New England in 1885 as "Beverage Moxie Nerve Food," it was considered a tonic. The original label touted it as a cure for "brain and nervous exhaustion, loss of manhood, helplessness, imbecility and insanity." After these claims were dropped, it continued to be a popular soft drink and outsold Coca-Cola for years. It is still available in New England with gentian as one of its ingredients.[5]

In the language of flowers the gentian signifies constancy. But when sent in a Victorian bouquet it conveyed the message "you are unjust"— perhaps for doubting the lover's constancy? In other lists it signifies ingratitude, reflecting the elusive quality of this proud beauty, which has a reputation for resisting the efforts of gardeners to cultivate it.

The famous fringed gentian of the eastern United States is the occidental flower emblem of autumn. Its intrinsic beauty has earned it a place in the hearts of flower lovers and in literature. Thoreau wrote that it surpassed the color of a bluebird. And William Cullen Bryant was inspired to write an "Ode to a Fringed Gentian," in which he calls its color "heaven's own blue: / Blue—blue—as if that sky let fall / A flower from its Cerulean wall."

Bluebonnet

Legume Family (*Leguminosae/Fabaceae*)

Common Names: Buffalo Clover,
Lupine, Wolf Flower, Conejo

When President Theodore Roosevelt visited Austin on April 6, 1905, thousands of schoolchildren lined the road, singing "America" and tossing bluebonnets in his path. Like the Lone Star flag and the longhorn, the bluebonnet is a symbol of Texas. It seems such a perfect choice for the state flower that few people realize it had to win out in hot competition with the open cotton boll and the blossom of the prickly pear cactus.

In 1901 when a resolution proposed by the Colonial Dames of Texas to adopt the bluebonnet as the state flower was introduced in the Texas House of Representatives, a business leader suggested that the open cotton boll, "the white flower of commerce," be adopted instead. Jack Garner, future vice president of the United States, rose to support with glowing praise the prickly pear, a prominent inhabitant of the area near his Uvalde home. The Dames marshaled their forces to lobby the representatives, and as a visual aid they brought into the House a bluebonnet picture painted by Miss Mode Walker of Austin. The opposition, including "Cactus Jack," was overwhelmed, and the bluebonnet won the day.[1]

The question of the state flower, however, was not at rest. The bluebonnet named in the legislators' resolution was *Lupinus subcarnosus,* not considered by most bluebonnet lovers to be the most attractive of the six species discovered so far in the state. Many argued that *Lupinus texensis,* known as the Texas bluebonnet, which creates lush blue carpets through-out Central Texas each spring, should be the official designee. Finally, seventy years later, in 1971, the Texas congress passed a new resolution that added the Texas bluebonnet and also "any other variety of Bluebonnet not heretofore recorded." We have, therefore, as Jean Andrews points out, six state flowers and the possibility of others if new species are discovered.[2]

Whether they are the plains bluebonnets of the Panhandle or the tall bluebonnets of the Big Bend region, each species works its own magic, and many Texans agree with J. Frank Dobie, who said: "No other flower—for me at least—brings such upsurging of the spirit and at the same time such restfulness." He described the bluebonnet's fragrance, "the evanescences of petal and leaf mingling into an aroma that is at once delicate and as tonic as a heifer's breath. What else in the world can be like passing a field of bluebonnets in a spring night and sensing them only by smell!"[3] Others have described the bluebonnet aroma as "subtle" and "intoxicating."

It is easy to see how the bluebonnet got its most common name, as the little flowerets resemble the bonnets worn by pioneer women. *Conejo*, the Mexican name, refers to the white top that resembles the white tail of the cottontail rabbit. Other names arose because of mistaken beliefs. Bluebonnets were called "buffalo clover" into the twentieth century because native peoples and early settlers thought the buffalo liked to eat them. We now know that only goats and sheep relish bluebonnets; cattle and horses avoid the plants, and deer eat them only when nothing better is available to them. Past generations sometimes called bluebonnets "wolf flowers" because they seemed to rob the soil and make it poor, just as wolves robbed shepherds of their sheep. The scientific name *Lupinus* (from the Latin *lupus,* meaning wolf) arose from the same erroneous belief about lupines. Today we know that lupines actually enrich the soil by putting nitrogen into it.

There are a number of legends about the origin of the bluebonnet, and several were recorded in 1964 by the Texas Folklore Society. In one of them the Indians who had gone to the Happy Hunting Grounds engaged in a terrific battle in which they knocked chunks from the blue sky. These fell to the earth and shattered into tiny pieces that became bluebonnets.

In many Native American myths, the idea of sacrifice is important, and this Aztec myth is an example: Once when a terrible pestilence dev-

astated the land of the Aztecs, nothing they could do brought relief. Their prayers and pleas remained unanswered until at last the Great Spirit spoke. He proclaimed that the wickedness of the people could be atoned for only by a living sacrifice of some sinless human. An Aztec maiden offered herself, and as she was led up the hillside to the sacrificial altar, her blue headdress fell unnoticed to the ground. The next day the ground near the altar was covered with blue flowers in the shape of her headdress and each was splotched with her spilt blood. The pestilence passed, but the blue flowers returned each year as a reminder of the bravery of the Aztec maiden.[4]

The best known of the bluebonnet origin myths is the one told by Dobie in *Tales of Old-Time Texas* and more recently made into a children's book by Tomie DePaola. This legend says that the native people had suffered through a great flood followed by a greater drought and a bitter winter of sleet and ice. They were starving, and a dreadful disease was devastating the tribe. Clearly, the Great Spirit was angry with them, and he refused to be appeased by anything they could do, although the medicine men chanted incantations and danced to the beat of tom-toms day and night. Warriors cut their own flesh with flint knives and sent up wild cries of supplication in vain. Finally the Great Spirit spoke to the medicine men, telling them that the tribe must make a burnt offering of their most valued possession and scatter the ashes to the four winds to atone for the selfishness that had brought his wrath upon them.

A young girl sat listening in the darkness on the outer edge of the council meeting. Hidden in the folds of her skirt was her beloved doll. Dressed in a soft deerskin robe, it had long, black horsehair braids and a headdress made of the bright blue feathers from the bird that calls "Jay! Jay!" Her heart grew heavy as she realized what she must do. Late that night after everyone else had gone to sleep, she crept from her tepee, hugging the precious doll to her chest. Taking a burning coal from the council fire, she went to a nearby hill, where she gathered sticks and started a fire. As the flames leaped up, she held up her doll, surely the tribe's "most valued possession," and asked the Great Spirit to accept it. Then she quickly threw it into the fire and watched as the greedy flames consumed the body and the face, the deerskin robe, the horsehair braids, and the beautiful blue feathers of the headdress.

When the ashes had cooled, the little girl scooped them up. Turning to the north and south, east and west, she let them blow through her fingers. In the morning the tribe awoke to find the barren land covered with a blanket of beautiful blue flowers, and they knew it was a sign that the Great Spirit had forgiven them. Their land became green and lush, and the little girl who was the most unselfish of them all was given the name One-Who-Dearly-Loves-Her-People.[5]

Because they are not self-fertilizing, bluebonnets depend largely on hungry bees as pollinators. Attracted by the white spot on the banner, or upper petal, the bee alights on the keel formed by the two lower petals, and pollination is triggered as the petals open. The pollen-bearing reproductive organs are thrown against the bee, which transports the pollen to a nearby blossom. According to Jean Andrews, the dramatic change of the spot on the banner petals from white to red is not (as is commonly thought) a sign that pollination has taken place. It is instead an indication of the age of the flower, and on the fifth day after the flower opens, the spot will turn red no matter what the sexual activity of the flower has been.[6]

The main uses that have been made of bluebonnets have been related to their aesthetic appeal. Although many large natural bluebonnet colonies have been covered over with concrete in towns and cities, the Texas Department of Transportation has worked diligently seeding and reseeding bluebonnets along roadways to give motorists vistas of blue to enjoy in the spring. Also, many towns and cities have beautification programs that encourage planting bluebonnets, and there are numerous bluebonnet festivals and pageants throughout the state as well as bluebonnet trails for motorists to follow. The sight of bluebonnet fields has inspired countless painters and photographers, as well as poets and songwriters—with varying degrees of success.

In the language of flowers, the bluebonnet means "voraciousness" and "imagination," and there seem to be no limits to the imaginations of those who use the bluebonnet as a decorative motif. Texas gift shops carry an endless array of bluebonnet souvenirs, including fine china and crystal, pottery, napkins and tablecloths, placemats, pillows, fabrics, towels, stationery, and almost anything a bluebonnet can be painted, printed, or sewn on.

No amount of manipulation, however, can spoil the genuine pleasure of experiencing again each spring the time when the sky seems to fall on Texas as the bluebonnets return for a few weeks to refresh our spirits.

Broomweed
Sunflower Family (*Asteraceae*)
Common Names: Snakeweed, Kindling Weed, Turpentine Weed, Matchweed, Matchbrush

I f broomweed is "the smiles of God," as the Native Americans called it, then God truly does smile on Texas in autumn, when the plants create unbroken sheets of shining yellow gold in fields and on hillsides—sometimes for miles. Its favorite habitat seems to be anywhere, in any kind of soil, throughout most of Texas.

Not palatable to livestock (or wildlife), broomweed sometimes robs grass of precious water and is generally despised by ranchers as a nuisance weed. It is, however, valued by bee keepers as one of the best sources of honey for winter storage. The honey from broomweed is strong, dark, and slightly bitter.[1]

Broomweed's dainty sprays of tiny yellow flowers make attractive fresh bouquets as well as lasting dried arrangements. In addition to being decorative, broomweed is a useful plant. Its name derives from the fact that early settlers gathered it in bunches and tied it to sticks for use as brooms to sweep hearths, porches, and hard-surfaced yards. Because broomweed's high resin content makes it extremely flammable, the settlers also found it useful as kindling.

Common broomweed, which originally bore the scientific name *Gutierrezia* in honor of a Spanish nobleman, has been rechristened with the mouth-filling title *Xanthocephalum dracunculoides,* indicating that it is a yellow-headed plant resembling tarragon. It is an annual.

Its close relative, snakeweed (*X. sarothrae*), is a perennial. When its stems are crushed, it gives off an odor of turpentine. Also known by its Spanish name, *yerba de vibora* (viper's weed), snakeweed was used in making poultices to treat sheep that had been bitten by rattlesnakes. For humans, a folk remedy still used to ease the pain of arthritis is to steep a cup of the stems and leaves of snakeweed thirty to forty minutes in a quart of water, which is *not drunk* but rather strained and poured into hot bath water.[2]

The Navajo also chewed the plant and applied it as a poultice to alleviate the stings of insect bites, and they gave a tea made from the whole plant to women after childbirth to help expel the placenta.[3] This use affirms the belief of ranchers that the hated snakeweed aborts fetuses in pregnant cattle who happen to eat it.

Broomweed is used to make dyes in shades of yellow, green, gold, or dark brown, depending on the method and the mordant used. It is also one of the common plants that is high in hydrocarbons, compounds used to make fuels, rubber, plastics, and textiles; therefore, Delena Tull suggests that it may be a valuable future alternative to foreign sources.[4]

European broom, which is a member of the pea family, was introduced into North America as a garden plant. It is said that Thomas Jefferson was one of those to import it. The numerous small yellow flowers, which are shaped like pea blossoms, are followed by pealike pods. The plant's scientific name, *Cytisus scoparius,* means "resembling a broom," from the Latin for "floor-sweeper." It acquired this name in the Middle Ages, when its twigs and branches were used as brooms. During that period people attached superstitions to the use of broomweed in full bloom. According to an old English saying, "If you sweep the house with blossomed broom in May, you are sure to sweep the head of the house away." It was also thought to frighten witches away.

In Europe broom is associated with heraldry. Geoffrey, count of Anjou, is supposed to have adopted broom as a badge and fastened it to his helmet before going into battle. A century later, Louis IX of France founded a new order of knighthood, which chose broom as its emblem of humility.[5] The Plantagenet royal house of England derived its name from the Latin *Planta genista*, "sprig of the broom plant," and the Plantagenets wore sprigs of broom in their battle headgear. In the sixteenth century distilled water made from broom flowers was commonly used as a diuretic and purgative. Even Henry VIII is reported to have relied on it when he was ill.

In the language of flowers, broom represents both humility and neatness, perhaps referring to its humble usefulness as a sweeper.

Buttercup

Buttercup Family/Crowfoot Family
(*Ranunculaceae*)

Common Names: Crowfoot, Large Buttercup, Gold Cup

In Texas, evening primroses are often called buttercups, but the true buttercups of poetry and legend are the *ranunculus,* whose bright blossoms Thoreau in his *Journals* called the "gold of the meadow." The botanical name *ranunculus,* the diminutive of *rana,* which means little frog, probably came about because many species grow in soggy places where frogs abound.

Another source of the name is a Greek myth that tells of Ranunculus, a youth noted for his gorgeous clothing, always of green and yellow silk, and for his melodious voice that charmed everyone who heard him, including himself. One day while singing to a group of wood nymphs, he became so entranced with his own music that he expired in ecstasy, and Orpheus transformed him into the brilliant flower that bears his name.[1] The common name "crowfoot" comes from the shape of the leaves, whose deeply cleft segments suggested the toes of a crow to someone.

In addition to the various buttercups, several other well-known plants belonging to the *Ranunculaceae* family are found in Texas, including the anemone, larkspur, clematis, and columbine branches. The varicolored anemones (discussed in a separate chapter) are among our earliest spring wildflowers. Prairie larkspur occurs throughout most of the state. Its pale blue flowers, which grow on the upper part of the slender stems, are distinguished by one prolonged sepal that resembles a spur. The Carolina larkspur, with its deep blue flowers, is abundant in East Texas in spring. Two interesting clematis vines are common in the state. One, called virgin's bower or old-man's-beard, is noted for the masses of silky gray white plumes that trail from the seed covers. The other is the leather flower, which has no true petals but four thickened sepals with recurved tips that form a colored urn—red or purple, depending on the species.

The few species of the lovely columbine that are found in Texas are worth hunting for. Yellow longspur columbine is found near springs in the canyons of the Chisos Mountains in Big Bend, and the Chapline columbine, a rare plant of the Guadalupe Mountains has been found in McKittrick Canyon. The more prevalent red and yellow flowered columbine (*Aquilegia canadensis*) grows on limestone bluffs and shaded rocky slopes in the Hill Country. The common name for the plant comes from the Latin *columba* (dove) because of the fancied likeness of the five spurs to the heads of doves around a dish. Columbines were once thought of as being symbolic of sorrow and infidelity, but in time the decorative flower and distinctive leaf came to be valued motifs in the coats of arms of many historical houses. It is interesting that President Eisenhower, leader of Allied troops in World War II, chose this flower, whose name symbolizes peace, as the name of his official airplane. At least one variety of columbine blooms in every state, and Colorado has chosen as its state flower the elegant white and lavender columbine (*Aquilegia coerulea*).

Of the dozen or more native buttercup species in Texas, the most striking is the large buttercup (*Ranunculus macranthus*), found in Central Texas and other scattered locations. Its bright, waxy, yellow flowers may be up to two inches across.

All buttercups have an acrid sap that blisters tissue, and beggars reportedly used to rub themselves with the juice to produce ulcerous sores to arouse sympathy. Taken internally the juice causes gastric distress, and in his *Herbal* Nicholas Culpeper called it the "biting herb." In the language of flowers, the buttercup came to represent "ingratitude and spite." Although all parts of the plant are toxic, apparently at one time it was used as a weird stimulant. Pliny warned that eating it caused people to break into such gales of laughter they could hardly contain themselves and added that unless it was washed down with date wine the eaters might guffaw themselves to death.[2] The ancients used the plant externally to treat leprosy, plague, and insanity, and more recently people have used it to remove warts or to raise blisters (when blistering was a routine medical practice).

Hellebore and aconite, members of the buttercup family, have deservedly sinister reputations as both contain virulent poisons. According to Greek folklore aconite was created by Hecate, the queen of hell, from the froth of Cerberus, the three-headed dog that guarded the gates of the underworld. Under its common name, "wolfsbane," it is featured in werewolf tales, and Medea is supposed to have used it to poison Theseus. The juice was used to poison arrow tips and to murder people to such an extent that a law was passed in Greece prescribing the death penalty for so much as possessing it.[3] Keats's "Ode on Melancholy" mentions the "poisonous wine of wolfsbane." Today the powerful chemical aconitin is extracted from the roots for use in liniments and in medicines that affect the heart rate and the breathing center.

Poets have found use for buttercups in lighthearted and in serious verse. Edward Lear, in one of his nonsense poems for children, has a character request a feast of "eggs and buttercups fried with fish." While he was living in Italy, Robert Browning remembered the buttercups of England in April with nostalgia: "the buttercups, the little children's dower / Far brighter than this gaudy melon-flower!" And Wilfred Owen (who captured the inhumanity of World War I in his poems before he himself died in action a week before the Armistice) pictures soldiers dug into a hillside waiting for battle: "Hour after hour they ponder the warm field, / And the far valley behind, where the buttercup / Had blessed with gold their slow boots coming up."[4]

Their glossy gold petals have made buttercups the symbol of wealth. A folktale relates the story of a little boy who was determined to find the gold at the foot of the rainbow. He left his home, family, and friends and spent his life searching for the gold. He grew old and wrinkled and weary, but still he searched, paying no attention to anyone else. Then one night a beautiful woman in shining white robes appeared to him and told him he would find the gold he had spent his life looking for, but she warned him that since he had never stopped to help or care for anyone but himself, it would bring him no happiness. The next day after a gentle rain shower, a rainbow stretched across the sky. The old man followed it to the end, where he found the gold lying in a sack. Afraid that someone might ask to share it, he planned to bury it out of sight, and after dark he stole away with the treasure slung over his back, searching for a place to hide it. He did not notice when an elf slipped up behind him and cut a small hole in the bag so that one by one the pieces of yellow gold began to drop out onto the grass. Not until it had all slipped away did the old man realize that the treasure was gone. Then he flew into a fit of rage and disappeared, never to be seen again. The fairies decided to fasten stems to the gold pieces so they would not sink into the ground, and the next morning each shiny piece had become a golden buttercup.[5]

Many generations of young children have held buttercups under the chins of playmates to see if there is a yellow reflection indicating a love of butter. And older children hold buttercups under the chin of someone of the opposite sex to see if there is a glow indicating that he or she is "sweet on you." Happily, even on cloudy days there is always such a gleam from the waxy, golden petals of the buttercup.

Clover

Legume Family (*Leguminosae*)
Common Names: Shamrock, Trefoil, Beebread,
Cowgrass, Sweet Clover, Crimson Clover

In 1884 Emily Dickinson wrote: "The Pedigree of Honey / Does not concern the Bee / A Clover, anytime, to him is Aristocracy."[1] The elevation of common clover to celebrity status goes back, however, much further than the late nineteenth century. In ancient times Hope was represented as a child standing on tiptoe, holding out clover blossoms. Greeks used clover for garlands and decorations in their temples, and both Greeks and Romans cultivated red clover as an economically valuable plant. In England the leaves were worn as a charm against witches and evil, and in Ireland a species of clover known as the shamrock became the national emblem.

Long before St. Patrick arrived in the Emerald Isle to teach Christianity, the shamrock was a druidic mystical symbol associated with the sun wheel. Regarded as a sacred plant, second only in veneration to the mistletoe, according to tradition it was instrumental in persuading the Irish people to accept the Christian faith: As St. Patrick labored during the early days of his mission to explain the doctrine of the trinity to a clan of dubious natives, he had little success. Then one day a chieftain demanded, "How can there be three in one?" and St. Patrick, noticing the shamrocks growing at his feet, plucked one leaf and held it up. Using this old lucky symbol of the sacred sun wheel, he illustrated how three persons in the Godhead can exist and yet be one. The illustration was so simple and so forceful that the entire clan followed its leaders in accepting Christianity.

Through the years other religious interpretations attached to the plant. Early Christians fancied that the stem represented the path of life, the right-hand leaf Purgatory, the left-hand Hades, and the center Heaven. Another interpretation was that the three-part leaf represented faith, hope, and love. The stylized clover became a feature of ecclesiastical architecture in both interior and exterior decorations.[2]

In folklore the clover is associated with fairies: a four-leaf clover springs up wherever a fairy foot touches the ground, and whoever finds one is taken under the protection of the fairy folk and allowed to converse with them. The finder is also assured of good luck in love, fortune, and health as the ancient rhyme says:

> One leaf for fame,
> And one for wealth,
> One for a faithful lover,
> And one to bring you glorious health,
> Are in a four-leaf clover.

In dream lore to dream of a clover field meant good health and prosperity, and for a single person foretold a happy marriage. The plant was also used as a love charm: a man put a clover under his pillow to dream of his loved one, and a young woman secretly slipped a clover sprig into the shoe of her lover before he set out on a journey to ensure he would remain faithful to her.

The word clover comes from the Anglo-Saxon word for club, and the scientific name *Trifolium* comes from *tres* (three) and *folium* (leaf). The clover is supposedly the origin of the club (known as *trefle* in France) design for one of the suits in a deck of playing cards.

Although lawn owners might scoff, clover, which grows in some of its three hundred species in almost every part of the world, has been a beneficial plant to man and beast. Not only does it provide fine pasturage and superior fodder, but it also enriches the ground where it grows by adding about fifty to 150 pounds of nitrogen per acre to the soil and by increasing the availability of other nutritive elements for succeeding crops. At least fifty species of birds and mammals, including grouse, prairie chicken, quail, marmots, and woodchucks feed on clover. Many varieties of clover provide a fine-quality honey. Bumblebees and butterflies are the chief pollinators, as only they among the insects have tongues long enough to suck out the sweet nectar from the tiny tubular florets that make up the globular flowerheads. Children, too, enjoy sucking the sweet liquid, and a child who has not spent lazy hours creating long clover chains has missed one of the pleasant rites of spring.

Medicinal uses of clover go back many centuries. Ancient Egyptians made a tea from sweet clover to treat intestinal worms and earache. Anglo-Saxons in England as well as Native Americans used clover plants to make salves and poultices for treating burns, eye problems, and wounds and sores. Its demulcent action, which loosens coughs and lessens difficult breathing, made it popular with early settlers, who made a syrup from clover to treat bronchitis, asthma, and whooping cough.[3]

These pioneers gathered clover in full bloom in the summer, dried it in the shade, and stored it in a dry place to be used for making hot tea throughout the winter. Native Americans anticipated a late spring treat of boiled clover buds, and they ate the leaves as a vegetable. Pioneers learned to make a pleasing vinegar from clover blooms, and Irish immigrants brought along the tradition of adding a tablespoon of dried clover blossoms to a loaf of bread.[4] Clover was also used in its native Europe to flavor snuff and pipe tobacco.

Vermont, one of the first states to adopt a floral emblem, chose red clover in 1894. Over 150 years ago, crimson clover (*Trifolium incarnatum*) was introduced into East Texas to replenish nutrients in fields that had been depleted by overplanting in cotton. Today the Texas Department of Transportation uses it, especially in East Texas, in its roadside beautification program and for erosion control.

In addition to eleven species of *Trifolium*, Texas has three kinds of sweet clover or *Melilotus* (honey lotus). These tall bushy plants resemble their relative alfalfa more than common clover. They are notable for their fragrance which is like that of sweet, newly-mown hay and for the delicious mild, light-colored honey that bees manufacture from them. They are also important as cover crops as they enrich the soil with nitrogen and are useful as hay or forage. White sweet clover (*M. albus*) grows from one to four feet high with racemes up to six inches long bearing numerous small white flowers. Yellow sweet clover (*M. officinalis*) frequently grows in the same area. Its crushed leaves have a vanilla fragrance and are often used in making sachets; they have also been used as a flavoring. Sour clover or Indian clover (*M. indicus*) is very similar to yellow clover in appearance except for having smaller flowers. The new leaves may be used in salads.[5]

In the language of flowers, red clover represented industry, white clover meant "think of me," and a four-leaf clover begged "be mine."[6] Even before that code was devised, the expression "to live (or be) in clover" meant to live luxuriously. It apparently came from the fact that clover is obviously highly palatable as well as nourishing to livestock, and to be in the middle of a field of clover must be a pleasing situation for the animals.

Many writers in old England and in New England sang the praises of clover. Shakespeare (who called it "honey stalks"), Burns, and Tennyson all paid it tribute as did Emerson and Thoreau. John Burroughs wrote, "There is nothing else like that smell of clover. It is the maidenly breath of summer; it suggests all fresh, buxom, rural things."[7] It seems appropriate, however, to let the Irish have the last word in praise of their national emblem by way of James Whitcomb Riley's "The Clover":

> *And so I love clover—it seems like a part*
> *Of the sacredest sorrows and joys of my hart;*
> *And wherever it blossoms; oh, thare let me bow*
> *And thank the good God as I'm thankin' Him now;*
> *And I pray to Him still fer the stren'th when I die*
> *To go out in the clover and tell it good-by,*
> *And lovin'ly nestle my face in its bloom*
> *While my soul slips away on a breth of purfume.*

Coral Bead

Moonseed Family (*Menispermaceae*)

*Common Names: Margil Vine, Snailseed,
Coral Vine, Moonseed*

The decorative vine known as coral bead or moonseed (*Cocculus carolinus*) can be found in East and Central Texas climbing over fences and small trees and trailing in vacant lots and backyards as well as in fields and pastures. The minute, creamy white or greenish yellow flowers are followed by brilliant clusters of scarlet fruit about a quarter of an inch in diameter. The leaves vary from heart-shaped to round to distinctly three-lobed.

Moonseed refers to the crescent shape of the seeds of the fleshy red berries. Ellen Schulz says the berries of *Cocculus carolinus* are edible, but Delena Tull warns that the foliage and berries may be toxic. The Chinese have proved that the berries of the Indian moonseed are potent by using their acrid poison to catch fish, which it temporarily intoxicates or stuns.[1]

Another family member, *Menispermum canadense*, Texas sarsaparilla, does have poisonous berries. Blue black in color, they are easily mistaken for wild grapes and have caused accidental deaths. The root, however, is the source of a tea recommended by modern herbalists as a tonic, diuretic, and laxative, and the plant was listed in *The Pharmacopoeia of the United States of America* at the turn of the century.[2]

Texans in the San Antonio area call coral bead "Margil vine" after the venerable Fray Antonio Margil, first *padre presidente* of the Texas missions. A man of great ability, he was renowned as an orator and chosen to serve as the president of three colleges in Mexico. He is buried in the National Cathedral in Mexico City. An enduring legend illustrates his humanity and connects him with the coral bead.

In 1719 at Christmas time at the Missión San Antonio de Valero, now known as the Alamo, Fray Antonio Margil (who established the mission) wanted to impress the converts with the meaning of the season. The missionaries set up a realistic nativity scene, using native mosses and foliage, and invited the native children to bring gifts for the Christ child in the manger. Some brought strings of beads and animal claws, bright birds' feathers, colorful bits of cloth, furs of small animals, and painted horns of buffalo.

But one small boy, Shavano, whose family was very poor, had nothing to give to the infant. Finding Shavano crying bitterly, Father Margil comforted him and went with him in search of a gift. Finally they found a little vine with green berries and leaves, which they dug up and planted in a clay pot. Although Shavano was not satisfied with his spindly offering, he presented it, asking the Christ child to accept it and make it beautiful. The next morning, the story goes, Shavano heard people crying *"Milagro! Milagro!"* (Miracle! Miracle!). Hurrying to the manger scene, he found that the vine had grown and twined itself around the crib. Its leaves had become a glistening dark green, and the berries had turned bright red, making it the most beautiful of all the gifts around the Christ child.[3]

The vine, with its scarlet berries and bright green leaves, still grows wild around San Antonio. And the natives still call it the Margil vine in honor of Padre Margil, who witnessed the miracle of that early Christmas at the Alamo.

Daisy

Composite Family
(*Compositae/Asteraceae*)

Common Names: Marguerite, Whiteweed, Gowan,
Moon Flower, Oxeye Daisy, Fleabane Daisy

In the language of flowers, the daisy can mean both deceit and innocence. Two origin myths may account for these contradictory messages.
According to a Roman myth, the daisy (*Bellis perennis*) originated with
the nymph Belides, a dryad. While dancing one day with other nymphs,
she attracted the attention of Vertumnus, the deity of the orchards, and
to escape his pursuit, she transformed herself into the flower *Bellis*—clearly
a case of dissembling. On the other hand, a Celtic origin myth tells of the
grief of Malvina, whose infant son was taken from her. The maidens of
the court of the King of Morven came to her and told her they had seen
her beautiful child looking radiantly happy as he floated above the fields,
dropping on them a new flower with a golden disk, which was surrounded
by silver leaves like the rays of the sun. As the blossoms stirred in the breeze,
they looked like infants playing in the green grass—the very essence of
innocence.

Shakespeare, who seems to have known the meaning of everything,
uses the daisy to represent both these meanings in Hamlet. In the mad
scene in which Ophelia hands Queen Gertrude a daisy, it seems to signify
that her fickle love cannot expect constancy from her deceitful husband,
but when Ophelia weaves daisies into the garlands of flowers she drapes

around herself before drowning, they appear to symbolize her innocence.

The name *daisy* comes from two old Anglo-Saxon words, *daeges* and *eage*, which mean "day's eye" or "eye of the day," referring to the flower's habit of closing in the evening and opening in the morning. In France it is known as the "Marguerite," or pearl, after Margaret of Anjou, unhappy wife of Henry VI, who chose the daisy as her flower emblem when she was young. A happier Margaret, sister of the French king Francis I, also loved the daisy, and the people of her country wore it in her honor. Her brother, Francis I, who was very fond of his sister, liked to call her "the Marguerite of Marguerites."[1]

In Italy in 1868, when Prince Humbert, first king of United Italy, took Margaret to be his wife, celebrants wore wreaths and bouquets of daisies to honor their new queen. Victor Emmanuel's wedding present to his daughter-in-law was a necklace of gold and pearls set to look like daisies.[2]

The daisy is the quintessential English flower, and Britain's best poets have been charmed by this most common of common flowers. It was Chaucer's favorite flower. In his *Legends of Good Women* he tells of Alceste, who saved her husband's life by sacrificing her own and was changed into a daisy because of her goodness, with each petal representing one of her virtues. In *Queen Mab* Percy Bysshe Shelley speaks of the "daisy-spangled lawn." And in "To a Daisy," Wordsworth calls it a "chearful" flower that we come upon "like a pleasant thought."

Often the poets use the beauty of the daisy to soften the harshness of death. In *Cymbeline* Shakespeare has the Roman general Lucius give instructions for burying a fallen soldier: "let us find out the prettiest daisied plot we can, and make him with our pikes and partisans a grave . . ."[3] Keats, anticipating his early death from tuberculosis, told his friend Joseph Severn: "I shall soon be laid in the quiet grave . . . the daisies growing over me . . . O for this quiet . . . it will be my first."[4]

After inadvertently crushing a daisy with his plow, Robert Burns wrote a poem, "To a Mountain Daisy," in which he compared his own destiny to that of the luckless flower, lamenting that his own bloom would be crushed by "stern ruin's ploughshare."

In all of western literature, only the rose has been used as a symbolic flower more often than the daisy. Dante, Ben Jonson, Dryden, Goethe, and Schiller have all made use of it. Many writers have used it in simile and metaphor to show admiration. After Frederick Marryat coined the phrase "fresh as a daisy" (in *Peter Simple*, 1834), it quickly became a cliché.

In the nineteenth century Daisy was common as a girl's name, and the song "Daisy Bell" ("Daisy, Daisy, give me your answer do! I'm half crazy, all for the love of you!") became popular as soon as it appeared at the end of the century.

The ubiquitous flower even made its way into sports terminology. A "daisy cutter" became a name for a horse that lifts its feet only slightly above the ground while trotting. And in tennis it means a serve that fails to rise properly, while in baseball or cricket it indicates a ball bowled or batted so as to skim the surface of the ground.

The daisy has been exalted in religious literature and history. According to a Christian legend, Mary's tears on the flight to Egypt became the first daisies. Dante, in a vision of Paradise, saw it as one of the flowers of the blessed, with its face turned toward God. It is the flower of St. Margaret of the Dragon, whose day of remembrance is June 20. And it is recorded that when St. Augustine came to England and saw a field covered with daisies, he fell on his knees, exclaiming, "Behold! A hundred pearls, so will the spirits of the blest shine in heaven." He also used a daisy chain in a sermon to illustrate the strength in unity of Christians and the purity and goodness reflected from heaven on them.[5]

In some European countries daisies were dedicated to John the Baptist and called St. John's Day flower. In countries along the Rhine River they were hung indoors, as the yellow centers were thought to have the power to ward off thunder and lightning. In Germany the daisy is called *tausendschon,* "one thousand times beautiful."[6]

The oxeye daisy (*Chrysanthemum leucanthemum*) immigrated along with early settlers from Europe to North America, where it took over crop fields to the dismay of farmers, who called it whiteweed. Many of today's chrysanthemum varieties have been developed from it. In Texas the oxeye daisy grows wild only in the northeastern corner. This is the "loves-me, loves-me-not" daisy of folklore. The odds of the fortune seeker receiving a favorable answer are good because over 90 percent of the flowers of the oxeye daisy have an uneven number of petals. To go a step further, the would-be bride might pick another daisy, reciting "this year, next year, sometime, never" to discover when the wedding will be. Again, because of the likelihood of an uneven number of petals, the odds are in her favor. And finally, the betrothed can squeeze the yellow center of a daisy into the palm of her hand and toss it into the air; catching the falling grains on the back of her hand, she counts the number to learn how many children she will have.

Three of the daisies found in Texas are named after early botanists in the state—Engelmann, Lindheimer, and Berlandier. Engelmann's daisy is widespread, and its rough hairy stems topped by bright yellow flower clusters are common on vacant lots and prairies and along roadside ditches. Texas A&M University has released "El Dorado," an Engelmann cultivar especially adapted for Texas and Oklahoma.[7] This plant is also known as cut-leaved daisy because of the deeply cleft lower leaves. Lindheimer's daisy is commonly called Texas yellow star because the yellow flower heads have five ray flowers, corresponding to the five points of the Lone Star emblem of Texas. Found in open grassy areas, it is one of our most common early composites. Berlandier's daisy is found in several varieties in different parts of the state. Because the yellow ray flowers surround a center of disk flowers that have a green appearance, the plant is often referred to as Texas green-eyes.

The yellow sleepy daisy and the white lazy daisy are other popular

Texas daisies, although as their names indicate, they prefer not to open up to greet the day until it is nearly half over. The lazy daisy, with its crisp white face, is like a smaller version of the oxeye daisy.

The hardy blackfoot daisy (*Melampodium leucanthum*) is becoming increasingly popular. It is exceptionally drought resistant, sprouting out of caliche and rocky cracks like refreshing bouquets in the summer heat. Under each white ray flower is a foot-shaped bract that turns dark when it matures. The blackfoot daisy's preference for rocky places gives it another common name: rock daisy.

The attractive fleabane (*Erigeron*), which is often called a daisy, may be white, pale pink, or pale lavender. Its single, leafy stem branches mostly in the upper half. At the end of each stem is a flower head bearing 150 to four hundred threadlike rays that form a delicate fringe around the conspicuous yellow disk center. The name fleabane comes from the insecticidal properties of some species of the genus. Native Americans applied the crushed blooms to dogs to chase away fleas, and settlers hung in it in their country homes to keep out insects. Philadelphia fleabane traditionally was dried and crushed to make a tea to ease sore throats and stomach ailments.[8]

Fleabanes as well as daisies have long been used to make poultices to apply to swellings and bruises. In fact, crushed daisy leaves were such a popular remedy for bruises in Europe and among early American settlers that the plants were sometimes called bruisewort.[9] In addition to bruises and swellings, daisies were used in a variety of medicines intended to cure eye ailments, warts, insanity, small pox, tumors, jaundice, and boils and to relieve symptoms of headache, gout, whooping cough, asthma, and night sweats. The oxeye daisy in particular has been used as an antispasmodic, a diuretic, and tonic.

Europeans and Native Americans ate the roots of daisies as potherbs and used the tender leaves in salads. Engelmann's daisy has been used to obtain a yellow dye.

Daisies had a part in chivalry: knights stuck daisies in their scarves before taking part in tournaments, while the privileged women wore daisy wreaths upon their brows.

Since the late 1880s Vassar College has carried on a tradition in which selected sophomores carrying a daisy chain escort the graduating seniors. Originally the chains were made by the sophomore girls of daisies growing in the fields surrounding the school. Six solid inches in diameter, the chains might be 200 feet in length and were quite heavy. Wearing identical white dresses and daisy wreaths in their hair, the chosen students bore at least twenty pounds of weight on their shoulders each. After a series of protests, the selection of the bearers of the daisy chain became less of a beauty contest, and the chosen sophomores were required to be in good academic standing and to have made contributions to college life as well as to be attractive. Since 1971 men, wearing blazers and white trousers, have been included in the daisy chain ceremony. The chain itself is now made by florists.

An old English saying is that spring has not come until you can set your foot on twelve daisies. Traditionally an unmarried English woman put daisy roots under her pillow so she would dream of her lover. In dream lore, to dream of daisies in spring or summer is a sign of good luck, but to dream of them in fall is a bad omen.

No matter what the imaginary or practical uses of the daisy, its best virtue has always been to bring visual pleasure and to remind us that the earth is renewing itself again. Of all the tributes paid to its tribe, no one has expressed the spiritual uplift of its commonplace beauty better than Chaucer:

The Daisy

Of all the floures in the mede
Than love I most these floures white and rede
Soch that men callen Daisies in our town.
To Hem I have so great affection
As I sayd erst, when comen is the Maie,
That in my bedde there draweth me no daie,
That I n'am up and walking in the mede
To see this floure ayenst the Sunne sprede;
When it up riseth early by the morrow,
That blissful sight softeneth all my sorrow.

Dandelion

Sunflower Family (*Asteraceae*)

Common Names: Blowball, Puffball, Texas Dandelion, False Dandelion, Priest's Crown, Swine's Snout

The bright blossoms of the common dandelion (*Taraxacum officinale*) and the Texas or false dandelion (*Pyrrhopappus multicaulis*) appear at almost any time of the year in almost all parts of Texas. Usually they are the first wildflowers recognized by Texas children, who soon learn to make use of them in their play. The hollow stems make fine bubble blowers; the stems can also be split and joined to make flower chains; and when the flowers go to seed, they become puffballs to blow away with a breath of air. If all the little seed heads fly away on their parachutes with one puff, a wish will be granted. Or the number of seeds left on the stem can be used to make predictions: "How many years until I marry?" "How many children will I have?" or any other number-type question the puffer chooses. Also the number of puffs necessary to blow away all the seeds may be manipulated to tell the time of day.

When the child grows up and becomes a lawn owner, a dramatic attitude change occurs: the plaything becomes a pesky weed, a despised enemy against which an unending war must be waged. It's a losing battle because the clever plant has a bagful of survival tricks. Even if children do not scatter them far and wide, the tiny parachute seed heads are easily disseminated by the wind. The roots are almost indestructible and exceedingly deep and can themselves produce new plants. Like the "golden tramp" it is sometimes called, the ubiquitous dandelion adapts easily to various habitats. On lawns, in pastures and fields, and along roadsides, the dandelion makes itself at home, seeming not to care whether conditions are wet or dry. Promiscuously it welcomes the attention of butterflies, bees, flies, wasps, and beetles, and if they fail to pollinate every floret, the neglected floret is capable of reaching backward with its styles to pollinate itself.

The common name *dandelion* is a corruption of the French *dent-de-lion* (lion's teeth) and comes from the fancied resemblance of the jagged leaves to the canine teeth of a lion. The nickname "swine's snout" comes from the appearance of the mature head when all the florets close up within the sheath of green bracts before opening to become the gossamer ball that gives it the nickname "blowball."

Finally, when all the seeds have been blown away, all that remains is a speckled disk like a medieval priest's shorn head, giving it the nickname "priest's crown." Because of the well-known diuretic effect of an extract of its roots, the French called it *pissenlit,* which the English translated as "piss-a-bed." The botanical name *Taraxacum officinale* derives from the Greek words for "disorder" and "remedy," and *officinale* indicates that it was an herb sold by apothecaries. Until recently the United States and British pharmacopoeias listed the dandelion as a medicinal plant.

It may be difficult for lawn owners to imagine, but European settlers carefully packed dandelion seeds to bring to the New World because they valued the plant both as medicine and as food. The virtues of the dandelion have long been recognized and recorded. Some biblical researchers believe that the "bitter herbs" mentioned in Exodus 12:8 ("And they shall eat the flesh in that night, roast with fire, and unleavened bread; and with *bitter herbs* they shall eat it.") and Numbers 9:11 (" . . . eat it with unleavened bread and *bitter herbs*") were leaves of plants like chicory, endive, and dandelion—eaten as a salad.[1] A tenth-century Arabian physician mentions the use of dandelions as medicine, and in addition to using the root extract as a diuretic, the Chinese used it as an antibacterial and antifungal agent.

Seventeenth-century English herbalist Nicholas Culpeper recommended dandelions as "very effectual" in treating obstructions of the liver, gall, and spleen as well as for other "evil dispositions of the body" and concluded that "Great are the virtues of this common herb."[2]

Other early European herbalists recommended dandelion juice as a tonic or laxative and also as a remedy for skin diseases such as impetigo and the itch. A persistent folklore belief is that rheumatism can be prevented by drinking a cup of dandelion tea morning and night. In her *Modern Herbal* (1931), Maud Grieve gives dandelion prescriptions for treating liver and kidney ailments, hemorrhoids, and gall stones, among other problems.[3]

The Dutch brought along to America the idea that eating dandelion salad on Maundy Thursday kept one healthy all year long. Native Americans appreciated the dandelion, using it to make a tea for heartburn and as a general tonic. Today scientists are studying the plants as a source of lecithin, which may help prevent cirrhosis.[4]

Dandelion roots, leaves, and blossoms are all useful as food. Delena Tull says, "They outrank just about any garden vegetable in nutrition." The leaves are rich in vitamins, especially A, and the flowers contain beta-carotene and ascorbic acid. In research initiated by Euell Gibbons, scientists discovered that dandelions are excellent sources of iron, calcium, phosphorus, and potassium.[5] The English make dandelion sandwiches out of the young leaves, and for centuries Europeans have used them in spring salads. They do become more bitter as they age, but even then they can be parboiled (changing the water once or twice) to use as potherbs and in soups. The French not only cultivate the plant to use as a vegetable but also revere it as a symbol of wisdom.

Midwestern bee keepers used to sow large quantities of dandelion seed as a source of honey as it is a favorite bee food and has a long growing season. Small birds also like the seeds. During the Great Depression and again during shortages of coffee in World War II, dandelion roots were roasted and ground to make a palatable substitute, said to taste somewhat like chicory coffee.

Probably the best known use of dandelions is in making a delicious golden wine, a use immortalized by Ray Bradbury in the title of his story "Dandelion Wine" (1957). The wine, made from the fermented blossoms, tastes like a slightly flat sherry and has the reputation of being an excellent tonic, especially good for the blood.[6]

Scots are said to have made a magenta dye from the plant for their tartans. In America, however, experiments have shown that the plants grown here yield only a yellow dye.[7]

Texas lawn owners may consider their state number one in dandelion production, but Vineland, New Jersey, which produces dandelions commercially, is known as the "dandelion growing capital of the United States." Much of its produce is sold to ethnic markets in New York City.

There are several Native American legends concerning dandelions. One of the most charming is this Algonquin tale: Shawondesee, the fat, lazy South Wind, resting in the shade of a tree, saw a beautiful golden-haired young girl in a nearby meadow. Although he admired her very much, he was too indolent to pursue her. Day after day he idly watched her from a distance. One day he looked out across the meadow and saw in the place where the maiden had been an old woman with fuzzy white hair. He heaved a big sigh of disappointment and was astonished to see her white hair fly away. From her hairs each spring other golden-haired maidens appear, but they too grow old and white-headed. And the South Wind still fervently sighs for his lost love and sends their white locks flying.[8]

In books on the language of flowers, dandelions are called "oracles of time and love" because of the superstitions connected with the game of blowing away the seed heads. Their symbolic message is "faithful to you." Texas gardeners would have to agree, but perhaps instead of fighting nature they should learn to emulate Opus, the comic strip penguin who goes and sits among the flowers, taking "a dandelion break" when life becomes stressful.

Some of America's most famous writers have paid their respects to the common dandelion. Henry Ward Beecher called them "Golden kisses all over the cheeks of the meadow." Thoreau said they were the gold he had on deposit in country banks on which he could draw interest in the shape of health and enjoyment. Walt Whitman described the dandelion's trustful face: "innocent, golden, calm as the dawn."[9] And in "Ode to a Dandelion," James Russell Lowell wrote:

> *My childhood's earliest thoughts are linked with thee*
> *Dear common flower, that grow'st beside the way,*
> *Fringing the dusty road with harmless gold.*

Dogwood

Dogwood Family (*Cornaceae*)

Common Names: Flowering Dogwood,
Virginia Dogwood, Rough-leaf Dogwood, Tupelo,
Sour-Gum, Black-gum, Silk-tassel

Native to North America, dogwood is found from Maine to Florida and west to Texas, usually as shrubs or small understory trees but sometimes reaching almost forty feet. When the lovely white or pinkish blossoms of the flowering dogwood appear in the spring before or just as the leaves begin to show, thousands of visitors come to East Texas to follow dogwood trails. The showy blooms are not made of petals but are four enlarged, notched bracts, and the real flowers are the small clusters in their centers that look like the French knots used in embroidery. Dogwood is also attractive in the fall when brilliant red fruit almost half an inch long appears in clusters and the leaves turn red to match the fruit.

Cornaceae is a small family of shrubs and trees known mainly for the dogwoods, or *cornus*, which comes from the Latin *cornu* (horned), referring to the hardness of the wood. In England and some other countries, they are called cornel trees, and *cornel* is related to *crenel*, meaning having a notched or indented edge. The English also call them "dagwood" (perhaps from the Old English *dagge*, from which "dagger" derived) and "skewerwood" because butchers used the wood for meat skewers. Another theory is that they are called dogwood because the English used a decoction of the species *C. sanguinea* to wash mangy dogs.

Cornel trees were said to have grown in Apollo's sacred grove on

Greece's Mount Ida, and according to myth Apollo became terribly angry when the Greeks cut down the trees for wood to build the Trojan horse; consequently, in an effort to appease Apollo, an annual festival was instituted in his honor in Greece. Cornel wood was used by the ancients in making the handles of spears and lances, and another myth says that when Romulus wished to enlarge the boundaries of Rome, he hurled his spear, and where it struck the ground on Palatine Hill, the handle grew into a cornel tree—an event foreshadowing the strength of the Roman state.[1]

In addition to handles for weapons and tools, many other uses are recorded for the hard, heavy, fine-grained wood of the dogwood. These include furniture, arrows, dowels, backs for brushes, mallets, wedges, golf club heads, knitting needles, and especially bobbins and shuttle blocks used in weaving. In the early twentieth century, it was the wood of choice for this purpose as it grows smooth with use, and approximately four million shuttle blocks were made from dogwood in 1926.[2] In the language of flowers, the dogwood was designated to represent durability, an appropriate recognition of its lasting quality.

In 1729 explorer William Byrd reported that he had used dogwood bark with "good success" to cure a malaria outbreak among members of his boundary survey party. Long before these Westerners appeared, Native Americans had been making good use of an extract of dogwood as a tea to promote sweating in order to break fevers. They also used the plant to treat chronic diarrhea and to relieve sore and aching muscles. Colonists steeped the flowers, fruit, and bark in warm water to make a decoction to treat intermittent fevers, and during the Civil War when Southern ports were blockaded and Cinchona bark, the source of quinine, was not obtainable for treating malaria, dogwood bark tea was used as a substitute.[3]

Both the natives and pioneers in America used the twigs of the dogwood as "chewing sticks," forerunners of toothbrushes, and it is reported that they were effective in whitening the teeth and hardening the gums. Flowering dogwood (*C. florida*) was listed as an official medicine in *The Pharmacopoeia of the United States of America* (1820–94) and in the *National Formulary* (1916–36).[4]

When ink was in great demand, the inner bark of the dogwood was used to make black ink. Native Americans gathered the roots of dogwood and extracted the red sap to use as a dye. Delena Tull says that a rusty

brown dye may be made from the root, bark, or prunings and a bright yellow dye from the leaves and twigs.[5]

Whatever its practical uses, the flowering dogwood's chief value is as an exceptionally beautiful ornamental. Two famous Virginians appreciated its beauty: George Washington had a "circle of dogwoods" planted in his south garden, and Thomas Jefferson planted dogwoods at Monticello as early as 1771. When selecting their official state flower, Virginians were torn between the famous Virginia creeper and the flowering dogwood, but when the final vote was taken in March of 1918, the dogwood won by a single vote. North Carolinians, who for many years regarded the daisy as their unofficial state flower, also made the flowering dogwood their official choice in 1941.[6]

In Texas, in addition to the well-known flowering dogwood (*Cornus florida*), we have three other *Cornus* species, including the rough-leaf dogwood (*C. drummondii*), a twiggy shrub or low, round-headed tree with somewhat malodorous true white flowers that are massed in clusters. According to the National Wildflower Center, at least forty types of birds dine on the small white drupe, or globular fruit, of the rough-leaf dogwood, including bobwhite quail, wild turkey, and prairie chicken.

The *Nyssa,* tupelos, sour-gums, or black-gums, are large trees found in the woodlands of East Texas, where birds enjoy their rather bitter berries. And the silk-tassel (*Garrya*) are shrubs or small trees with flowers hanging in tassels found on the Edwards Plateau and in the Trans-Pecos, where the plants are browsed by deer and the purplish fruits eaten by numerous birds.

There is a legend to explain why the bracts of the flowering dogwood are notched: Because the dogwood was Adam's favorite tree in the Garden of Eden, naturally the devil hated it and wanted to blight it. One dark night he climbed a honey locust tree and swung by his tail over the wall of the garden, intent on tearing off all the lovely blossoms. But he was shocked to find that because every flower was in the shape of a cross, it was beyond his powers to pull them off. In a rage and wanting to do the worst he could, he bit a piece out of the edge of each snowy leaf and then jumped back over the wall and climbed down the honey locust tree. Ashamed that she had helped the Devil, the locust grew a bristling necklace of strong spikes to wear so no one would ever be able to climb her again. It was, however, too late to save the dogwood bloom from harm, and the bites never healed, as can be seen to this day.[7] As a matter of fact, the bracts start out as dark purplish bud covers. In early spring they break away at the tips and begin to grow, turning green and then white or pink, and the small brown notch on each bract indicates where it was originally attached on the bud.

Although dogwood was unknown in biblical lands in the days of Christ, a widespread belief grew up that it was the tree of which the cross on Calvary was made. According to another legend, in those days the dogwood was as large and strong as the oak until Jesus, sensing its sorrow at being used for such a cruel purpose, promised that it would never again grow large enough to be used for a cross. And since then it has had a slender trunk, bent and twisted, and blossoms in the form of a cross, with a crown of thorns in the center of each flower and on the outer edge of each petal nail prints brown with rust and stained red.[8]

Foxglove/ Penstemon

Figwort Family (*Scrophulariaceae*)

Common Names: Beardtongue,
Fairy Thimbles, Dew Flowers

A bewildering number of different penstemon grow wild in North America, and they are especially abundant in the Rocky Mountain area. Texas has its share of these beauties with over twenty species. The most famous member of this useful and ornamental family is foxglove (*Digitalis*), often grown in gardens as a stunning ornamental, with large tubular blossoms in shades of lavender purple, yellow, white, or pink on tall spikes. Even if its medicinal value had never been discovered, *Digitalis purpurea* would no doubt have been cultivated for the beauty of the large, bell-like mauve pink flowers with dark, pink spots interlining the throat. Although the juice of foxglove leaves was used in ancient Greece and Rome to ease the pain of sprains and bruises, and the leaves were crushed and bound to wounds as poultices by early herbalists, it wasn't until late in the eighteenth century that its value as a source of digitalis—a vital medicine for treating heart disease—became known to European physicians.

Two women—one young and the other very old—deserve credit for making possible its discovery by a young English physician named William Withering. He began to collect herbal plants for a young woman patient whom he later married, and they settled in Shropshire, where their interest in plants continued. Here Withering learned of an old herbal woman who had a secret cure for dropsy caused by heart disease. Obtaining her mixture of herbs, he recognized foxglove as the important ingredient and began to study its use in treating the edema of congestive heart failure. After ten years of experimentation, he standardized procedures for gathering, preparing, and administering digitalis. In 1785 he published his findings in a paper that became a classic in medical literature: "An Account of the Foxglove and Some of its Medical Uses." By 1834 European doctors were prescribing digitalis to strengthen and regulate the heart. Today *D. purpurea,* grown on herb farms in the United States, is the basic source of digitalis, a valuable cardiac glycoside used to stimulate heart muscle contractions and to slow the rate of heartbeat.[1]

The Shoshone called the American variety of foxglove "bad disease medicine," and hundreds of years before Withering's discovery, native North Americans were using it correctly as a cardiac stimulant.[2] Writers have made use of Withering's findings. For example, in *Silas Marner* George Eliot tells us that Marner learned the use of common herbs from his mother, and after he prescribes a simple preparation of foxglove for the cobbler's wife who has dropsy, he is hounded by the villagers to cure all kinds of ailments.

It should be noted, however, that although foxglove is among the most important of medicinal plants, it is also among the most dangerous if used without proper professional supervision. A leaf chewed and swallowed may cause sudden heart failure or paralysis, and children have been poisoned by drinking water from a vase that held foxglove plants.[3]

The genus name *penstemon* indicates a flower having five stamens, and it is characteristic of the penstemons to have four regular stamens and a fifth broader stamen lacking an anther and covered with fine fuzzy yellow hairs. From this hairy or "bearded" stamen comes the common name beardtongue. Another characteristic is a line or arrangement of dots that lead visiting insects to the honey trove. Growing throughout most of the state, our best-known penstemon, wild foxglove (*P. cobaea*), is a tall perennial with lined lavender flowers. Often found in colonies, it is also called dewflower, perhaps named by children who discovered that drops of nectar can be sucked from the corolla tubes early in the morning. Cows are also fond of this herb. Early settlers called it balmony and brewed a laxative tea from its leaves. Virginia Scully mentions a number of other medicinal uses for penstemon discovered by Indian medicine men and taught to the newcomers, including a tea of boiled white penstemon for childhood stomachs, poultices for treating skin ailments, a distillation of mashed leaves for use as an eyewash, and a syrup made of dry or fresh flowers sweetened with honey for whooping cough.[4]

There are several showy red penstemon in Texas, including the Harvard penstemon in West Texas and the scarlet penstemon in East Texas. Also attractive is the Hill Country penstemon with its long cherry-red blossoms. Another favorite is the pink plains penstemon, which has long, dark pink to white blooms and forms large mounds in sandy soils in the western part of the state.

Other notable members of the figwort family found in Texas include toadflax, wild snapdragon, and cenizo as well as Indian paintbrush and mullein, which are discussed in separate chapters. Toadflax is a pretty, delicate, fragrant blue flower that doesn't deserve its nickname, which Ellen Schulz suggests came about because some of the early settlers thought it was real flax and, upon discovering it was not, expressed their disgust by giving it the ugliest name they could think of.[5] Another explanation is that the open flower supposedly resembles a toad's mouth.

Climbing snapdragon is a delicate vine that climbs over fences and also on shrubs, making them appear to have lavender blooms. Sometimes called monkey flower, it is widespread and especially attractive in the summer and fall on islands along the Gulf Coast.

There are at least three wild species of cenizo (commonly called purple sage, Texas silver-leaf, Texas ranger, and senisa) in Texas. The genus name *Leucophyllum* means white leaf, and the plant's silvery gray leaves, which are covered with a dense layer of fine hairs, give it an ashy appearance. It is known as the barometer bush because it is sensitive to moisture, and after a rain the low bushes are covered with a mass of delicate blossoms. It is not, however, a dependable weather forecaster as it may sprout flowers at any time, and ranchers sometimes call it "liar's bush." When there is widespread rainfall in west Texas, perhaps every six to ten years, the cenizo can be spectacular. Naturalist Benny Simpson tells of coming across cenizo in bloom "by untold millions across thousands of acres from the southern Rio Grande Plains, across the Trans-Pecos to Big Bend National Park" and on to El Paso. He describes seeing colors from the familiar pinkish violet to all shades of purple to shell pink to white. Early settlers used the leaves to make a tea to treat jaundice. The bushes provide cover for wildlife and nesting space for birds.[6]

In Old English "foxes-glofa" literally means foxes' gloves, and a couple of fables explain how the name came to be. One says that at one time foxes' tails were considered potent charms against the devil, and foxes were constantly hunted. Reynard, king of the foxes, appealed to the gods for help, and they gave him the belled plants to hide in the fields so that when hunters came into the fields and brushed against the bells they would ring and alert the foxes to run to safety to protect their brushes. Another fable says that the bad fairies gave the flowers to the foxes so they could muffle their footfalls and slip into chicken coops to steal the sleeping fowls.[7] Perhaps this is why in the language of flowers the foxglove came to symbolize insincerity.

In Germany, where the foxglove plant was called *fingerhut*, finger hat or thimble, the name suggested to botanist Leonhard Fuchs the specific Latin designation of *digitalis*, "pertaining to the finger," when he officially classified this genus in the 1500s. The finger-shaped blossoms have given rise to fanciful nicknames in the folklore of many countries. Some say the name was folks glove—the glove of the good folk or fairies, and the Irish called digitalis fairy thimbles or fairy fingers and believed the fairies used them as gloves and caps. The Welsh called them goblin gloves, and the French called them shepherd's gloves or Virgin's finger. In Scotland they were called dead man's bells, and if you heard them ring you were thought to be doomed. In rural England foxgloves were called poppers because when the broad end of the flower is held closed between finger and thumb and the small end blown full of air, it can be struck with the other hand to make a loud crack or pop.[8]

Poets have used the stately spires of foxglove to suit their needs. Sir Walter Scott wrote in "Lady of the Lake" (I, xii): "Fox-glove and nightshade side by side / Emblems of punishment and pride." And in "In Memoriam" Tennyson laments that spring is slow in coming and begs her to bring "the foxglove spire" to cheer him.

Gaillardia/ Indian Blanket

Composite Family
(*Compositae/Asteraceae*)

Common names: Blanket Flower, Firewheel, Sunburst, Bandana Daisy

J ust as fields of bluebonnets are a sign of spring in Texas, fields of Indian blanket or gaillardia are a signal that summer is about to begin. Like gaudy Fourth of July pinwheels, the showy red and yellow flowers spread themselves over large areas of up to forty or fifty acres in impressive displays. *Gaillardia pulchella,* the most widespread and best-known Indian blanket, grows throughout most of the state. *Pulcher* means beautiful or handsome.

Despite its French name the gaillardia is native to North America. When it was introduced into Europe from Louisiana in early colonial days, the plant was named in honor of Gaillard de Marenlonneau, an eighteenth-century French patron of botany. The common names—firewheel, sunburst, bandana daisy—are efforts to describe the vivid coloring of the plant.

Gaillardias are good performers indoors and out. Almost as drought resistant as desert plants, they thrive in poor soils. The long-lasting quality of the cut flowers make them ideal for indoor arrangements, and they are cultivated in the North and East, where they are sold in flower shops.

In addition to variations of *G. pulchella,* such as the deep red-flowered gaillardias that thrive in sandy soils, there are distinctive gaillardias in other parts of the state. In the Big Thicket, Winkler gaillardia grows with prominent yellow centers and white ray flowers that are tubular at the base and flare out into three deeply cut lobes. Farther west are fragrant gaillardia (*G. suavis*), noted for their sweet fragrance and their odd appearance. Sometimes called pincushion daisy, globe flower, or perfume ball, the naked flower stalks end in round flower heads whose fringes of ray flowers (yellow to orange or red) fall off, leaving only rayless heads on the bare stems.

The reddome blanketflower (*G. pinnatifida*), which grows in the Trans-Pecos area and up into the plains of northern Texas, has a rounded dark red dome of disk flowers and yellow ray flowers with purple veins on the underside of the lower petals. The reddome has a history of being used in folk medicine. It was believed that a tea made from the dried flowers, if drunk seven days in a row, would increase fertility. The tea was also drunk as a blood tonic and diuretic. Poultices made from the entire plant were applied to the forehead to relieve sinus headaches, and powdered flowers were inhaled to relieve other headaches.[1]

Eliza Johnston liked to paint the wildflowers of Texas and to collect their legends. In the wildflower book she made for her husband, General Albert Sidney Johnston, she tells this Mexican legend about the gaillardia:

> Originally a bright gold, the flower was a favorite of the Aztec. Young women decorated their jet black hair with crowns of the golden flowers, and young children delighted in playing among the bright blossoms. Then Cortez came, and the lovely land was drenched with the blood of the trusting inhabitants. The much-loved flower in pity caught the blood of the innocents as it fell. And to this day the red stains remain on the flower. When the tiny butterfly, which is the color of the flower, is seen flitting around it, the Mexicans say it is the spirit of the Aztec "watching in gratitude their favourite flower."[2]

Where they grow in masses, Indian blanket resemble the bright tapestries of western Native Americans. There are at least two native legends about how the flower came into being. One is told by Ellen Schulz in *Texas Wild Flowers:*

> Once the braves of a certain tribe went on the war path, leaving their wives and children at home. The wife of the greatest chief of the tribe spent long hours weaving a blanket for her warrior husband. Her little daughter loved to play in its folds, pretending she and her father were together. Into the blanket the mother wove bright hues of red and orange, each pattern a symbol of a prayer to the Great Spirit to protect her husband and bring him safely home. One day the little girl, who considered the birds and flowers and insects her playmates, chased after a butterfly and became lost in the woods. Night came on and although she searched and searched, she could not find her way out of the woods. Worn out, she lay down in a clearing and asked the Great Spirit to send her the blanket belonging to her father to keep her warm during the night. Then she fell asleep. The next morning when she opened her eyes, she found herself covered over with flowers of the same bright hues as those of her father's blanket—flowers new to the land. When her father and the other braves found her, she showed them her blanket of flowers, and the people decided to name the flowers Indian Blanket.[3]

The other Native American legend tells of an old blanket maker with such extraordinary skill that members of faraway tribes traveled many moons to trade their pottery, jewelry, and basketry for one of his beautiful blankets. But the blanket maker was getting very old and realized he had only a little time left to live. He began to weave his own burial blanket, which he intended as a gift to the Great Spirit when they should meet. Determined to make it more beautiful than any he had ever created, he wove into it intricate designs using his favorite reds, yellows, and browns. When he died, according to his instructions, his family wrapped him in the blanket. The Great Spirit was pleased with the exquisite gift but sorry the tribe could not also enjoy its beauty, so he decided to share the gift with them. And the next spring, wildflowers of the design and colors of the old man's last blanket covered his grave to bloom and spread forever.[4]

In the language of flowers, the gaillardia symbolizes bravery.

Goldenrod

Sunflower Family
(*Compositae/Asteraceae*)

*Common Names: Yellow Weed,
Farewell Summer, Woundwort*

*A*fter the Boston Tea Party, during which they had dumped the taxable British tea into Boston Harbor, rebellious American colonists found themselves without their favorite beverage. Luckily they discovered that a tasty tea could be made from the leaves of the native American goldenrod, and they dubbed it Liberty Tea.

Goldenrod is a prized garden plant in England and other European countries, but in America for a long time it suffered an undeserved bad reputation as a cause of hay fever, until it was discovered that the real villain is the inconspicuous ragweed that blooms in the same locations during the same season. In fact, the heavy, sticky pollen of goldenrod is not easily wind-borne, nor does it need to be as myriad insects happily perform the task of pollination for it.

Other folk beliefs surrounding goldenrod say that where the flower grows there is buried treasure and that whoever carries its flowers will have good fortune. It was also said that if the plant grows near a house where it has not been planted, it will bring good fortune to the inhabitants. Another belief is that goldenrod may be used as a divining rod (by the right person) to locate underground water or minerals.[1]

An old legend tells of the origin of goldenrod: An ugly old woman walking in the woods became tired and footsore. She asked the trees for a walking stick, but they all refused to help her. Finally an old broken stick humbly offered its services. Emerging from the woods, the old woman turned into a beautiful fairy, who asked the stick what it wanted most in the world. The stick replied it would like most to be loved by children everywhere. The fairy turned it into a flower and sprinkled it with gold dust, declaring it a golden rod that would always be loved by children.[2]

Since ancient times goldenrod has been used extensively as a healing herb. Its genus name *Solidago* means "to make whole." It was in use during the crusades. In his *Herball* John Gerard says of goldenrod: "It is extolled above all other herbes for the stopping of blood in bleeding wounds." Sailing vessels took huge cargoes of goldenrod to England from the American colonies to be sold in apothecary shops. In Queen Elizabeth's time herb women sold it in powdered form in the marketplace in London for up to half a crown an ounce, as it was in great demand for dressing cuts and wounds.[3]

Native North Americans found many uses for goldenrod, including treating ulcers, boils, kidney diseases, colds, rheumatism, and relieving pain and nausea. The leaves were chewed to relieve sore throats, and the roots were chewed to relieve toothache. It was also used as a pleasant-tasting disguise to cover the bitter taste of other herbal medicines. Some tribes called it "sun medicine" and used it as a component in medicinal steam baths. The pot of herbs was boiled and the patient and the pot covered with a tent of blankets until the medicine man deemed that all pain and evil spirits had left the patient's body.[4]

Modern herbals still recommend goldenrod as a carminative (to alleviate intestinal gas) and as a diaphoretic (to promote sweating) in cases of fever.[5]

More than twenty species of goldenrod grow in Texas, with many more varieties that are sometimes classified as species. The plants may be branched and feathery or slim and rodlike with innumerable tiny yellow flower heads in plumelike clusters. The lower leaves are often coarser and larger than the middle and upper ones. Although goldenrod grows best in damp places, it is a highly adaptable plant, and its height may vary from ten inches to over six feet, depending on the soil. The many common names, which are descriptive of differing characteristics, include tall goldenrod, rough goldenrod, prairie goldenrod, dwarf goldenrod, stiff goldenrod, three nerved goldenrod, and downy goldenrod.

Sweet goldenrod (*Solidago odora*), which grows in east and southeast Texas, has showy, plumelike clusters of small blossoms. The fresh green leaves and the flowers taste like licorice or anise, and a tea made from either the leaves or flowers has the same delicate aroma and taste. In the late 1700s sweet goldenrod was exported to China from the United States as a choice tea plant. A licorice-flavored jelly can be made from the fresh leaves and flowers of sweet goldenrod.

In addition to food and medicine, goldenrod has other uses. Oil extracted from sweet goldenrod leaves has been used in perfumes. And most goldenrod species make good dyes for wool. Gold, orange tan, olive, and gray hues may be obtained by using the flowers, buds, and leaves and different mordants. Delena Tull says that tall goldenrod (*S. altissima*) contains enough hydrocarbons to have commercial potential.[6]

If synthetic rubber had not been invented, we might be riding on tires made from goldenrods. Thomas Edison experimented with making rubber from the latex of the plant. Harvey Firestone collaborated with him in making one fantastically costly set of goldenrod rubber tires, which Henry Ford used on his own personal Model-A touring car.[7]

Since goldenrod and purple asters frequently grow side by side, they have traditionally been paired in folklore. There is even a legend telling of their simultaneous origin: At the edge of a pine forest lived a very old woman who was believed to have magic powers. It was thought she could talk to all things in the forest in their own language and that she could change human beings into animals, birds, or plants. One day late in summer two young girls came to her hut. One of them had beautiful golden hair, and the other had beautiful deep violet-blue eyes. When the old woman asked what they wanted, the golden-haired girl asked to be made into something that would please everyone, and the blue-eyed girl asked only to be always near her friend. The old woman invited them into her hut and gave each of them a magic corn cake to eat. After that time neither girl was ever seen again, but the next morning two new flowers bloomed side by side where the girls had walked. One was like a golden plume, and the other was like a little purple star, and goldenrods and asters have been companions ever since.[8]

A native of almost every state, goldenrod has been adopted by both

Kentucky and Nebraska as their state flower. In the language of flowers, goldenrod means good fortune and encouragement. American poets including Longfellow, Whittier, Lowell, and Celia Thaxter (who grew them on her island garden) have praised the goldenrod in verse. In "The First Autumn" Marshall Schacht wrote: "Where God had walked / The goldenrod / Sprang like fire / From the burning sod."

Holly

Holly Family (*Aquifoliaceae*)

Common Names: American Holly, Possumhaw,
Winterberry, Black Alder, Inkberry, Yaupon, Gallberry

D ecking the halls with boughs of holly is an ancient custom dating back to Roman Saturnalian festivals (673–40 B.C.), which began on December 17. During these carnival-like celebrations in honor of Saturn, Roman god of seed sowing, citizens sent boughs of holly accompanied by other gifts to each other as tokens of friendship. Pliny recorded several Roman superstitions connected with holly: planted near a dwelling it warded off lightning and witches; the flowers caused water to freeze; a stick of holly thrown after an unruly animal would compel it to return and lie down by the holly branch.[1]

When early Christians adopted the custom of hanging greenery around their homes and meeting places, the church issued an edict forbidding Christians to decorate with green boughs at the same time as the pagans. Obviously the edict had little effect, and there is an ancient carol that says: "Now with bright holly all the temples strow."

As frequently happened in the evolution of Christianity, when the church encountered a pagan custom it could not overcome, it encompassed it. So in Christian symbolism holly became a symbol of Christ's sacrifice and supposedly grew up in his footsteps on the way to the crucifixion. The spiny leaves recall his crown of thorns and the scarlet berries the blood he shed on the cross. Holly remains an evergreen symbol of everlasting life, and in the languages of northern Europe it is called "Christ's Thorn" or "Holy Tree."[2]

In Britain Druids decorated their huts with holly and other evergreens in winter to provide a refuge for sylvan spirits. English churches began to use holly and ivy at Christmastime during the first reign of Henry VI (1422–61).[3]

In his *Herball* John Gerard described the holly, holme, or hulver tree of England: "The leaves are of a beautiful green colour, smooth and glib . . . and cornered in the edges with sharp prickles . . . the floures be white, and sweet of smell. The berries are round, of the bignesse of a little Pease, of colour red, of tast unpleasant, with a white stone in the midst . . . the root is wooddy."[4]

The hollies of North America and Texas essentially fit Gerard's description, and although their leaves and berries are less brilliant than European holly, they are still quite attractive as ornamental plants in the wild, in gardens and in hedges, and used as yuletide decorations. In East Texas American holly (*Ilex opaca*) may reach forty feet in height, but other Texas hollies are usually shrubs with either evergreen or deciduous leaves. Male and female flowers develop on separate bushes, and fertilization is effected mostly by bees. Possumhaw (*I. decidua*) is a particularly striking plant with bright red berries that cling to the bare branches of the female plant after the leaves drop off, providing excellent winter food for many birds, including bluejays, robins, mockingbirds, and cedar waxwings. Inkberry, gallberry, or bay-gall hollies (*I. glabra* or *I. coriacea*), common in East Texas, have small shiny black fruit and dark, stiff, lustrous leaves. Winterberry or Black Alder (*I. verticillata*) grows along swamps, stream banks, and damp thickets in East Texas, where it is enjoyed not only by birds but also by other small creatures. Thoreau, observing the winterberries near Walden Pond in 1857, wrote: "What pretty fruit for the mice these bright prinos [an old name for *Ilex*] berries! They run up the twigs in the night and gather this shiny fruit, take out the small seeds, and eat their kernels at the entrance to their burrows. The ground is strewn with them."[5]

The most abundant of our Texas hollies is yaupon (*I. vomitoria*). The botanical name was supposedly given by early Anglos who witnessed Native Americans using yaupon leaves as the main ingredient in a ceremonial "black drink," which they made strong enough to act as an emetic and purgative for purification ceremonies.[6] The leaves of a related South American species of holly, Paraguay tea (*I. paraguariensis*), are used to make the popular drink *mate*, a caffeine-rich tea. The leaves and berries of yaupon may be used to make dyes in shades of yellow, tan, or gray, but their chief value is in the decorative Christmas touch they add to the woods of Central and East Texas and the feast they provide for birds.

Although the fruits are considered poisonous for humans, in the past holly was used to treat many ailments. American Indians chewed the berries for colic and indigestion. In folk medicine holly leaf tea was used to treat measles, colds, flu, pneumonia, and externally for sores and itching, and holly bark tea was used to treat malaria and epilepsy.[7]

In England the white, hard, close-grained wood of holly trees is used as inlaid hardwood (especially in Tunbridge ware) and for making mathematical instruments and blocks for calico printing. Straight holly sticks are used to make the stocks of light driving whips and also for walking sticks. Until recent times holly bark was much used to make birdlime, a sticky substance used to trap small birds. After the bark is allowed to ferment, it is beaten into a paste, washed, and fermented again; then it is mixed with a little oil, preferably from goosefat, and stored in earthen vessels ready for use.[8]

In the language of flowers, holly represents foresight and defense. Sent in a nineteenth-century nosegay, it bore the message, "I dare not approach." Holly is the flower of December on the occidental calendar.

In *As You Like It* (act II, sc. vii, line 181) Shakespeare associates holly with lighthearted festivities in a song that says: "Sing heigh-ho unto the green holly, / Most friendship is feigning, most loving mere folly. / Then heigh-ho! the holly! / This life is most jolly!"

Ancient English Christmas carols are full of references to holly and ivy. In these carols holly represents the male and ivy the female spirit. One says: "Christmastide comes in like a bride, / With holly and ivy clad." And another old carol, "The Holly and the Ivy," tells us, "The holly and the ivy, / When they are both full grown / Of all the trees that are in the wood, / The holly bears the crown."

Honeysuckle

Honeysuckle Family (*Caprifoliaceae*)

Common Names: Woodbine, Japanese Honeysuckle,
Trumpet Honeysuckle, Virburnum, Elderberry

Members of the honeysuckle family range from trees to perennial herbs, with shrubs and vines in the majority. For most Texans, though, the word honeysuckle conjures up an image of a vine with sweet-smelling, long tubular white flowers that have protruding stamens. Or they may think of the deep red blooms of trumpet honeysuckle. The familiar Japanese honeysuckle (*Lonicera japonica*), with its sweet fragrance and white blooms fading to yellow ivory as they age, is a native of Asia that has escaped cultivation. Although it is condemned by respected botanists such as Correll and Johnston as a "rampant pernicious weed" that endangers native vegetation, the plant does have its uses.[1]

The Latin name for honeysuckle is *Caprifolium* (goat's leaf), signifying that the herbage of the plant is a favorite of goats. Old herbals recommend using honeysuckle to treat various ailments. Nicholas Culpeper said he knew no better cure for asthma than a conserve made of the flowers, and he claimed that an ointment made from the plant would clear the skin of "freckles, sunburnings, and whatever else discolours it."[2] Children especially like the plant, knowing it as a sweet-smelling flower that offers a delectable treat to those who have learned the secret of carefully pulling the pistil down through the funnel until it emerges bearing a drop of pure nectar.

In Japan the leaves and flowers are made into a beverage tea, and in

Asia Japanese honeysuckle is generally respected as a plant with a wide variety of medicinal uses, including treating bacterial dysentery, enteritis, laryngitis, fevers, and flu, and for use externally as a wash for rheumatism, sores, boils, scabies, and swellings. Extracts of the flowers are being tried experimentally there to lower cholesterol.[3]

White honeysuckle or honeysuckle bush (*L. albiflora*) is popular with Texas gardeners as it is a climbing shrub with fragrant white flowers similar to Japanese honeysuckle but without its aggressive and invasive habits. Coral or trumpet honeysuckle (*L. semper-virens*) is a Texas native with the most brilliant color of all the honeysuckles. Although it lacks the fragrance of the white honeysuckles, it is cultivated as an ornamental and as a source of nectar for migrating hummingbirds. It is also loved by butterflies and by cardinals and purple finches when the fruit ripens into crimson berries. The genus name, *Lonicera,* honors Adam Lonitzer, a sixteenth-century German botanist and physician, and the specific name *semper-virens* means evergreen. Native Americans and early settlers smoked the dried leaves of coral honeysuckle to relieve the symptoms of asthma.

The graceful twinflower (*Linnaea borealis*), one of the loveliest of Texas' honeysuckles, is found in East Texas growing around the base of trees in dry woods. Its delicate, trailing stems send up shoots that bear pairs of dainty, bell-shaped, pink-tinged fragrant blossoms. The minuscule fruits are covered with bristles that catch in the fur of passing animals, which disperse the seeds. The plant is named for Linnaeus, the father of systematic botany, who is often represented holding a spray of the blossoms.[4]

Several viburnums (from Latin, the wayfaring tree) grow in Texas, including those called black haw and arrow wood. Typically they have small, cream white flowers in clusters at the end of short branches and bluish black edible berries, enjoyed by hikers in the fall. James Whitcomb Riley was among those who appreciated them, and he wrote: "What is sweeter, after all, than black haws, in early fall?" European settlers brought along their tradition of treating women's problems with extracts from black haw bark, and it was listed in *The Pharmacopoeia of the United States of America* from 1882 until 1926.[5]

The elderberry or elder (*Sambucus*) is by far the member of the honeysuckle family with its roots deepest in history and folklore. Elderberries are found in different species in East and Central Texas as well as in the Trans-Pecos area and in the Chisos Mountains. There is evidence that the

elder was cultivated in prehistoric times in Switzerland and in Italy, and ancient Romans used the juice from the fruit to color the statues of Jupiter red on festive occasions.[6]

Conflicting traditions gave the elder both good and bad connotations: In *Love's Labour's Lost* Shakespeare refers to the common belief that Judas hanged himself on an elder, but a different tradition was that the Cross of Calvary was made of elder wood, and an old couplet says that it became "ever bush and never tree / Since our Lord was nailed on thee." The elder became a symbol of sorrow and death, and in the *Shepheardes Calendar (November),* Spenser says: "The Muses that were wont green baies to weave, / Now bringen bittre Eldre braunches seare." In Europe drivers of hearses carried whips made of elder wood; green elder branches were buried in graves to protect the dead from evil spirits; and elder bushes trimmed into the form of crosses were planted on new-made graves. If they bloomed, the belief was that the spirit of the dead would find happiness.[7]

Ancient heathen myths connect the elderberry with magic. It was a common superstition that in its branches dwelt a dryad, the Elder-tree Mother, whose permission had to be asked before cutting it. If the tree was cut without her permission, she haunted the owners and was even said to torment babies placed in elderwood cradles. In *The Book of Herbs,* Lady Northcote lists some of the many other superstitions connected with the elder: "The Russians believe that Elder-trees drive away evil spirits, and the Bohemians go to it with a spell to take away fever. The Sicilians think that sticks of its wood will kill serpents and drive away robbers, and the Serbs introduce a stick of Elder into their wedding ceremonies to bring good luck. In England it was thought that the Elder was never struck by lightning, and a twig of it tied into three or four knots and carried in the pocket was a charm against rheumatism. A cross made of Elder and fastened to cowhouses and stables was supposed to keep all evil from the animals."[8]

In Germany men doffed their hats when passing elder trees in deference to the spirit that supposedly lived within. And in northern Europe a long-lasting superstition was that "common people need to gather elder leaves on the last day of April and affix them to their doors and windows in order to prevent witches from entering their houses."[9]

The soft pith of the elder pushes out easily, and the tubes were used as pipes (hence its nickname of pipe tree). Both Europeans and Native Americans discovered that a kind of flute or musical whistle could be made from the stems, and small boys for centuries have enjoyed using the hollow stems as pop guns. The wood was once used to make shoemakers' pegs, butchers' skewers, and needles for weaving nets.[10] A black dye can be produced from the bark and roots, a green dye from the leaves, and a purple color from the berries.

Although the bark, roots, leaves, and unripe berries are toxic, both Europeans and Native Americans found many medicinal uses for the elderberry plant. They made a tea of the inner bark that was a diuretic, strong laxative, and emetic and used it poulticed on cuts, sore or swollen limbs, and boils to relieve pain and swelling and also to relieve headaches. A poultice made of the leaves was used on bruises or cuts to stop bleeding, and a tea with peppermint in water was a folk remedy for colds, to induce sweating and nausea. In 1644 a book (translated from the Latin), *The Anatomie of the Elder,* entirely devoted to the praise of the elder appeared in England. It dealt in great detail with the medicinal virtues of the flowers, berries, leaves, roots and bark, pith, and even a fungus of the plant called "Judas's ear."[11]

The British pharmacopoeia listed elderflower water as an official preparation for use in mixing medicines and making eye and skin lotions.

Commonly used in the nineteenth century to remove freckles and sun-
burn, elderflower water had the reputation of keeping the skin white, soft,
and free of blemishes.[12]

Immigrants to America from Europe were pleased to find the elderberry growing here. In addition to using it medicinally, they used the plant
as food in many ways: they made the berries into ketchup, vinegar, chut-
ney, pies and jellies; they made pickles of the buds; and they beat the small
flowers into their pancake batter and fritters. They also made a decoction
from the leaves to sprinkle over their choice plants to prevent caterpillars
from eating them.[13]

An old custom brought to this country was the making of "Elder-
blow" wine from the juice of the berries. Europeans considered it an infe-
rior wine, and in the eighteenth century the practice of doctoring port
wine with elderberry juice became so widespread that it was forbidden in
Portugal to cultivate the elder tree.[14]

In Texas elderberry wine has never really caught on, but many species of song birds relish the fruit, as do red squirrels, raccoons, mice, and
rabbits, and deer browse the foliage. The Indian currant or snowberry,
another member of the honeysuckle family, is useful in controlling soil
erosion and in providing wildlife food and cover, especially in West Texas.

Honeysuckle is the flower for the month of June. In the language of
flowers it acquired many meanings, including devoted affection, generos-
ity and gaiety, fidelity, bonds of love, and sweetness of disposition. Included in a nosegay, it carried the message, "I will make you happy."

Poets have made metaphors of the curling habit of honeysuckle, which
twines clockwise. Morning glories (also called woodbine) twine counterclockwise, and when the vines meet they join in a tight embrace, as
Shakespeare notes when he has Titania wind Bottom tightly in her arms
as "doth the woodbine the sweet honeysuckle entwist."[15]

Philip Freneau, America's first important lyric poet, immortalized the
honeysuckle in a sensitive nature poem called "The Wild Honey Suckle,"
in which he says:

> *Fair flower, that dost so comely grow,*
> *Hid in this silent, dull retreat,*
> *Untouched thy honied blossoms blow,*
> *Unseen thy little branches greet . . .*

Iris

Iris Family (*Iridaceae*)

Common Names: Flag, Fleur-de-lis,
Blue-eyed Grass, Celestial, Southern Iris,
Dixie Iris, Herbertia, Crocus, Orrisroot

In addition to wild irises, celestials, and blue-eyed grass, the large iris family includes such popular garden favorites as gladiolus, freesias, crocuses, and numerous domesticated irises. Typically irises have six petal-like segments: the lower drooping trio called the *falls* and the upper curved, domelike trio called the *standards*. Most common garden irises are of the tall bearded variety, and they are continuously being hybridized to produce hardier, taller plants with larger blossoms. Like their tame relatives, wild irises come in different sizes and colors ranging through many shades in combinations and blends. The distinctive leaves, which fold lengthwise embracing the stem and a new, young leaf, have a lancelike appearance that has inspired such common names as "daggers" and "Jacob's sword."

According to Plutarch the word *iris* means "eye of heaven" and so was given to both the rainbow and the membrane surrounding the pupil of the human eye. *Iris* comes from the Greek word for *rainbow,* and in Greek mythology the rainbow is personified in the swift golden-winged goddess Iris, a messenger of the gods and particularly of Hera (Juno), who is supposed to have commemorated Iris's beauty and purity by naming the flowers that bloom in the colors of the rainbow after her. The rainbow was said to be the path Iris traveled between the gods on Mt. Olympus and favored mortals on Earth. Shakespeare refers to this duty in *II Henry VI* (act III, scene ii, line 407) when Queen Margaret says to her banished lover, the Duke of Suffolk: "Whereso'er thou art in this world's globe I'll have an Iris that shall find thee out."

Another of Iris's duties was to lead the souls of dead women to the Elysian Fields, and in token of that belief Greeks planted purple irises on the graves of women. In the nineteenth-century language of flowers, iris in a bouquet promised that the sender had a special message for the recipient.

Among the plunder King Thutmose III (d. 1450 B.C.) brought back to Egypt from his conquests were many special plants. After planting them in his gardens, he had some of his favorites, including irises, carved on a wall of the great temple of Amon-re with an inscription that said in part: "All these plants exist in very truth. My Majesty hath wrought this to cause them to be before my father Amon, in this great hall for ever and ever."[1] Also over three thousand years ago in Knossos on the island of Crete, an unknown artist painted irises on a wall of the great Minoan palace.

Fleur-de-lis, a common name for iris, translates as "flower of the lily," and there has been over the years considerable argument as to whether its source was the lily or the iris. Since "lily" has been used loosely for so many flowers, and since the fleur-de-lis looks most like a stylized iris, it is the plant generally accepted today. Ruskin called it the flower of chivalry, with "a sword for its leaf and a lily for its heart," and its three-partite form came to represent faith, wisdom, and valor.

The fleur-de-lis is inextricably woven into the history of France, where for twelve hundred years it was associated with the French crown. There are half a dozen tales explaining why the Frankish king Clovis I (d. 511) chose the iris to adorn his victory banner. One is that during an important battle when his army was trapped on one side by an enemy army and by a river on the other, he noticed yellow flag iris growing halfway across the water and realized the river was shallow enough for his army to cross to safety. Other versions say he crossed the river in order to pursue the enemy. Another tale relates that his wife, Clotilda, tried for many years in vain to convert Clovis to Christianity. On the eve of a great battle he told her that if he won he would be baptized, and after winning he kept his promise, embracing Christianity and exchanging the three toads on his banner for three irises. The banner of the great Charlemagne (742–814) is said to have had a banner showing golden fleurs-de-lis on a blue background.[2]

Louis VI used the fleur-de-lis on his seal and had it engraved on coins; Louis VII adopted it as his blazon during the Crusades; Louis VIII wore blue vestments embroidered with gold irises at his consecration. A blue shield sprinkled with numerous golden fleurs-de-lis became the royal banner, until Charles V decreed that the number of fleurs-de-lis be three in honor of the Holy Trinity. As the symbol of France, the fleur-de-lis was used as a conventional ornament and featured on everything from upholstery, drapery, and wallpaper to clothing and jewelry. English kings included irises in England's coat-of-arms from 1340 to 1801 to represent their claims to French sovereignty. And a messenger in the opening scene of Shakespeare's *Henry VI* relates the crumbling of the French empire won by Henry V by saying: "Cropped are the flower-de-luces in your arms; / Of England's coat one half is cut away." With the coming of the French Revolution the fleur-de-lis along with other signs of royalty became a hated symbol which the rebels tried to obliterate by destroying sculpture and carvings depicting the flower, and men wearing a fleur-de-lis on their clothing or jewelry were likely to find themselves on the way to the guillotine.

Yellow flag (*Iris pseudacorus*), which can be found growing in water in the Big Thicket, is related to the yellow iris that Clovis took as his emblem. It has proved a useful as well as a pretty plant. The flowers yield a beautiful yellow dye, and the roots, which contain sulphate of iron, yield good brown and black dyes as well as black ink. In the nineteenth century it was discovered that the ripe seeds, well roasted, make a palatable coffee substitute.

Several varieties of blue irises grow in East Texas, but Edna St. Vincent Millay was probably referring to the regal larger blue flag (*I. versicolor*) so visible east of the Mississippi River when she wrote in "The Blue Flag in the Bog": "Never loved I anything / As I loved that tall blue flower! . . . Rearing up so blue and tall—It was all the gallant Earth / With its back against the wall!"

This is the blue flag of folk medicine and herbal usage that was listed in the United States *National Formulary* until 1947, and which is still used by English herbalists and medical communities in the Orient. Native Americans poulticed the root of blue flag to use on swellings, sores, and bruises and to treat rheumatism. Although it is sometimes called poison flag and considered potentially toxic, it has been used in the form of a root tea as a cathartic, diuretic, and emetic. Also known as "liver lily," blue flag was traditionally considered good to cleanse the blood and to treat diseases of the liver.[3] In his *Journals* Thoreau accused the larger blue flag of being "loose and coarse in its habits" and complained it was "a little too showy and gaudy, like some women's bonnets." Yet, he admitted, "it belongs to the meadow and ornaments it much."

One of Texas' most alluring irises is the purple pleat-leaf or pinewoods lily (*Eustylis purpurea*) so charmingly illustrated and described by Eliza Griffin Johnston: "The small petals of this plant have the appearance of Butterflies hovering round the flower. The sheath encloses buds in different stages of development, each one as it arrives at maturity escaping from its protection, expands its rich petals to light and life, and leaves its unperfected fellows snugly wrapped in their envelope, until the season of their perfection arrives."[4] Unlike the majority of the iris family members, the purple pleat-leaf grows from a bulb. Its short-lived flowers have three cup-shaped segments of pale to deep purple, three crimped violet-colored segments, and white throats flecked with brown or gold.

The well-named celestials (*Nemastylis geminiflora*) also grow from bulbs on prairies from North Central Texas to the Edwards Plateau to South Central Texas, where their sky blue flowers appear out of grasslike sheaths. As the name *gemini* indicates, they often appear in pairs. The bulb is edible, and Eliza Johnston noted that when boiled it tastes like boiled chestnuts. Closely related is another small bulb iris called herbertia (*Alophia drummondii*) which is endemic to South Texas where it sometimes appears in blue or purple carpets. The Wasowskis call it an "extraordinarily pretty" wildflower.

Another attractive member of the iris family is blue-eyed grass (*Sisyrinchium*), with at least fifteen species in Texas growing over most of the state except in the Panhandle and Far West. The common name comes from its grasslike leaves and dainty blue flowers with yellow centers. But the scientific name for this dainty flower has the unlovely translation of "pig's snout" (Greek *sys,* a pig, and *rhynchos,* a snout) probably because pigs were observed digging up the wiry, yellow roots.

The crocus, a tame member of the iris family, is valued by Texas gardeners for its cuplike bloom, which grows close to the ground, surrounded by leaves that look like broad blades of grass. The plant was once believed to bloom at dawn on St. Valentine's Day, and love potions have been made from it. According to a Greek myth, Crocus was a noble youth in love with a beautiful woman named Smilax who tended sheep. Because of their difference in rank, he was not allowed to marry her and killed himself from grief. The heartbroken Smilax wept so much that the goddess Flora felt sorry for her and turned the lovers into flowers: Crocus into the flower that bears his name and Smilax into a beautiful vine whose tendrils were used to bind together garlands of crocus used by Greeks as decorations at marriage festivals.[5]

Crocus is synonymous with *saffron,* which is obtained from the aromatic, pungent dried stigmas of a blue-flowered crocus (*C. sativus*) and was once widely used in medicines and in making a brilliant yellow dye as well as to add color and flavor to food. It is still very popular in India, especially for use in curries. Saffron is mentioned in the Song of Solomon (4:14) among the "chief spices." In ancient times it was used in potpourris, scattered on the floors of theaters, and sprinkled over the clothes of guests as they entered a house.[6] Among his many eloquent personifications of the Dawn, Homer refers to her as "saffron-robed." Saffron has been used in more recent times to lend color to confectionery, butter, cheese, liquor, and varnishes. In the nineteenth-century language of flowers, spring crocuses symbolized youthful gladness and saffron was connected with mirth.

Orrisroot, obtained from the dried rhizomes of some irises, has a long history of usefulness. Of the several species of iris that yield orrisroot, the finest is *I. florentina,* a plant so important in Italy that the city seal of Florence bears its likeness. The fresh roots have a fine violetlike fragrance that gradually develops during the drying process, intensifying as the roots age. In ancient times people used it in sweet-smelling unguents and threw it into the fire to produce a pleasant aroma. Because orrisroot has the quality of strengthening the odors of other substances, it became a popular fixative in powders and perfumes. In the days when bathing was considered an unsafe practice, cloth makers and drapers trimmed clothing with iris roots to give them a pleasant odor. Elizabethans put orrisroot in their wash water to give their linens a sweet smell and gave it to their male servants to chew to neutralize the effects of liquor, garlic, and tobacco. They also used it in powdered form as snuff and to perfume their wigs.[7]

Orrisroot has long been used in the manufacture of soaps and dentifrices as well as sachets and pomanders. It also has played a role in making beverages. The Germans used to suspend it in beer barrels to keep the beer from getting stale, and in France it was hung in wine casks to enhance the bouquet of wine. The English used orrisroot to flavor artificial brandies, and the Russians in Czarist days used it to flavor a soft drink made of honey and ginger.[8]

After the schoolchildren of Tennessee voted for the wild maypop or passionflower in 1919, it remained the state's unofficial floral emblem until 1933, when a group of passionate iris breeders persuaded the state legislature to replace it with their favorite flower. The Nashville Iris Association lobbied for the change by holding iris shows and iris festivals, and Peabody College presented an iris bulb to each graduating student. Wisely, the legislators did not designate a specific iris, so the citizens of the Volunteer State may consider either wild or tame irises as representing them.[9]

The beauty of the iris has inspired many painters and writers. After it was recognized as an emblem of royalty, Dutch and Italian old masters often introduced it into paintings of incidents in the life of Christ to signify his royal descent, and along with the lily it appears in fifteenth-century Flemish altarpieces and religious paintings. In *Childe Harold* Byron described a sunset: "all colours seem to be / Melted to one vast iris of the West, / Where the day joins the past Eternity." And in "Locksley Hall," Tennyson wrote his famous lines: "In the spring a livelier iris changes on the burnished dove / In the spring a young man's fancy lightly turns to thoughts of love."

In "Flower-de-luce" Longfellow praises the iris: "Born in the purple, born to joy and pleasance." He believes it bears "the message of some God," calling it "fair among the fairest" and begging:

> *O flower-de-luce, bloom on, and let the river*
> *Linger to kiss they feet!*
> *O flower of song, bloom on, and make forever*
> *The world more fair and sweet.*

Lily

Lily Family (*Liliaceae*)

Common Names: Madonna Lily, White Lily,
Lily of the Valley, Wood Lily, Carolina Lily, Day Lily,
Tiger Lily, Dog's Tooth Violet, Fawn Lily, Trillium, Wake Robin,
Wild Hyacinth, Wild Onion, Crow Poison, False Garlic,
Solomon's Seal, Aloe Vera, Smilax

According to ancient Semitic tradition, the lily sprang from the tears of Eve when she was expelled from the Garden of Eden and found that she was to become a mother. In later Christian lore it was said that the lily had been yellow until the Virgin Mary stooped to pick it. In Christian symbolism the lily came to represent purity, chastity, and innocence and to be the symbol of the Resurrection and of Easter. However, thousands of years before the white lily came to be called the Madonna lily, it was an important religious symbol—a sacred flower of motherhood and the flower emblem of the chief goddesses of ancient religions. In the prehistoric Minoan period of Crete (3000 B.C.), it was the sacred symbol of Britomartis, a goddess of birth and health. In ancient Greece it was the flower of Hera, the goddess of women and childbirth. And in ancient Rome it was the emblem of Juno, goddess of marriage and motherhood. The Romans called the lily "Juno's rose" and told this myth to explain its creation: When Jupiter had Hercules by Alcmene, he wanted his son to be nourished by the milk of the great Juno, so while she slept he had Hercules put to her breast. When Hercules had drunk his fill, there was still an abundance of milk falling from the goddess's breasts, and the portion that spilled into the heavens created the Milky Way, while the portion that fell down to earth created the lilies.[1]

The Madonna lily (*L. candidum*) may be the oldest domesticated flower. Cretan artists used lilies as motifs in wall paintings and in abstract geometrical designs on vases during the Middle Minoan period (2100–1580 B.C.). Romans cultivated lilies, and it was Virgil who gave them the name *candidum* "pure white, shining." Greek and Roman brides and grooms were crowned with wreaths of lilies and wheat, symbolizing a pure and fertile life, and white lilies placed on Christian altars had their stamens and pistils removed "so that they might remain virgin." The association of the lily with the Virgin Mary dates from a tradition that when her tomb was visited three days after her burial, it was found empty except for the roses and lilies that filled it. In England the Venerable Bede (637–735) made the lily the emblem of the Resurrection of the Virgin—the pure white petals signifying her spotless body and the golden anthers her soul glowing with heavenly light.[2] Great artists of the Middle Ages, including Titian, Murillo, Botticelli, Correggio, and Fra Angelico painted the white Madonna lily in their representations of the Annunciation and in other pictures depicting the Virgin.

Lilies come in many guises, some of them false, and they have a number of close relatives, some quite elegant and others distinctly odd. Common names can be misleading, and botanists using scientific names do not always agree on classifications. Lilies are closely related to the Amaryllis and Iris families. Yuccas and agaves sometimes appear in the Lily family, but in other places they are classified in the Agave family. (In this book they appear in a different chapter). To add to the confusion, rain lilies, spider lilies, and copper lilies belong in the Amaryllis family, but dog's tooth violets belong in the Lily family. Calla lilies and water lilies, however, do not, and there are other plants called lilies that belong in other families. Many cultivated plants in the family such as the vegetables asparagus, onion, garlic, and leeks are economically important as are a number of ornamentals, including tulips, hyacinths, day lilies, lily of the valley, aspidistras, Turk's caps, and snowdrops.

At one time the Madonna lily was imported and cultivated as the Easter lily, but nurserymen found another white lily (*L. longiflorium*) easier to make bloom at the proper time. This lily comes mostly from Japan

and China, where people eat the sweet and sugary bulbs and make ointments from them to treat tumors, ulcers, and external inflammations.

Dedicated scholars who have spent countless years trying to decipher
exactly what flowers are meant in the numerous biblical references to lilies have come up with different answers. The Moldenkes, authors of one
of the best-researched books on biblical plants, believe it is most prob-
able that several different kinds of plants, perhaps five or six, are referred
to under the name "lily" in the *Authorized Version of the King James Bible.*
They note that there is a definite tendency among modern translators to
broaden the concept of "lilies" (at least in the Matthew and Luke references) to embrace wild flowers in general. In the references to lilies in the
Song of Solomon, again, the Moldenkes believe more than one kind of
flower may be meant, including the cultivated Madonna lily (that a wealthy
king like Solomon might have in his garden) and also the deep blue and
fragrant wild hyacinth.[3]

The plant we call lily of the valley (*Convallaria majalis*) does not occur in Palestine, but it does grow wild in some parts of Texas as an escape
from gardens where it is prized for its beauty and its fragrance. The delicate white flowers hanging like bells from the long flower stalk inspired
the name "our Lady's tears," and Medieval monks noting the steplike arrangement of the blossoms on the stalk called it "ladder to heaven." Its
sweet scent was said to attract nightingales. Culpeper placed the plant
under the dominion of Mercury and claimed it "strengthens the brain and
recruits a weak memory and comforteth the heart and vital spirits."[4]

According to a Greek myth, the lily of the valley was found by Apollo
and given to Aesculapius for its medicinal properties. Water distilled from
the flowers was once thought to possess such great curative virtue that it
was called *Aqua aurea* (golden water) and kept in vessels of gold and silver. In the twentieth century a drug resembling digitalis in action, although
less potent, has been obtained from the lily of the valley plant and used to
treat soldiers who suffered from being exposed to poison gas in World
War I.[5]

In France, Germany, and Holland, lilies of the valley are called
"mayflowers," and in some parts of England they are called "may lilies"
or "conval lilies" from *convallis* (of the valley). The writer Colette described
the French adoration of the flower: "Its cult excites the entire populace of
a capital city to a pitch of effervescence . . . Come to Paris on May Day and

watch the flower sellers' frontal attack in the streets, twenty francs the sprig, a thousand francs the bunch.[6] The French make a toilet water, *eau d'or*, (water of gold) from the flowers. In the language of flowers, the lily of the valley signifies a return of happiness, and sent in a bouquet in Victorian times, they carried the message "let us make up."

In Texas two colorful species of *Lillium* are found on opposite sides of the state. The wood lily (*L. philadelphicum*), which Barton Warnock calls one of the most attractive lilies in the United States, grows in the Trans-Pecos in the canyons of the Guadalupe Mountains, while the Carolina lily (*L. michauxii*), a favorite of monarch butterflies, is found in pine and oak woods in southeastern Texas. Both plants have orangy red, purple-spotted blossoms.

Another showy orangy lily, the common day lily (*Hemerocallis fulva*), is a popular garden plant that has escaped cultivation to bloom along roadsides and borders of fields and thickets. Although individual flowers collapse and decay after expanding for a day, the plants bloom so prolifically they make a continuous colorful show. The Greek name *Hemerocallis* indicates that it is a flower "beautiful for a day," and *fulva* describes its tawny color. Because they reproduce by dividing off rootstock to create new plants, Dr. Harold Moldenke speculates that millions of day lilies growing today are actually still living parts of plants that grew in Asia centuries ago. The Chinese have grown day lilies as a food crop for thousands of years. The entire plant is edible, but the young buds and flowers are considered a delicacy in China, where half-kilo packages of day lily flowers are sold in shops. Called *gum-tsoy*, "golden vegetable," they are enjoyed with noodles or in soups. The dried flowers are also used in Chinese medicine. The great variety of day lilies available in the United States is due mainly to the efforts of Dr. A. B. Stout, who worked at the New York Botanical Garden, collecting and hybridizing the day lily to produce a wide range of colors.[7] In the language of flowers, the day lily represents coquetry.

Still another favorite showy orange lily is the black-spotted tiger lily (*L. tigrinum*), which William Kerr, a collector from Kew Gardens, brought from the Orient to England. In Japan it is called the "ogre" lily, and in *Through the Looking Glass* Lewis Carroll depicted them as having disagreeable traits. When Alice says to the tiger lily, "I *wish* you could talk!" the tiger lily snaps, "We *can* talk when there's anybody worth talking to," and the character is also quite rude and domineering toward the other flowers.

There is, however, a Korean legend about the creation of the tiger lily that gives it a better character: A hermit removed an arrow from the fore-leg of a tiger, and they became fast friends. When the tiger was about to die, it begged the hermit to use his magic to keep it near him after death. The hermit turned the body of the tiger into the tiger lily, and when the hermit drowned some time later, the lily spread over the land looking for its kind friend.[8]

At least three varieties of dog's tooth violet (*Erythronium*) are found in thickets and on hillsides over the eastern half of Texas and from the central to the northern and western parts of the state. White dog's tooth violet (*E. albidum*) has long, white-petaled, lilylike blossoms, often tinged with lavender, nodding singly on slender leafless stems. The edible bulbs were roasted and relished by both Native Americans and early settlers. The American naturalist John Burroughs thought the dog's tooth violet one of the most beautiful wildflowers and lamented that it had "no good and appropriate name." In addition to being misnamed a violet, it is also called trout lily, adder's tongue, and fawn lily, names deriving from the imaginations of people observing the markings and shapes of the leaves and flowers.

Trillium is Latin for "triple," and it was Linnaeus who created this apt name to describe the threeness of this unusual wildflower: three large leaflike bracts surround flower scapes that consist of three sepals, three petals, and six stamens; the ovaries are three- or six-winged and the berries three-sided. Wake robin is another common name, indicating that the plant is an early spring bloomer. In late March or early April before the leaf canopy has become thick enough in East Texas forests to shut out the sunlight, trillums show their pretty faces. The erect petals of the prairie wake robin (*T. recurvatum*) vary from yellowish green to purple, while the petals of Texas trillium (*T. texanum*) pass through stages from white to pink and finally to a reddish color. The other two species of trillium found in Texas, *T. gracile* and *T. viridescens,* usually have purple flowers that emit a distinct odor, sometimes described as musty or like rotting fruit. They are not nearly so odoriferous, however, as their relative *T. erectum,* found in many other states and often referred to as stinking Benjamin or wet dog trillium. The smell, reminiscent of carrion, is a sensible one for the plant as it depends on flies to do its pollinating. When the doctrine of signatures was in vogue, this distinctive odor led medical practitioners to make an ointment from the roots to treat gangrene. Another common name for this plant is birthwort because it was used to stop hemorrhaging after childbirth, and it remains a popular folk remedy for bleeding, snakebite, and skin irritations.[9]

In sandy or rocky soils from Central Texas northward in the spring, the pale blue spires of wild hyacinth (*Camassia scilloides*) sweetly scent the air with the distinctive hyacinth perfume. *Hyacinthus orientalis* is indigenous and quite common in Palestine and Lebanon, and in the springtime the blue, fragrant blooms literally cover some hillsides in Galilee. The Moldenkes have concluded that in several verses of the Song of Solomon (2:1–2 & 16, 4:5, and 6:2–3), the most plausible translation is to substitute "hyacinth" for "lily."[10]

In Greek myth the origin of the hyacinth, like that of the narcissus, is connected with the death of a beautiful youth: Apollo was passionately attracted to a fair-haired youth named Hyacinth. One day as they were playing at throwing the discus, the god's throw accidentally went past its mark and struck Hyacinth a fatal blow in the forehead. As the weeping Apollo held the dying boy in his arms, from the bloodstained grass sprang the purple flower that was to bear his friend's name forever. In some versions of the myth it was Zephyrus, the West Wind, who blew the discus off course and made it strike Hyacinth because Zephyrus was jealous that the handsome youth preferred Apollo to him.[11] In the language of flowers, the hyacinth symbolizes sorrow and sadness.

In his *Herball* John Gerard extolled the virtues of the bulbous root of the hyacinth, claiming it was full of "a slimie glewish juice, which will serve to set feathers upon arrowes instead of glew, or to paste bookes with," and he added "Here of is made the best starch next unto that of wake-robin roots." And indeed it was used to fix feathers on arrows and by bookbinders as well as being a source of starch in the days when stiff ruffs were in fashion.[12] Native Americans and early settlers relished the onionlike bulbs of the wild hyacinth, which they roasted in pits lined with stones, and one war was caused by the white settlers trespassing on the ceremonial camas fields of the Nez Perce Indians. Unfortunately, the death camas (*Zigadenus*) grows in the same areas as the edible camas and has similar onionlike bulbs, but true camassia have blue flowers while the death camas has creamy white, greenish, or yellowish flowers. If eaten they may cause death to sheep, cattle, and even humans, although numerous insects enjoy their pollen and nectar with impunity.

Water hyacinth, which belongs not to the lily but to the pickerelweed family, has been called a beautiful, noxious weed. Introduced from South America, this aquatic herb forms large masses of lovely bluish purple blooms that clog waterways and destroy native vegetation in South Texas as in other southern states.

Although detractors have called them "stinking lilies," the *Alliums* are very valuable members of the lily family. Onions, garlic, and leeks all belong to the genus, and among the several species of wild onions growing in Texas, Drummond wild onion (*Allium drummondii*) is the most common. It has attractive white, pink, or reddish flowers, and its bulbs are edible as are the bulbs of the other wild onions. But as so often happens in nature, a dangerous look-alike often blooms in the same area. Both the common names, crow poison or false garlic, and the scientific name, *Nothoscordum* (bastard, spurious) reveal the true character of this poisonous imposter. One method of identification is that it lacks the onion odor of the edible plants.

Onions, garlic, and leeks have inspired much folklore and many superstitious beliefs through the ages. Odysseus supposedly escaped being changed into a swine by Circe because he kept with him the herb moly, which is usually identified as wild garlic. Ancient Egyptians revered the onion; they took oaths on onions and presented them to their gods as sacrificial offerings and also enjoyed them as a favorite vegetable. According to the Bible, when the Israelites were wandering in the wilderness, among the foods they expressed a longing for were the leeks, onions, and garlic they had enjoyed in Egypt (Numbers 11:4–6). According to the Greek historian Herodotus, nine tons of gold were spent to buy onions to feed the builders of the pyramids, and soldiers in the Roman legions ate garlic in the belief that it gave them courage. The English, however, fed garlic not to themselves but to their gamecocks to increase their fighting spirit. In the *Canterbury Tales* Chaucer's Pardoner, the most unpleasant character of all the pilgrims, is described as loving well "the garlic, onions, aye and leeks." Nevertheless, garlic enjoyed a long reputation for white magic and as a defense against vampires and the plague. In 1609 Sir John Harrington wrote in "The Englishman's Doctor": "Garlic then have power to save from death / Bear with it though it maketh unsavory breath, / And scorn not garlic like some that think / It only maketh men wink and drink and stink." Sailors in the seventeenth century found a practical use for garlic by cooking their stale and rotting meats with it. Early explorers in America were happy when they found wild onions to supplement their diet. Today cows savor the tender, juicy plants in the spring after a long winter's diet of hay, but since the plants taint their milk and the butter made from it with a strong onion flavor, needless to say, Texas dairymen are not pleased to see clusters of wild onions appear in their pastures.

In his *Natural History* Pliny lists sixty-one different disorders that garlic was useful in treating, and over the years among the powers credited to onions and garlic have been the abilities to ward off germs and diseases, to stimulate stomach and gall bladder secretions, to help with cardiovascular problems, and in poultice form to treat colds and other respiratory infections. In 1858 Louis Pasteur verified the antiseptic properties of garlic, and in both World Wars I and II it was used as an antiseptic. Garlic and onion bulbs contain active sulphur compounds as well as vitamins

B_1 (thiamine), B_2 (riboflavin), and C. Today scientists are exploring the possibility that the ancients knew what they were doing when they used these plants to reduce hypertension and are also trying to establish their effectiveness in lowering cholesterol and fat content in blood.[13]

The emperor Nero is said to have followed Aristotle's recommendation to eat leeks to improve his voice. According to tradition the leek became the national flower of Wales after Welsh soldiers were directed by St. David to pluck leeks from a field to wear in their caps to distinguish their own men from the Saxons they were preparing to battle on March 1, 640. The Welsh army was victorious, and the leek was adopted as the national flower and worn by loyal Welshmen on March 1, the anniversary of St. David's day of victory.

Solomon's seal is the common name for a group of plants that have pendulous flowers on simple erect or arching stems and creeping roots that spread horizontally under the surface of the soil rather than growing straight down. Great Solomon's seal (*Polygonatum biflorum*), which grows in shady places in rich soil in eastern and north-central Texas, has greenish white flowers usually in pairs drooping from its slender arching stems. The species name *biflorum* indicates the pairing of the elongated, bell-shaped blossoms, and the genus name *Polygonatum* ("many knees") describes the knobby appearance of the rhizomes. The common name, Solomon's seal, has various interpretations. Each year where the stem breaks off, an enlarged scar is left, and the age of the plant can be determined by counting the number of stem scars. These supposedly resemble King Solomon's official seal, and one legend is that originally Solomon set the markings on the roots as testimony to their value. The story is that when workers were unable to quarry the extremely hard rock needed to build his temple, King Solomon himself, armed with the roots of this plant as his tool, ripped up the necessary blocks of stone. According to another explanation, when the flower is lightly dipped in ink and pressed on paper, it leaves an impression of a six-pointed star made up of two interlaced triangles like the Jewish Star of David—also known as the Seal of Solomon.[14]

Gerard believed the name came about because of the plant's effectiveness in sealing or closing up "wounds, broken bones and such like." He claimed that the crushed root of the plant "taketh away in one night or two at the most, any bruise, blacke or blew spots gotten by falls or women's wilfulnesse, in stumbling upon their hasty husbands fists."[15] The roots of Solomon's seal were eaten as survival food by the Iroquois and other Native American tribes. A flour was made from the pounded dried roots, and the plant was used as a pot herb. Medicinally, tea made from the roots was drunk to relieve stomach ailments and as a general tonic.

The aloe vera plant growing wild in the Rio Grande Valley and in many Texas home garden plots and pots is related to the aloes that were valued plants hundreds of years before the Christian Era. When the Old Testament poet Balaam surveyed the tribes of Israel, he was moved to exclaim, "How fair are your encampments, O Israel! Like valleys that stretch afar, like gardens beside a river, like aloes that the Lord has planted" (Numbers 24:5–6). In the New Testament (John 19:39–40) we are told that according to the burial custom of the Jews the body of Jesus was bound in linen cloths with a mixture of myrrh and aloes "about a hundred pounds' weight" before it was laid in the tomb. In the first century A.D. Pliny cited many uses for aloes, both externally and internally, and through the years it has been used to sooth minor burns, insect stings and bites, small wounds, and rashes. In fact, its ability to regenerate damaged tissues with dramatic swiftness has caused it to be called "the burn plant," and in recent years it has been used to treat even radiation burns. The emollient (skin softening) ingredient in aloe vera makes it popular as an ingredient in skin lotions, creams, salves, and shampoos, and several cosmetic companies have aloe vera plantations in Texas.

Smilax appears in at least ten different species in Texas, sometimes as a low-climbing shrub and sometimes as a high-climbing rampant vine. Common names for the plant indicate some of its characteristics: green brier, cat brier, sarsaparilla vine, stretchberry, and blaspheme vine. Where it forms dense tangles, its prickly thorns can cling like cat's claws when brushed against by fur or clothing or bare skin. The roots of some species provided the essential ingredient in sarsaparilla, an old-fashioned soft drink similar to root beer. The roots have also been used to make beer and to fatten hogs, and the stems have been used to make baskets. Smilax is useful in covering trellises and fences and is one of the best vines for providing wildlife cover; it is an important browse plant for deer, and many birds eat its fruit. Children used to add the ripe berries of green brier to chewing gum to make it pop. Since it does not wither quickly, smilax is useful in decorative arrangements.

Many of the genera of the lily family are of extreme beauty, and their main use is in horticultural display. In this category perhaps the most popular plants in the family are tulips, with their vast range of showy hybrids. The sego or mariposa (butterfly) lily is an example of a lily that is both beautiful and useful. Its petals look like butterfly wings with pansy markings; it blooms prolifically in Utah, where it has been named the state flower, and many historians believe that in the spring of 1848, when early Mormon pioneers ran out of food, they might have starved to death if it had not been for the bulbs of the sego lily.

From the useful *Alliums* to the beautiful *Lilliums* and *Trilliums*, lilies have been a blessing and an inspiration to humanity. Thirteenth-century encyclopedist Bartholomew of England wrote: "The lily is next the Rose in worthiness and nobleness. . . . Nothing is more gracious in fairness of color, in sweetness of smell and in effect of working and virtue."[16] In German folklore, after death souls take the form of a lily or a rose, and from the grave of those who were unjustly executed white lilies spring as a token of their innocence.

Keats called the lily the "queen of flowers," and Shakespeare (who often mentioned lilies) made popular the expression that to "paint the lily" is as wasteful and ridiculous an excess as gilding refined gold (*King John,* act I, scene ii, line 9). In the language of flowers, the lily represents purity and majesty, qualities that Julia Ward Howe no doubt had in mind as she wrote the stirring words that begin the fourth verse of *The Battle Hymn of the Republic:* "In the beauty of the lilies, Christ was born across the sea / With the glory in His bosom that transfigures you and me."

In ancient times lilies were often called hyacinths, and the great Persian poet of the thirteenth century, Sa'di, advised that one who was "bereft" of all worldly good except two loaves should: "Sell one, and with the dole / Buy hyacinths to feed the soul."

Mallow/ Winecup

Mallow Family (*Malvaceae*)

Common Names: Poppy Mallow, Cheeseweed, Hibiscus, Rose of Sharon, Althea, Indian Mallow, Globe Mallow, Wild Hollyhock, Turk's Cap, Pavonia

Mallows belong to an enormous family of more than seventy-five genera and a thousand species, ranging in color from scarlet to purple, pink, yellow, and white. The family includes such useful members as cotton and okra and such popular ornamental ones as hibiscus, althea, hollyhock, and turk's cap. The old-world marsh mallow is a member of the same genus as our garden hollyhock. Centuries ago the French learned to candy marsh mallow roots by boiling the spongy, sweet pulp to soften it and adding sugar, and from this confection descended our white marshmallow pillows. Marshmallow sweets continued to be made using the mucilaginous juice of the marsh mallow roots until gum arabic was found to be a cheaper substitute and gelatin in turn a still cheaper substitute for gum arabic.[1]

The name mallow derived from the Greek word *malakos*, meaning soft, which may refer to the plant's soft, downy leaves or to its demulcent and emollient properties. Babies were given the roots, which look like thin yellow carrots, to chew on when they were teething. As the baby chewed, the root softened and released mucilage, which had a calming effect.[2] This same quality made it a popular herb for treating upper respiratory irritations and inhibiting coughing, as well as for soothing digestive and urinary tract inflammations.

For orgy-prone ancient Romans a popular restorative was a drink made from high or common mallow (*Malva sylvestris*), a plant that grows in East Texas. In the first century the Roman naturalist Pliny thought so highly of the beneficial effects of this mallow that he recommended a teaspoon a day of a drink made from it to keep *all* diseases at bay. Sixteenth-century Italian herbalists also considered the high mallow plant an *omnimorbia,* or cure-all. Native Americans made poultices from the plant to relieve pain from swellings and insect bites, and modern herbalists follow this practice.[3]

Native Americans also used mallows in other ways. The Hopi called the globe mallow the "sore eye poppy" and used it for curing or relieving eye maladies. They chewed the stems of the globe mallow like chewing gum, and from winecups they produced an orange dye. In addition they taught the white pioneers the value of using the fresh crushed leaves as shoe liners for sore feet.

The leaves, flowers, and fruit of a number of mallows have been used for food. Our common or dwarf mallow (*Malva rotundifolia*), a small plant with rounded, heart-shaped leaves and small purplish flowers, was known to the ancients. Egyptians cultivated it to be boiled with meat and considered it a valuable potherb for poor people. Although authorities disagree about which plants are meant in each wildflower reference in the Bible, both the *King James* and the *Revised Standard Version* say that after Job fell on hard times, he pictured himself as being despised by those people who were themselves so destitute as to eat "mallows and juniper roots" (Job 30:4). The fruits of the malvas, or cheese mallows, are like little flattened disks and are safe enough for children's doll tea parties. In the Victorian code of flower symbolism, the mallow represents mildness.

In Texas, pavonia, or rose mallow (*Pavonia lasiopetala*), is becoming increasingly popular as a hardy, undemanding ornamental garden plant. It produces attractive pink blossoms that resemble miniature hibiscus in prolific quantities throughout much of the year. First discovered in Brazil, this plant is named in honor of Spanish botanist José Antonio Pavón (1754–1840), who collected extensively in South America. The species name, *lasiopetala* (shaggy petaled), refers to the minute hairs at the base of the petals. Spanish explorers called pavonias *las rosas de San Juan,* the roses of St. John. The bark was a source of fiber for Native Americans. Butterflies find pavonia especially attractive.[4]

Children and hummingbirds enjoy sipping the nectar of turk's cap or red mallow from the blossoms resembling Turkish fezzes. Early comers to Texas ate the flowers, fruit, and young leaves of turk's cap either raw or cooked and sometimes made a tea of the dried flowers. The fruit, which tastes a little like watermelon or apples, can also be made into a jelly or syrup that Delena Tull recommends as having a "distinctive but subtle flavor."[5]

Texas has almost a dozen species of the lovely hibiscus or rose mallow genus, which have a sturdiness that belies their delicate appearance. They include althea or rose-of-sharon and the swamp rose mallow or mallow rose. And we have at least six species of poppy mallows or winecups, *Callirhoe,* the name of a princess in Greek mythology. Ranging northward and eastward, the handsome flowers are generally red, rose, or purple, and sometimes white.

A legend from India describes the origin of the winecup: There was once a great ruler, well loved by his people for his wisdom and for his kindness. When he became very ill, everything possible was done for him, but nothing helped, and the doctors despaired of his life. A favorite dance in India was the "Dance of the Wine Cup," in which a goblet of wine was balanced on the hand of the dancer. When the dying ruler asked Ivan, his favorite servant, to perform the dance for him one last time, Ivan rejoiced that he could do something to please his master, and he determined to dance as never before. The next morning while the dew was on the grass, the ruler sat at a window watching as Ivan performed the "Dance of the Wine Cup" as it had never been done before. Moving with great speed and grace, he refused to stop until he finally stumbled from exhaustion, dropping the fragile goblet, which shattered on the ground, splattering the wine far and wide. Ivan was distressed, but his master comforted him, telling him that the dance had restored his strength and started him on his way to recovery from his illness. Then Ivan gathered up the bits of the goblet and left, and the next morning the people of the court were astonished to see the lawn dotted with a new flower of a rich red wine color in the shape of the goblet Ivan had broken.[6]

Even though most Texans today don't make use of mallows as medicines or foods, the great variety of the plants across the state affords a smorgasbord of visual pleasure. From the stately copper mallows of West Texas to the burgundy winecups of Central Texas, to the bright clumps of turk's cap in East Texas, to the delicate pink of the lovely swamp mallows of South Texas, there is something for everybody.

Milkweed

Milkweed Family (*Asclepiadaceae*)
Common Names: Antelope Horns, Silkweed, Butterfly Weed

A t the Centennial Exposition in Philadelphia in 1876, thousands of visitors were attracted to a large bed of brilliant reddish orange flowers imported from Holland. They admired and praised the plants as gorgeous foreigners until it was discovered they were only a Dutch edition of our own native butterfly weed.[1]

Of the thirty-five different species of milkweed growing throughout Texas, orange butterfly weed (*Asclepias tuberosa*) is undoubtedly the most spectacular, and the white flowered milkweed (*A. variegata*) which grows on the edges of woodlands and thickets in the eastern part of the state is a good candidate for the most beautiful. The rosy showy milkweed (*A. speciosa*), which is at home in the Panhandle, has the most massive flowers, with seed pods so large that Native Americans used the dried pods as utensils. Several green flowered varieties with distinctive ball-shaped heads are common in the Hill Country and throughout Central Texas from late spring through early fall. One of these is antelope horn (*A. viridis*), named for the shape of the seed pods, which begin to curve as they lengthen, resembling antelope horns. Other species in Texas include pink and purple milkweeds and climbing vine milkweeds.

The genus name *Asclepias* honors Asklepios, the Greek god of medicine, who is better known by his Latin name, Aesculapius. A son of Apollo, he was raised by the centaur Chiron, who taught him so much about medicinal herbs that he was able to restore the dead to life. His insignia, a staff entwined by a snake, remains the symbol of healing. *Asclepias* is an appropriate name as there are many recorded medicinal uses for milkweed, especially among native North Americans.

A common name for Texas milkweed (*A. texana*) is rattlesnake milkweed. Ellen Schulz relates this incident: A Native American chief and five braves stopped at a ranch home in the Boerne area to ask for food. While they were eating, a family member rushed in to say that one of their party had been bitten by a rattlesnake and was extremely ill. The chief motioned to his men, who dashed off in different directions. One returned with some Texas milkweed, and a poultice was made of the mashed roots and applied to the wound; a liquid was also made from the roots and given to the victim, who recovered in a remarkably short time.[2]

Native Americans taught early settlers to use the thick milky sap exuded by most species of milkweed to treat warts, ringworm, poison ivy, and other skin problems and to make a salve out of the ripe seeds to treat sores.[3] Women drank an infusion of the milkweed plant to increase lactation and as a contraceptive. Some tribes boiled the roots and used the extract for various problems including dysentery, rheumatism, dropsy, tapeworms, asthma, heart palpitations, and syphilis. In the 1880s American doctors used both the sap and the root of milkweed in treating respiratory diseases.[4]

Because it was so widely used to treat lung inflammations, butterfly weed is also known as pleurisy root. It does not have the milky latex characteristic of other members of the milkweed family, but early-nineteenth-century American medical writers could hardly find words to praise the plant enough. In the second volume of his *American Medicine Plants* (1887), Dr. Charles Millspaugh summed up its various uses, noting that pleurisy root was regarded "almost since the discovery of this country as an anti-spasmodic, anti-pleuritic, anti-rheumatic, anti-syphilitic" and he added it was recommended in "low typhoid states, pneumonia, catarrh, bronchitis, pleurisy, dyspepsia, indigestion, dysentery and obstinate eczemas."[5] Butterfly weed was listed in *The Pharmacopoeia of the United States of America* from 1820 to 1905 and in the *National Formulary* from 1916 to 1936.

Early settlers in America also used the milkweed plant as food. They ate the young leaves and shoots of some species as potherbs, and they boiled the young seed pods like okra and ate them with buffalo meat. They found that boiling with several changes of water eliminated the slight bitterness and toxicity of the milky juice of the broken stems and leaves. They also dipped the flowers in boiling water, coated them with batter, and fried them to make fritters. Some native tribes made a crude sugar from boiled milkweed flowers, and some collected the sap, let it harden, and chewed it like gum.[6]

In *A Practical Guide to Edible and Useful Plants,* Delena Tull warns that at least eight Texas milkweeds are deadly poisonous to livestock and that some Texas species contain toxic levels one hundred times greater than the levels of species in the eastern states. Fortunately, in general livestock avoid eating the bitter milkweed as long as other forage is available.

The monarch butterfly has found a fantastic way to make use of the toxic glycosides in milkweed. The female monarch lays her eggs on the leaves of the plant. When the caterpillars emerge they feed on the leaves, and the bitter poison is incorporated into their bodies—to remain forever. Birds soon learn to avoid the monarch as they find it is a snack that will make them sick. The monarch-milkweed connection was proved in the 1840s when some milkweed plants were introduced to the Hawaiian Islands (then called Sandwich Islands) and monarch butterflies that had never been seen in that part of the world appeared and began breeding. The viceroy butterfly is an opportunist with a color pattern that mimics that of the monarch and so is able to fool birds into leaving it alone also although its body contains none of the toxic poison found in the monarch and would be a tasty morsel for them.[7]

One of the remarkable features of the milkweed family is a sophisticated pollination system equaled only by that of the orchid family. In return for a drink of its abundant sweet nectar, visitors (butterflies, bees, wasps, and flies) are forced to do the work of fertilization for it. The large spherical head of the milkweed plant is composed of an inner circle of tiny upright sacks called hoods and an outer circle of flat triangular petals. Milkweed pollen comes in tiny teardrop masses called pollina. If a needle is inserted in one of the slits in the crown of a milkweed flower and pulled upward, it will have two pollen masses hanging on it, joined by a thread. When an insect straddles the slippery flower, it must struggle to get a foothold, and invariably a leg will slip into the tiny groove where the pollina lie waiting to attach themselves to it by the cross thread when the insect jerks its leg out of the crevice. The next flower presents the same trap, and in the struggle to free its leg, the insect deposits its load of pollen.

The milkweed plant is just as clever at repulsing undesirable visitors, such as ants who want the sweet nectar for their winter store but do not help with the fertilization process. Before these pilferers can reach the nectar, the sticky juice of the milkweed entangles them, and they are lucky if they can drop to the ground without becoming fatally embedded in the goo.

As fall sets in, the warty banana-shaped seed pods become more conspicuous, until one day they suddenly split open, releasing hundreds of seeds that become airborne on long, silky parachutes. It is these fluffy tufts that give milkweed its common name of silkweed. Goldfinches line their nests with the soft down, and children use the empty pods as doll cradles and fairyboats. Fiber from mature milkweed seed pods can be spun like cotton and once was used to make candlewicks. Clothing made from the fibers over ten thousand years ago has been discovered by archaeologists. In the 1940s schoolchildren were asked by the government to help the war effort by filling bags with milkweed fluff so that life jackets could be stuffed with it instead of kapok, which came mainly from Japanese-controlled Java.[8] Fibers of swamp milkweed (*A. incarnata*) are extremely tough and can be made into twine and cordage. A strong yellow dye can be produced from the whole milkweed plant.

Milkweed has been called a mystery plant. Mysterious or not, it is certainly versatile, skillful at propagating itself, attractive, useful, and interesting. In "The Tuft of Flowers" Robert Frost wrote of the feeling of kinship he had for the mower whose scythe had spared a butterfly weed beside a reedy brook, "a leaping tongue of bloom," to be enjoyed by butterflies—and poets.

Mistletoe

Mistletoe Family (*Viscaceae*)

Common names: Golden Bough, Birdlime

In 1892 everybody was talking about the gigantic World's Fair to be held in Chicago to mark the 400th anniversary of Christopher Columbus's discovery of America. The planning got so involved that the Fair opened a year late—in 1893—but nobody seemed to mind; there would be so many exciting new things to see and experience, such as the first Ferris wheel, created especially for this fair. Each state or territory was to prepare its own building, so women in the Territory of Oklahoma quickly got together and petitioned the legislature to name the mistletoe as the floral emblem of the territory so they could use it to decorate Oklahoma's building.

The "flower" adopted by the Sooners is unusual for several reasons. First, it is not the small yellow flowers but the pearly white berries that are its main attraction. Second, it does not grow from roots in the ground but rather lives its entire life high up in the branches of trees. Third, it makes its best showing in winter when other flowers have gone to sleep. And fourth, it is the only state flower that is a parasite. Its roots dig into the vascular system of its host, depleting the sap, and it may eventually kill the limb it is attached to or weaken the entire tree until it dies. Also, despite the fact that the mature berries are very poisonous, the plant has traditionally been considered an important and valuable medicine.

Legendary mistletoe is *Viscum* of the Old World, similar to American mistletoe, which is sometimes called "false mistletoe." The genus

Phoradendron, meaning "tree-thief" in Greek, is common in the southern states and can be found on oak, ash, elm, mesquite, sycamore, and many other trees. In Texas, there are five species and several varieties of *Phoradendron,* including a pretty pinkish berried mistletoe that grows on juniper in western Texas.

The mixture of beauty and destructiveness in this strange little plant has always fascinated. From ancient times people have credited it with magic power, and in Roman mythology it was the "golden bough" that men risked their lives for. In Norse mythology it was a mistletoe dart that caused the death of Balder the Beautiful, the most beloved of the gods. The myth relates that after Balder had a dream that left him with a feeling of great and imminent danger, his mother, Frigga, thought of a plan to save him. Rushing over all the earth, she got everything to promise never to harm Balder; the only thing she overlooked was the mistletoe, which was hidden up in the branches of an oak tree. When the other gods learned that Balder could not be hurt, they played a game of throwing rocks and arrows and darts at him, roaring with laughter as these things bounced off him and rolled harmlessly away. Balder enjoyed the game as much as the others, daring them to hurl their spears and arrows at him. The only one who wasn't enjoying the game was sly Loki, who hated Balder for his goodness and beauty. Loki persuaded Balder's blind brother, Hodur, to join in the game, and giving him a dart made of a twig of mistletoe, Loki said, "I will guide your aim." He did, and when Hodur threw the twig it flew straight to Balder's heart, killing him instantly.[1]

In many lands mistletoe was treated as a sacred plant. Because it flourished in the branches of trees that seemed dead in winter, some ancient people thought it was the tree's soul, and it seemed to spring to life mysteriously, like a gift from heaven. They apparently did not know that birds eating the berries and flying from tree to tree left the seeds in their droppings and in the sticky residue of the berries as they brushed them from their feet and bills. Druids, priests of the ancient Celts, worshipped the oak tree and the mistletoe growing in it, which they harvested in a special ritual. Wearing white robes, they entered the oak groves, where one priest climbed a tree and cut the mistletoe branches loose with a golden sickle. Below the tree the other priests held up a white cloth to catch the falling sprigs so that they would not touch the ground and lose their special magic. They sacrificed two oxen under the trees and said prayers of thanksgiving for the plant, which was called all-heal because it was thought to be a remedy for all diseases.[2] The priests gave the Celtic people sprigs of mistletoe to carry for good luck and to hang over their doorways to attract good spirits and drive away evil ones. The Norse believed that mistletoe in the house protected the house from loss by fire, and Swedes placed mistletoe in stalls to keep witches from riding or injuring their horses.

In Christian legend the mistletoe was a tree until its wood was used for the cross on which Christ died, when it shrank to its present size. Monks, who called it "wood of the cross," swallowed water in which it had been steeped and wore fragments of mistletoe around their necks to cure disease.[3]

Over the years hanging branches of mistletoe came to symbolize peace and love. Seventeenth-century English boys hung mistletoe clusters over doorways and claimed kisses from any young girl who walked under it. In the nineteenth century people in Britain combined mistletoe branches with other greenery to make "kissing boughs" as decorations. And the idea of kissing under the mistletoe became a firmly entrenched Christmas tradition after Dickens promoted the idea in *The Pickwick Papers* by describing a kissing spree at Dingley Dell:

> As to the poor relations, they kissed everybody, not excepting the plain portions of the young lady visitors, who in their excessive confusion ran right under the mistletoe, as soon as it was hung up, without knowing it![4]

In America, Washington Irving recorded in his *Sketch Book:* "The mistletoe is still hung up in farmhouses and kitchens at Christmas; and the young men have the privilege of kissing the girls under it, plucking each time a berry from the bush. When the berries are all plucked, the privilege ceases."[5]

Europeans called mistletoe birdlime and used the resin in the plant to catch small birds. They used mistletoe as a panacea to treat many ailments, including tuberculosis and palsy, and considered it a specific for epilepsy. Curiously, while European mistletoe has been used to treat high blood pressure for centuries, experimental data shows that American mistletoe actually raises blood pressure.[6]

Native Americans used it to cause abortions, and modern herbalist

Michael Moore points out that the dried plant has ergotlike effects on the uterus, stimulating contractions and lessening bleeding after childbirth, but he cautions that further testing is needed.[7] The U.S. Food and Drug Administration lists mistletoe as an "unsafe" plant to use as a medicine.

Today mistletoe remains a popular decoration during the Christmas and New Year's holiday season and several southern states, including Oklahoma and Texas, do a big business gathering and shipping tons of the curious plant to places throughout the world where it does not grow in such abundance.

In the language of flowers, mistletoe represents affection and love and is assigned the motto "I shall surmount all difficulties."

Morning Glory

Morning Glory Family (*Convolvulaceae*)

Common Names: Bindweed, Tievine, Dodder, Love Vine

The family name for morning glories comes from the Latin *convolvo*, meaning "to intertwine," and the genus name *Ipomoea* comes from a Greek word meaning "wormlike." Humans have always had a love/hate relationship with these wildflowers, which have been called the courtesans of the plant world—both beautiful and bad. Some members of the family, particularly the bindweeds, can be found in very bad company, growing alongside poison ivy, and the truth is that most family members are not particular where they are found, twining their tendrils around hedges, corn stalks, cotton plants, fences, telephone poles, and chain link fences with equal enthusiasm. Several folk names for the family members known as dodder express the exasperation this plant aroused among rural people, who called them old man's nightcap (old man being a name for the devil), devil's guts, devil's garters, and hellweed.

Nancy Ranson tells this myth about how the morning glory became a vine:

At first it was only a small plant with a great curiosity about what was happening around it, and when it heard baby birds chirping in a nest built in a nearby shrub, it was eager to see them. Creeping and stretching, it crawled along until it got near the shrub. Then it stretched and reached until it got hold of a branch. Encouraged, it began to wind itself around the branch and climbed upward until at last it reached the edge of the nest and peeping inside was pleased to get to see the three little birds almost ready to fly. Since that day the plant has been able to run along the ground and to climb.[1]

Another legend about how morning glory flowers were created is told by both Ranson and Ellen Schulz:

When the earth was still young and fairies lived everywhere, the fairy children loved to play in meadows and running streams. The children often displeased their mother by getting their pretty dresses, which were made by the rainbow fairies, wet and muddy. One bright morning, after promising to stay clean, the children went out to play. At first they ran happily in the meadows collecting flowers and chasing butterflies, but as the sun got hotter, they thought they heard the babbling brook calling to them. Soon they left the meadows and were splashing in the cool water, completely forgetting their promise to their mother. When they realized that their dresses were soaked, one bright fairy suggested they take them off and hang them up to dry. This they did, hanging the colorful frocks on a vine that stretched over the bushes along the bank. But when they tried to pull the dry clothes off the vine, they found they were stuck tight. No matter how hard they pulled, the dresses would not come loose, so they had to leave them hanging there. Ever since, the delicate pleated flowers that look like tiny, frilly skirts blooming in the bright morning hours have been called morning glories.[2]

In the wild and in cultivation, morning glories grow profusely with attractive funnel-shaped flowers on twining and trailing hairy stems, in colors ranging from white to pink to blue, purple, and scarlet. One species called heavenly blue (*Ipomoea violacea*), a native of tropical America, has vines with heart-shaped leaves and seeds containing acids that are similar to those found in LSD. These seeds are consumed during secret ceremonies among Native Americans in Mexico and in some South American countries in order to produce hallucinations that are used to foretell the future and in curative rites.[3]

In North America some tribes also found uses for native morning glories. An infusion of bush morning glory was used to treat heart problems, and different types of bindweed were used to treat jaundice and gall blad-

der ailments or to increase bile flow.[4] It was apparently known to Native Americans as well as to Europeans that all members of the *Convolvulus* family have purgative properties to some degree.

Common bindweed (*Convolvulus arvensis*), which grows in many parts of Texas, has become established and cursed in many languages over most of the world. *Arvensis* comes from the Latin *arvum,* "a cornfield," indicating the habit of the plant of taking over cultivated fields, where it strangles the stems of the crops and grows so prolifically it shuts out sunlight. It is extremely difficult to extirpate as its long roots run deep into the ground and extend over large areas. Because the roots are brittle and snap readily, it is easy to leave in the ground small pieces that soon grow as vigorously as ever, sending up shoots to the surface. The creeping stems swing in slow circles until they come in contact with something they can climb upon. No wonder one of the common names of bindweed is possession vine. These ruffians of the wildflower world are deceptively pretty, with dainty pink or white flowers that have a faint perfume of vanilla. In the language of flowers, morning glories represent affection, and bindweed represents humility—which surely must refer to the condition of the person who struggles to be rid of it rather than to the militant plant itself.

A useful member of the family is the wild sweet potato, which has morning glory type blossoms and large tuberous roots. Native Americans called these wild potatoes "man-of-the-earth" and ate them dried or roasted. Shakespeare mentions the wild sweet potato in *The Merry Wives of Windsor* and in *Troilus and Cressida*.

Also useful is the attractive rose-purple goat-foot morning glory (*Ipomoea pes-caprae*), which helps stabilize shifting coastal sand dunes. Both its common and scientific names come from the shape of the leaf, which resembles a goat's hoof. *Pes* is from the Latin *pediculus* (foot) and *caprae* from the Latin word for goat. Widespread on tropical shores, it creeps along dunes, laying down an extensive deep root system. Also called railroad vine, it may sprawl for thirty feet. Beach morning glory (*I. stolonifera*) with its white blossoms is often seen alongside goat-foot morning glory, twining over Texas' Gulf Coast dunes, helping to anchor them.

Texas has about two dozen species of dodder (*Cuscuta*), which is a total parasite. Starting from seeds in the ground, the slender stems wave about and soon attach themselves to a host plant by minute disks that sink into its tissues. The dodder then severs its connections with Mother Earth as its roots and seeds become detached, and it lives for the rest of its life entirely on the food it draws from its unfortunate host. The flowers—tiny, white, waxy, fleshy, and bell-like—grow in clusters along the curling leafless orange or yellow stems. As the dodder matures it looks like tangled orange or gold masses of threads sprawling from plant to plant. Its hosts may be bluebonnets, verbena, or vetch, or it may choose flax, clover, or alfalfa to sponge on, in which case a farmer may lose a crop as the intruder lives up to its common names of strangleweed and tangle-gut.

Much folklore attaches to this strange plant. Because it shines like spun silk in bright sunlight, dodder is sometimes called angel's hair. But it also has been associated with witches and with the devil. "Witches' shoelaces" indicates one use supposedly made of it, and "devils' thread" was a name it acquired because of the belief that the devil spun dodder at night in order to destroy clover, one of God's favorite plants. Another superstition caused it to be called "love vine," and it was said that if a man swung a bit of the vine three times around his head and then threw it backwards, he could find out if his sweetheart loved him. After three days, when he returned to the spot, if he found that the dodder had attached itself to another plant or bush and was growing, the person named when it was thrown returned his love, but if the vine had died, that person did not love him. The fact that the vine usually thrives probably accounts for the popularity of this test.[5]

Some practical uses have been found for dodder. The Chinese used the seeds to treat urinary tract infections. In England it was used to treat urinary complaints and kidney, spleen, and liver diseases. The Cherokees crushed the stems to make a poultice for bruises, and other tribes used dodder as a contraceptive and also made a bath from it for patients with lung complaints. In addition, the vines can be boiled to produce a clear yellow dye.

In England the names woodbine and withywind were given to different plants at different times, and sometimes they were applied to morning glories. Shakespeare seems to have known that members of the morning glory family twine counterclockwise and members of the honeysuckle family twine clockwise, and when they meet they join in a tight embrace. In *A Midsummer Night's Dream* Titania promises to wind Bottom in her arms as tightly as "doth the woodbine the sweet honeysuckle gently entwist" (act IV, scene i, line 44).

Thomas Hardy makes symbolic use of morning glories in *Noble Dames* (scene ii, line 90) when he says of a character that he was "One of those sweet-pea or withy-wind natures which require a twig or stouter fibre than its own to hang upon and bloom." And in *The Return of the Native* one character tells another: "You could twist him to your will like withywind, if you only had the mind."[6]

The morning glory is the floral symbol for September, and the Japanese consider the morning glory the symbol of mortality. In rural England the plant was called the "life of man" because it was thought to illustrate in a day the stages of human life: childhood in bud form in the morning; maturity in the fully opened blossom at midday; and old age as the flower wilts in the evening.[7]

Mullein

Figwort Family (*Scrophulariaceae*)

Common Names: Velvet Plant, Flannel Plant,
Blanket Herb, Great Mullein,
Common Mullein, Moth Mullein

*A*lthough mullein made its way to America as a stow-away with early European immigrants and followed in their footsteps as they moved westward, it has been here so long and made itself so completely at home throughout the United States that its origin is often forgotten. Britons who cultivate mullein in their gardens call it American velvet plant.

Looking out over a field covered with mullein, Thoreau wrote in his *Journals* (July 8, 1851) that just three years earlier none were noticeable, and he noted: "Where millet was planted, mulleins sprung up. Millet did not perpetuate itself, but the few seeds of mullein accidently brought in with the grain are still multiplying." In America mullein is more apt to be called a weed than a wildflower, but in England it is given more respect. On a trip to Britain, naturalist John Burroughs mused: "I have come 3,000 miles to see the mullein cultivated in a garden and christened the 'velvet plant.'"[1]

In Texas woolly or great mullein (*Verbascum thapsus*) is a common plant, especially in neglected fields and waste places. During its first year the plant forms a large rosette of thick, whitish green, woolly leaves and establishes a deep taproot system. The following spring a single thick leafy stalk topped by a spire of yellow flowers arises from the rosette to a height of two to seven feet.

The entire plant is covered with a soft felt made up of branched hairs that have given it the name mullein, from the Latin *mollis* (soft), which is also the root for the term for the invertebrate, soft marine creatures called mollusks. *Verbascum* is a corruption of the Latin *barbascum* (with beard), and the name *thapsus* derives from the fact that the plant species was supposed to have originated in a place of that name on the Mediterranean Sea.

Moth mullein (*V. blatteria*) grows in the same habitats as common or great mullein but appears less frequently in Texas. *Blatteria* comes from the Latin word for the order of cockroaches, and it was once thought that this plant was effective as an insect repellant. The English name "moth mullein" derived from the fancied resemblance of the corolla to a moth, the lower three hairy stamens being the tongue and antennae. The stem is much slimmer than that of common mullein, and the pretty fragile flowers may be yellow, white, or light pink, with violet tufts of wool on the stamens.

The names Aaron's rod, Jupiter's staff, or Jacob's staff and Shepherd's club reflect the tall ramrod appearance of common mullein, while its downy nature has earned it such folk names as Adam's flannel, beggar's blanket, hare's beard and bunny's ears. Other nicknames reveal some of the ways in which mullein has been used. Romans, who dipped the dried stalks in tallow and used them as torches in funeral processions and in other ceremonies, called them *candelaria*. Greeks soaked the leaves in oil to use as lamp wicks; the thick down is still used in parts of Europe as candle wicking, and dried down from the leaves and stems is used as tinder; consequently, mullein has been called torches, high taper, hedge taper, and candlewick.

Other uses both practical and frivolous have been found to take advantage of the peculiar qualities of the plant. The velvety leaves have been used as shoe liners in cold weather and rubbed on rheumatic joints like flannel to create a soothing warmth. Hummingbirds have been observed lining their tiny nests with the downy hairs from mullein. Children have found their own uses: girls use the leaves as soft doll blankets, and boys hurl the dried stalks as javelins, their light weight and pointed roots making them sail straight and far.

Roman women used the yellow flowers cosmetically, to create a dye for their hair when a golden hue was in fashion. More recently, when the use of rouge was frowned upon, women rubbed the leaves on their cheeks to create a rosy glow, and the plant acquired the name "Quaker rouge." Today flower arrangers make use of the attractive rosettes of basal leaves as a base for floral arrangements. An exotic use for the seeds, which are slightly narcotic, has been to throw them into water to intoxicate fish and make them easy to catch.

In possibly the earliest medical treatise written in America, Cotton Mather wrote: "Our Indians cure consumptions with a Mullein-Tea."[2] During the Civil War mullein leaves soaked in hot vinegar and water were used as poultices to treat wounds.

The plant's common folk names, cow's lungwort or bullock's lungwort, indicate the widespread use of the plant to treat pulmonary congestion in cattle. And the name lungwort reflects the fact that mullein is an old and favorite remedy for respiratory complaints in humans, including East Texans who for centuries have stuffed the chopped dried leaves into corn cob pipes and smoked them to relieve coughs and asthma.[3] Another folk remedy for asthma is to burn mullein roots and inhale the fumes. For ear aches an oil made from the flowers has been a longtime favorite treatment. Homely mullein tea has been used as a panacea for numerous ailments including coughs and colds, and fomentations of the hot tea have been used externally to relieve ulcers, mumps, and glandular swellings as well as swollen joints.

The Choctaws applied mullein leaves directly to the head to relieve headache, and Barton Warnock says the Hopi used the plant to treat "mental aberrations."[4] Mullein leaves and flowers were official in the *National Formulary* (1916–36), in which it was classified as demulcent, emollient, and pectoral.

Among mullein's many aliases are witch's candle and hag's taper. One superstition suggests that witches used mullein stalks to illuminate their sinister meetings, and people who had dealings with the devil were thought to use mullein torches to light their way. On the other hand, mullein was thought to be a potent protection against witches and warlocks. Another superstition was that the plant could be used to make a love potion, and in the nineteenth-century language of flowers, mullein was called "herb of love."

Mustard

Mustard Family (*Cruciferae/Brassicaceae*)

Common Names: Black Mustard,
White Mustard, India Mustard, Tansy Mustard,
Tumble Mustard, Hedge Mustard Watercress, Wallflower,
Prince's Plume, Peppergrass, Bladderpod, Pennycress,
Spring Cress, Bitter Cress, Rock Cress, Charlock

Mustard gets its name from the Latin *mustum,* must or new wine, and *ardere,* to burn. Ancient Romans pounded the seeds and mixed them with grape must to make mustard, which they served with many different dishes, and almost certainly they introduced the plant to Britain. For many years the English prepared mustard by mixing the coarsely pounded seeds with honey or vinegar and a little cinnamon and then rolling the mixture into balls, until around 1729, when powdered mustard was invented by an elderly woman named Clements who resided in Durham. She ground the seed in a mill and passed the flour through several processes to free the seed from its husks. Keeping her recipe secret, she sold large quantities of powdered mustard through-out the country, and because she resided at Durham, it was called Durham mustard. When it was introduced to the royal table and George I gave it his approval, its success was assured.[1] Much farther south, at Tewksbury on the Avon River near Shakespeare's hometown of Stratford, mustard plants grew in abundance, and another famous mustard, called Tewksbury mustard, was developed. In part two of *Henry IV* (act II, scene iv), Falstaff says of another character, "His wit is as thick as Tewksbury mustard."

Biblical references to mustard are well known. Matthew and Luke relate parables in which Jesus uses a mustard seed as a symbol of faith that can move mountains or trees. Matthew, Mark, and Luke all tell the parable in which Jesus compares the kingdom of God to the mustard seed that a man sows in his garden and that grows to be a tree in which birds come to roost. Biblical scholars affirm that in those days the seed of the mustard plant probably was one of the smallest known, and there actually were mustard plants in Palestine that grew to be over ten feet tall with thick stems and branches strong enough to bear the weight of small birds attracted by the edible seeds.[2]

A distinguishing mark of the large and varied mustard family is that the flowers have four petals, which may be yellow, white, pink, or purple, in the shape of a cross; hence the original family name *Cruciferae* (marked with a cross). Another common characteristic is that the plants usually have peppery seeds, leaves, or roots. In addition to the numerous mustards, other well-known family members are peppergrass, watercress, and bladderpod as well as many common vegetables, including broccoli, cabbage, cauliflower, turnip, radish, rutabaga, kale, brussels sprouts, and kohlrabi, which are all varieties of *Brassica oleracea*, a mustard plant that can still be found growing wild in its primitive form around the Mediterranean Sea.

Various mustard plants were introduced into the United States as garden greens, and all the *Brassicas* growing wild in Texas are originally from Eurasia. These include the mustards known as India mustard, bird rape, charlock, and black and white mustard. Seeds of most *Brassicas* may be used to make mustard, but the best culinary mustards come from the spicy reddish black seeds of black mustard (*Brassica nigra*), which has been cultivated for at least two thousand years. In 1623 herbalist John Gerard wrote:

> The seeds of mustard pounded with vinegar is an excellent sauce, good to be eaten with any grosse meates, either fish or flesh, because it doth help digestion, warmeth the stomache and provoketh appetite.[3]

The oil of mustard seeds is edible, but it is used mainly in making lubricants and soaps. Long before it was discovered that mustard greens are rich in vitamins A, B$_1$, B$_2$, and C as well as minerals, calcium and potassium, they were relished for their crunchy, peppery qualities and used in salads or as potherbs and in soups. One of our common Texas weeds is peppergrass, named for its grasslike leaves and its peppery leaves and buds and equally peppery tiny flattened seed cases. The small fruits and young foliage were used by pioneers to add an aromatic snap to salads, and the dried seeds were used as a substitute for pepper.

Our watercress (*Nasturtium officinale*) is found around springs and in the cool, flowing water of creeks and streams, floating or creeping and sometimes forming dense mats. *Nasturtium* does not mean it is related to our popular garden flower but rather comes from the Latin *Nasi tortium* (nose twister), referring to its pungent quality. The leaves, which are rich in ascorbic acid (vitamin C), have long been valued in Europe as a protection against scurvy. The young leaves and stems are good in salads and sandwiches and are often used as garnishes for meat dishes and in soups. Unfortunately, because of pollution of our waters, it is no longer safe to freely gather and use the watercress that still grows abundantly in our streams.

Charlemagne included the cresses among the herbs he ordered his subjects to cultivate, and a sixteenth-century writer promised: "eating of watercress doth restore the wonted bloom to the cheeks of old-young ladies."[4] The seeds of pennycress, bladderpod, whitlow grass, tansy mustard, and hedge mustard can all be used as peppery seasonings, and the ripe seeds of many mustards are used in pickle recipes. The green pods of Shepherd's purse, which look like tiny replicas of the leather pouches in which shepherds carried their food, are a peppery spice, and the roots of spring cress or bitter cress are reported to taste like horseradish when grated and mixed with vinegar.

The medicinal uses of mustard have been as significant as its food uses. From cuneiform writings of Sumerians (who lived in what is now Iraq about 4000 B.C.), we know that their medicines included mustard. Ancient Greek physicians held the plant in such esteem that they attributed its discovery to Aesculapius, the first physician and son of Apollo, with powers so great he could restore the dead to life. The ancients knew that when mustard seeds were mixed with water they formed a powerful caustic substance, and they used mustard plasters for congestion. Dioscorides (ca. 40–90 A.D.), the Greek physician who studied plants and wrote the famous classical work *De materia medica*, said, "It is good in general for any pain of long continuance when we would draw out anything from the deep within to the outside of the body."[5] Based on his work people theorized that mustard seed oil was an irritant which caused blood vessels to dilate, resulting in an increased blood supply that carried away toxic products.

Along with mustard plasters, hot mustard foot baths have long been a popular treatment for relief of the congestions of colds, coughs, and headaches. In the first century Pliny listed forty-two medicinal uses for mustard, including some unusual ones: "[t]hat the smell of burnt Nasturtium drives away serpents, neutralizes the venom of scorpions . . . mixed with oil and applied to the ears with a fig in it, is a remedy for hardness of hearing."[6]

Apparently Nicholas Culpeper, who recommended that mustard seed be used inwardly and outwardly to "quicken the spirits," agreed with Pliny's notion of using it as an antidote, for he suggested taking a decoction of the seed in wine as it "resisteth poison . . . and the venom of venomous creatures if it be taken in time.[7] King Mithradates VI, who was said to have become immune to poisons by taking them in small increments, experimented with various substances and finally created a universal antidote, called mithridates. This elaborate compound, which was still used in the time of Elizabeth I, contained an extract of the mustard known as pennycress or Mithridates mustard (*Thlaspi arvense*), a plant that grows in Texas.

There is evidence that Victorians appreciated mustard as a common medicine. In an 1883 essay Coleridge wrote: "I have seen in an advertisement something about essence of mustard curing the most obstinate cases of rheumatism." And in 1858 in a letter to his sister-in-law, Miss Hogarth, Dickens wrote, "I got home at half-past ten and mustard-plastered and barley-watered myself tremendously."[8]

Texas has at least five species of whitlow grass (*Draba*), which was called nailwort by herbalists who used it to treat whitlows or felons. Hedge mustard (*Sisymbrium*), found in thickets and fields and waste places in Texas, has been called "singer's plant" ever since Pliny declared it to be a very good cure for coughs when mixed with honey, and herbalists through the years have recommended it as an excellent remedy for laryngitis.

When Shakespeare wrote of "lady smocks all silver white" in *Love's Labour's Lost,* he was referring to the *Cardamines*, members of the mustard family that we call bitter cress or spring cress in Texas. In England these plants were used in treating heart disease to strengthen the heart and also in treating hysteria and epilepsy. As the name implies they have been used like other cresses for salads. Sometimes the English refer to them as cuckoo flowers because, as Gerard says, they flower in April or May "when the cuckow begins to sing her pleasant note without stammering."[9]

Prince's plume or desert plume (*Stanleya pinnata*) is a shrubby perennial with several stout blue-green stems that are spreading and have feathery (as *pinnata* indicates) lower leaves. It is also called the "sentinel of the plains" because the sulphur yellow flower spikes glow on the western prairies and desert areas. It is an indicator of selenium-bearing soil, and the poisonous element selenium is absorbed from the soil in sufficient quantities to be dangerous to livestock feeding on it; small amounts cause severe damage to cattle and large amounts may kill them.[10] Apparently the hazard is not as great for humans, as Barton Warnock says that the Indians of the Terlingua area in the Big Bend used the leaves and stems as potherbs and made mush from the seeds.

Texas has three species of wallflowers (*Erysimum*) whose stiffly upright slender stems are crowned with showy, fragrant orangy yellow blossoms. As Gerard remarked, "Wallflowers groweth upon bricke and stone walls, in the corners of churches every where, and also among rubbish and other stony places."[11] Lacking ancient walls and decaying roof tops of ruined castles where they nestled in crannies in England, our native species make do with steep hillsides and narrow ledges of limestone bluffs. There is a romantic legend from Scotland that says that in the fourteenth century, Elizabeth, daughter of the Earl of March, dropped a wallflower from her castle wall to signal her lover, the son of an enemy clan, that she was ready to elope. But in making her escape she fell to her death, and her unhappy lover placed a wallflower in his cap and left Scotland forever.[12] In the nineteenth century young women who sat on the sidelines at social functions were called wallflowers because they, like the plant, clung to walls. Appropriately, in the language of flowers, the wallflower represents adversity in love.

In addition to those mentioned, Texas has several other species of mustard family members with interesting characteristics that are reflected in their common names. Bladderpods are also called popweeds because of their small bladderlike pea-sized seed pods that pop when stepped on.

Tumble mustards, which have loosely branched stems and pale yellow flowers, die after their seeds ripen and become tumbleweeds when their roots are dislodged from the soil by the wind. The spectacle pod has bilobed seed pods that resemble miniature spectacles, and the twist flower, found in far west Texas, has vibrant violet purple flowers with narrow twisted petals with wavy edges.

The expression "to cut the mustard" was originally a Western saying popular among cowboys during the late nineteenth century, and a genuine article was "the proper mustard." In a popular book, *Log of a Cowboy*, the author, Andy Adams, says of one character "for fear the two dogs were not the proper mustard, he had that dog man sue him in court to make him prove the pedigree." O. Henry described a pretty girl by saying, "She cut the mustard all right." And Carl Sandburg wrote, "Kid each other, you cheapskates. Tell each other you're all to the mustard."[13] The phrase took on new meaning in a twentieth-century pop tune in which the singer mentioned being "Too old to cut the mustard anymore."

Although people persist in calling mustard a weed, throughout the ages its family members have been our friends, providing relief for our aches and pains, nutrition for our bodies, spice for our food, and visual beauty in masses of golden blossoms that brighten our waste places.

Orchid

Orchid Family (*Orchidaceae*)

*Common Names: Yellow Lady's Slipper,
Adder's Mouth, Snakemouth, Coralroot,
Ladies' Tresses, Three Bird's Orchis, Water Spider,
Fringed Orchid, Beard Flower, Grass Pink, Rose Pogonia*

When Luther Burbank was asked if he had ever done any work to improve orchids, he stared at his questioner for a moment before replying: "Improve orchids? But who on earth would dream of wanting them improved?"[1]

The most beautiful, most grotesque, and strangest flowers in the world, orchids are members of one of the earth's largest, most complex plant family, ranging in size from plants that will fit into a thimble to a vine reaching a hundred feet. The flowers may be large single blooms or grow in clusters of hundreds on a spray and remain in flower for less than a day or for more than six months. Although some orchid plants are more notable for their attractive leaves than for their flowers, others have only a single leaf and some have no leaves at all. They grow at elevations from high mountain slopes to sea level, and a few grow beneath the ground and never see the light of day.

The idea of connecting sensual pleasure with orchids is ancient. The Greek philosopher Theophrastus (d. ca. 287 B.C.) in his *Enquiry into Plants* refers to plants called *Orchis*, the Greek word for *testis*, a reference to the testiculate tubers occurring in pairs. It was thought that these tubers when crushed and eaten stimulated sexual passion and also influenced the birth of male babies—beliefs that persisted into the seventeenth century. As usual the Greeks had a myth to explain the origin of the family name: Orchis, son of a satyr and a nymph, was a lustful character and an avid follower of Dionysius (Bacchus). At a Festival of Dionysius, Orchis, inflamed with wine, attacked a priestess. Immediately the whole congregation fell upon him and tore him limb from limb. When his father prayed to the gods to restore him to life, they refused but did agree to change his mangled body into flowers, each piece taking a different color and shape and all to be called by his name, Orchis.[2] These flowers were alleged to retain his temperament, and it was thought that to eat their roots was to suffer a temporary lapse into a lustful, satyrlike state. Orchis flowers were sometimes called "satyrion," and in France some varieties of orchids are still called satyrions.

Belief in the aphrodisiac power of orchids carried over into superstitions connected with witches, who were supposed to use the tubers in their philtres, the fresh tuber being given to promote true love and the withered to check wrong passions. Herbalist and inveterate astrologer Nicholas Culpeper perpetuated this idea by declaring that the roots should be used with discretion since they were "hot and moist under the dominion of Venus and provoke lust exceedingly which, they say, the dried and withered roots do restrain."[3]

In medieval England the folk names for many wild orchids were slang words for testicles: dog stones, fool's stones, goat stones, sweet cods, soldier's cullions. The early purple orchid (*Orchis mascula*) has tuberous roots divided into fingerlike lobes, and it is to these that Shakespeare refers in *Hamlet* when the Queen describes the "fantastic garlands" woven by the mad Ophelia: "long purples that liberal shepherds give a grosser name, / But our cold maids do dead men's fingers call them" (*Hamlet*, act IV, scene iii). In his *Herball* John Gerard calls orchids "fox-stones" and says it would require a volume to describe the "shapes of sundry sorts of living creatures" to be seen in their flowers, a few of which he lists: "some in the shape and proportion of flies, in others gnats, some humble bees, others like unto honey bees, some like Butter-flies, and others like Waspes that be dead."[4]

The most spectacular orchids are air plants found in tropical jungles, where they are either epiphyticus (growing on trees or shrubs) or epilithicus (growing on the surface of rocks). They are not parasites but use their hosts only for anchorage and take their nourishment from minute particles of organic matter in rain water or from the debris that collects around them. In temperate zones most species of orchids are not air plants but terrestrials growing from underground rhizomes. The flowers of orchids may range from large and showy to tiny and inconspicuous, but on close inspection they will be found to share the common trait of having one of the three petals, called the lip, that is larger and lower than the other two. Often grotesque in shape, frequently striking in color, this lip petal is sometimes fringed and sometimes has a spurlike appendage that secretes nectar.

As has happened in the case of other rare beauties, the history of orchids is filled with greed, envy, intrigue, and even death. In the seventeenth century, descriptions of exotic orchids sent back to England by missionaries and explorers from newly colonized tropical territories stimulated interest. When a few of the gorgeous specimens sent by ship survived the long trip, that interest ignited. As orchidomania spread, merchants and private individuals began sending orchid hunters out to the jungles of the world. In unfamiliar jungle settings, the collectors risked dysentery, fevers, snakebite, and attacks by hostile natives, and a number of them died from these causes. Some simply disappeared, never to be heard from again. But others took their places and sent back consignments of ten thousand plants of a single species, in some cases ruthlessly stripping areas of every orchid plant. At auctions in London and Liverpool, a "new" species might bring several hundred pounds. In order to mislead competitors, reports of locations were falsified by orchid buyers, and even botanical collectors concealed their sources by mislabeling, creating confusion that is still being sorted out.[5] When William Cattley, one of the first amateur orchid growers in England, succeeded in raising some large flowers with flamboyant trumpet-shaped lips, orchid lovers rejoiced, and the genus was named *Cattleya* after him.

Darwin was so impressed with the intricate pollination schemes of various orchids that in 1862 he published a treatise titled "On the Various Contrivances by which Orchids are Fertilized by Insects," and many other scientists have been fascinated by the sex life of these fantastic plants. The "sundry shapes" noted by Gerard are part of the plan to carry on the species. There are bee and butterfly orchids that look like these insects as well as fly, spider, lizard, bird's nest, swan, dove, and monkey orchids and one called *anthropophora,* or man orchid, that looks like the body of a man wearing a very big hat. Unlike most flowers, which release pollen in minute particles, orchids (like milkweed) concentrate their pollen in sticky, bloblike masses called "pollinia." Some orchids shoot the pollinia at the pollinating insect, and some orchids force the insect to pass through narrow spaces where it will brush against the pollen masses.

One genus, the Mediterranean *Ophrys,* assumes the appearance of a female wasp and emits a similar odor to attract the male moth. In his attempt to mate with the flower, the male picks up pollinia and eventually brushes it off onto another flower. Bees and spiders also pollinate by this pseudocopulation process. Another orchid mimics the insect prey of a wasp, which dives at the orchid to sting it and departs with a load of pollen glued to its body. In other orchids the lip has evolved into a pouch or slipper, and when a bee alights on the front edge of the pouch in search of nectar, it frequently tumbles into the pouch, from which it can exit only through a small opening next to the stamen. In squeezing through the opening it rubs against the pollinia, and when it visits the next flower and tumbles into its trap either accidently or through intoxication from the nectar, it can only escape by the same route, and this time it leaves the pollen on the stigmatic surface. Orchids pollinated by moths are generally glistening white and emit their scents only at night. Some tropical orchids have a fetid smell characteristic of decaying meat in order to attract carrion flies as pollinators.

For many years would-be orchid breeders suffered extreme frustration in trying to reproduce orchids from the dustlike seeds. Even after scientists discovered that the mature seeds of orchids germinate in a symbiotic relationship with a particular type of fungi (mycorrhizal fungi), the task was difficult. Finally in 1922 Dr. Lewis Knudson, a plant physiologist at Cornell University, came up with a formulae (known as the Knudson Formulae) consisting of various chemicals combined with cane sugar or glucose, agar, and water that eliminated the need for fungi, and the breeding went on apace.[6]

In addition to their aesthetic value, some species of orchids have been put to practical uses. Salep is the name for the dried tuber of some European and Indonesian species. They contain gum and starch and were used in medicines as a soothing agent. Imported to England under the Arabian name *sahlab* (the fox's testicles), which was corrupted in English into "saloop" or "salep," they were powdered and mixed with milk to make a nutritious hot beverage sold at stalls in London streets. Prepared like arrowroot, salep was considered a valuable diet for children and invalids. In the days of sailing ships salep was a part of the ship's stores on long voyages, as an ounce dissolved in two quarts of boiling water was considered sufficient subsistence for each man per day if provisions ran short.[7]

Vanilla is the name for a group of climbing orchids. Almost five hundred years ago, Spain's conquistadors found the Aztecs of Mexico adding bits of fragrant orchid seed pod to their cocoa. Soon *Vanilla planifolia* traveled to Europe and from there to Madagascar and other tropical islands where producing vanilla became a big business. The fruit pod of the vanilla plant is from five to ten inches long, with an oily black pulp that contains a large number of tiny, black seeds, fine as gunpowder. As the pods are dried or cured, they shrink, turning a rich, chocolate brown color and acquiring the flavor and aroma of vanilla as we know it. Vanilla extract is prepared by a complicated and expensive process that requires finely chopping or crushing the cured vanilla beans and percolating them with alcohol and water. On vanilla plantations in Madagascar and Tahiti, orchid flowers are pollinated by hand, as girls move from plant to plant lifting the little tongue on the flower column with a wooden needle and pressing the anther and stigma together in a process called "marrying the orchid."

In Texas, wild orchids can be found from the mountains and basins of far West Texas to the woodlands of East Texas. All are terrestrials, and, as might be expected, the Big Thicket area has the most variety with at least forty species. Undoubtedly the best known of Texas' orchids is the showy yellow lady's slipper (*Cypripedium*), also called moccasin flower and whippoorwill shoes because of its pouchlike, inflated lip. The botanical name refers to the sandal or slipper of Aphrodite (Venus), who was believed to have been born on the island of Cyprus. Bees are attracted by its pleasing apricot scent, and American Indians and pioneers used a chemical extracted from the boiled roots as a light sedative. For many years it was considered a favorite soothing herb for treating hysteria, irritability, delirium, and headaches.[8] Another lady's slipper, the beautiful pink and white *C. reginae* (slipper of the queen), is the state flower of Minnesota.

The *Habenarias* or rein orchids, which are characterized by spurs at the base of the lip petal, are sometimes called bog orchids because of their love of watery habitats. The water-spider orchid is found floating on mats of other vegetation on the surface of water in the eastern half of Texas, while other species such as the white or yellow fringed orchids and the snowy orchid thrive in marshes, swamps, bogs, and wet prairie lands.

Calopogon, the scientific name for grass pinks, means "beautiful beard," referring to the hairs and papillae lining the lip that occurs at the top instead of the bottom of the flower. Found in eastern and southeastern Texas from April through June, the royal grass pink (*C. pulchellus*) bears conspicuous rose-red flowers. Another pretty orchid is the rose pogonia which has a large pink flower at the tip of the stem with a fringed lip sporting a yellow "beard," and a solitary leaf near the middle of the stem.

There are at least thirteen varieties of ladies' tresses (*Spiranthes*) in Texas, usually with white flowers variously tinged with green, yellow, brown, or lavender. Growing in a more or less spirally twisted spike, they have common names alluding to their distinguishing characteristics such as slender ladies' tresses, nodding ladies' tresses, narrow-leaved ladies' tresses, fragrant ladies' tresses, lace-lip orchid (with a minutely toothed lip), and giant spiral-orchid. A beautiful member of the genus is scarlet ladies' tresses or flame orchid (*S. cinnabarina*), found in the Chisos Mountains in the Trans-Pecos. Its showy yellowish orange to scarlet flowers grow in a spire three to six inches long.

Coralroots (*Corallorhiza*) are strange little orchids with no chlorophyll or green color at any time. Like mushrooms and toadstools, they support themselves on the dead remains of other plants in the soil, and their underground rhizomes are much branched, pink in color, and in general coral-like. Coralroot grow in the decaying humus in pine-hardwood forests in the mountains and along streams of the Trans-Pecos and in cedar brakes and river bluffs in the eastern half of Texas.

Thoreau must have known that in the language of flowers the orchid represents a belle, for in his *Journals* (June 9, 1854) he notes that he has found a great fringed orchid, "a large spike of peculiarly delicate, pale purple flowers growing in the luxuriant and shady swamp. The village belle never sees this more delicate belle of the swamp . . . a beauty reared in the shade of a convent, who has never strayed beyond the convent bell." In "Aurora Leigh" Elizabeth Barrett Browning mentions "nooks of valleys lined with orchises," and in "In Memorium" Tennyson invokes Spring to bring him solace for his grief over the death of his friend, urging her to "bring orchis."

An ever-increasing number of orchid societies and amateur orchid growers attest to the continuing fascination with orchids. The task of registering and collating hybrids in stud books became so onerous that it was finally taken over by the Royal Horticultural Society of Great Britain. Orchid breeders have created over fifty thousand varieties; however, many people still prefer the natural species and agree with the Colombian orchid fancier who said, "*Allá la mano del hombre no ha medido la pata*," literally "There the hand of man has not put his foot into it."[9] In February of 1994 the San Antonio Botanical Gardens reported that more than twenty rare orchids had been stolen, probably for sale on the black market for rare plants.[10] Apparently intrigue is still rife in the world of this fabulous flower.

Paintbrush

Figwort Family (*Scrophulariaceae*)

Common Names: Scarlet Paintbrush, Texas Paintbrush,
Indian Pink, Painted Cup, Indian Paintbrush

Glowing with the colors of the most brilliant sunsets, paintbrush (*Castilleja*) ranges over the prairies and the mountains of the western states, and Wyoming has chosen the paintbrush as its state flower. The genus name *Castilleja* honors Domingo Castillejo, a Spanish botanist. In Texas this genus is represented by nine native species with colors varying from cream to yellow to orange to vermilion and magenta.

The eye catching part of all paintbrushes is not the inconspicuous yellowish green or yellowish pink flower but the colorful leaves (bracts) enveloping it and looking as if they had been dipped in paint. The chief pollinators of paintbrush are hummingbirds, which are attracted by the showy bracts to explore the nectar in the depths of the elongated tubular flowers.

Each year the Texas Department of Transportation sows thousands of pounds of the tiny seeds of Texas paintbrush (*Castilleja indivisa*) along Texas highways. There are well over five million seeds to a pound, which may cost as much as five hundred dollars, but a whole acre can be planted with several handfuls. The brilliant reds of this species, often mixed with the bright blues of another native Texan, the bluebonnet, create spectacular ribbons of color for motorists to enjoy each spring.

Recent studies at the National Wildflower Research Center in Austin have shown that paintbrush is hemiparasitic (drawing water and miner-

als from a host) and that it grows more vigorously when in contact with a host plant. The host used in the experiments was the bluebonnet, which has a compatible life cycle and is often seen growing with the paintbrush in nature as well as in highway plantings.[1] What this means for the bluebonnet is that in times of drought its paintbrush companion is apt to tap into its roots and steal water and minerals, causing it to wilt if not to die. If bluebonnets are not handy, the paintbrush uses other plants such as grasses, sagebrush, or oaks in time of need. No wonder that in the language of flowers the paintbrush symbolizes power.

Although paintbrush is potentially toxic, Native Americans reportedly made a weak tea from the flower to treat rheumatism and to use as a secret love charm in food and as a poison to destroy enemies. Laura Martin reports that according to the doctrine of signatures, paintbrush was used to soothe burned skin and ease the sting of centipedes and that women drank a concoction made from the roots to dry up menstrual flow. Virginia Scully says that a decoction of paintbrush roots was used as a blood purifier and that it was favored by some tribes as a remedy for venereal diseases, with small amounts of a solution made from the boiled roots being taken daily.[2]

Dyes were also made from the plant. The Zuni dyed deerskins black with iron minerals and the roots of paintbrush, and they obtained a greenish yellow dye from the stems, leaves, and flower of the plant when it was simmered with alum.[3]

An Indian legend describes the origin of the paintbrush: Each evening a young chief sat watching the sunset as the colors changed from rose to crimson to gold and then faded, leaving a gorgeous afterglow. He longed to be able to catch this beauty by painting it, but he had only his crude war paints made from pounded minerals and heavy, stiff brushes too clumsy to copy such nuances of color. Each night after the glorious tints faded into darkness, he went to his wigwam sad and heavy-hearted, and he prayed to the Great Spirit to give him the ability to capture the beauty of the sunset. One evening as he sat watching a sunset more beautiful than any he had ever seen, he heard a voice telling him to look down by his feet. There he found a graceful plant shaped like a slender brush wet with paint that matched the red of the sunset. When he held its tip to the soft buckskin, the color transferred perfectly. As other brushes sprang up dripping with the colors of the sunset, he worked feverishly at his picture, tossing aside each brush as he finished with it and plucking another. At last his heart was filled with joy for his picture was a true copy of the sunset. And in the morning he saw that every brush he had tossed away had taken root and multiplied, spreading the vivid beauty of the paintbrush over the land.[4]

Passionflower

Passionflower Family (*Passifloraceae*)

*Common Names: Maypop, Apricot Vine,
Water Lemon, Passiflora*

When Roman Catholic priests arriving in the New World found trees festooned with vines bearing strange, gorgeous flowers with large intricate purple and white blossoms, they immediately decided that nature had given them a wonderful tool for teaching Christianity. Here, it seemed to them, was a beautiful flower that exemplified the whole story of the divine passion of Christ. Specimens were sent back to Spain and Italy, and the remarkable vine soon flourished in Southern European gardens, where it was praised and venerated.

The scientific name given the plant, *Passiflora incarnata* (the flower of the passion incarnate), reflects the elaborate interpretation of symbols of the crucifixion assigned to it by the early Roman Catholic missionaries. Although there are variations, the symbolism is basically the same. Arising from the center of the flower is a column representing the cross. The corona is the crown of thorns. The three knoblike stigma are the nails, and the five stamens represent the five wounds of Christ. The bladelike leaves represent the spear that pierced Christ's side, and the curling tendrils suggest the whips and cords that tormented him. The ten sepals and petals account for the ten faithful Apostles—omitting Peter, who denied Jesus, and Judas, who betrayed him. The purple blossoms are the purple robe in which Christ was mockingly dressed, and the white blossoms represent the purity and brightness of Christ.

As time passed, theologians found further Christian symbolism in the complex flower: the starlike appearance of the partially open blossom was said to refer to the Star of the East that guided the three Wise Men; they also pointed out that like the vine of the plant, a Christian needs support to survive; and like the plant that grows again when it is cut down, so Christians also are not harmed by the evil in the world that attempts to destroy them.

When the passionflower reached England from its Virginia colony, its exotic beauty attracted attention and admiration, but the religious significance that had become attached to it was played down by the Protestant church leaders. Nevertheless, workers in stained glass and painters of church murals made use of it, and in the cathedrals at Lichfield and

Hereford, ironworkers enshrined the passionflower in beautiful choir screens.[1] In the nineteenth-century code of the language of flowers, the passionflower came to represent faith.

The nickname maypop arose not because the plant blooms in May, but as the anglicized version of the Native American word *maracock*, as the Virginia tribe called it. And *maracock* came from the South American Tupi term *maraca-cui-iba* (rattle fruit) because when the gourdlike fruit dries, the seeds rattle like a maraca.[2]

In Texas the splendid *Passiflora incarnata* with its large flowers is found in the eastern third of the state, while other, less showy members of the family grow in the Hill Country and in other areas. *P. lutea* is a smaller version with greenish yellow flowers. Its habitat may be along rows of fence, in pastures, along stream banks, and at the edges of woodlands and thickets. *P. foetida* (*foetidus:* bad-smelling, stinking) has velvety leaves, white or lilac flowers, and a rank smell. It is found in the Rio Grande Valley and on the Edwards Plateau. In some places passionflower vines may grow so thick that they choke crops just as bindweed does, but in general the attractive flowers make it a sought-after and frequently cultivated plant.

Many insects are attracted to passionflower blossoms, and several species of butterfly larvae thrive on the plant, so caterpillars are often found in abundance on it. The fruit is a large yellow egg-shaped berry with a slightly acrid flavor. Native Americans and pioneering explorers enjoyed sucking the flesh of the ripe fruit from around the seeds. Captain John Smith described the "maracocks" in Virginia as having a pleasant taste, much like lemons. The great naturalist, John Muir, praised the maypop (which he called the "apricot vine") as the "most delicious fruit I have ever eaten," but it should be remembered that Muir often subsisted on an extremely spartan diet.[3]

The general opinion seems to be that the best use of the maypop fruit is in making jelly or jam; however, Marjorie Kinnan Rawlings, an adventurous cook who liked to use the native plants around her Cross Creek, Florida, home, failed to produce an edible jelly. "Perhaps," she said, "I should have eliminated the skin or the seeds, but at any rate the exotic jelly on which I had set my heart did not materialize. The mixture jelled, but it tasted like a medieval poison, acrid and strange, and I threw it out in horror."[4]

Native Americans made poultices of the leaves of the passionflower plant to heal injuries. In folk medicine an extract of the fresh plant or powdered root or dried fruit and flower tops were used as a nerve sedative, to treat general restlessness, and to relieve insomnia and headache, dysmenorrhea, fever, and high blood pressure. Today, herbal medicine continues to use the plant and flower as a sedative and painkiller. Herbalist Michael Moore recommends a "simple, uncomplicated" sedative made from the passionflower to slow the pulse, decrease arterial tension, and quiet respiration and pulmonary blood pressure.[5] The *National Formulary* recognized passionflower as a tranquilizer/sedative source from 1916 to 1936.

At Queen Victoria's request a wreath of passionflowers was laid upon the last resting place of the martyred Abraham Lincoln, and it is still considered a suitable decoration for All Saints' Day.[6] The persistence of its religious symbolism and its exotic beauty make the passionflower a unique treasure among wildflowers.

Phlox

Phlox Family (*Polemoniaceae*)

Common Names: Drummond Phlox, Sweet William,
Prairie Phlox, Trailing Phlox, Standing Cypress

Many people, including Theodore Roosevelt, have written of their delight in coming upon large patches of the Texas wildflower known as Drummond phlox. In *Texas Wild*, Richard Phelan designates the lower end of the Post Oak country where it frays out into prairie as the "kingdom of the Texas phlox." He says that "hybridized and grown in flower beds, as it is now over much of the world, phlox is rather genteel and dull. Growing wild on hillside in the Post Oak country and also on the Gulf Coast, it is lively and cheerful."[1]

Drummond phlox became known throughout the world thanks to the efforts of an intrepid Scotsman, Thomas Drummond, who was a well-trained botanist. Drummond was among the naturalists Britain sent to study wildlife in the New World in the 1800s. On his way to Texas, he caught a fever that left him "skin and bone," and when he arrived at Velasco in the spring of 1833, he found Texas on the brink of a revolution against Mexico. Furthermore, a cholera epidemic was raging in the area, and in his weakened condition he succumbed to the disease; he attributed his survival to the medicine he had brought with him: opium. In addition to pestilence and threats of war, that was the year of a great flood that came to be called The Great Overflow of 1833. The Brazos River left its banks, submerging the prairies around Velasco up to fifteen feet—and it didn't recede for months.

By the summer of 1833, Drummond finally felt strong enough to travel to San Felipe, where he established his headquarters. From there he set out to explore the wilds of Texas without a guide or accurate maps or weapons other than his botanical tweezers and dissecting knives. In the spring and summer of 1834 he journeyed one hundred miles up the Brazos collecting specimens and seeds, which he wrapped and marked. Returning to Velasco for food and botanical supplies, he became seriously ill again with what he called "bilious fever," and again he was severely weakened. Despite the hardships he had suffered, he decided to apply for a land grant and move his family to Texas, explaining that in Texas he could be "more independent than I could ever hope to be in Britain." After packing up and dispatching his Texas collection of plant materials to his sponsors in England, he set out to return to Britain to collect his family. Going by way of Florida and Cuba, in Cuba he died of unknown causes.[2]

Many of the seven hundred plant species Drummond collected in Texas bear his name, but the star of the collection is the phlox he found growing so profusely in South Texas. Sir William J. Hooker, the first director of Kew Gardens, was Drummond's principal sponsor, and Hooker was so delighted with the results from the phlox seeds that he named the plant *Phlox drummondii* to honor the dauntless Scotsman in the hope it would "serve as a frequent memento of its unfortunate discoverer."[3]

In England at first Drummond phlox was of only one color—a brilliant rose red with a darker reddish purple eye or throat. English gardeners considered it highly desirable, and in the *Botanical Register* (London, 1837) John Lindley wrote:

> "A bed of this plant has hardly yet been seen; for it is far too precious and uncommon to be possessed by anyone, except in small quantities." Just three years later, Hooker described it as "the pride and ornament of our gardens."[4]

From England Drummond phlox soon spread all over the world, and it eventually became the rage of New England gardeners who thought of it as a fabulous European export for several years before they learned it was a simple native of the uncouth Republic of Texas. In 1979 Texas wildflower expert Carroll Abbott called it the most widely planted annual in the world.[5]

In Texas there are at least six subspecies of Drummond phlox ranging from pink to violet to carmine and occasionally variegated or bicolored. Usually there is an eye in the center shaped like a star or a ring. In addition to Drummond, other famous naturalists who explored Texas have had phlox species named after them. These include Berlandier phlox (bluish lavender) and Roemer phlox (varying from deep rose to purple or pink with yellow around the eye).

Prairie phlox (*P. pilosa*), sometimes called Sweet William or downy phlox, is notable for its delightful fragrance and flat-topped clusters of pink, blue, white, or lavender flowers. Unfortunately, trailing phlox (*P. nivalis*) is noted for being on the candidate list for endangered species in Texas.

The gilias, members of the Phlox family, are characteristically pale blue to lavender with yellow throats. Their genus name, *Gilia,* is in honor of Philipp Salvador Gil, an eighteenth-century Spanish botanist. They are found in various species abundantly in the western part of the state from the sandy regions of Northwest Texas to the Rio Grande plains. An especially attractive species is blue gilia (*G. rigidula*), a compact plant with blossoms whose bright golden eyes peer out of vivid violet blue petals.

Blue gilia grows in the harshest conditions, often springing dramatically out of a rocky caliche setting.

Texas has about ten members of the *Ipomopsis* group, including the impressive standing cypress (*Ipomopsis rubra*), also called Texas plume and red Texas star. Whether growing singly or in large colonies, this plant, with its wandlike stems featuring feathery foliage and clusters of scarlet trumpetlike flowers, is one of our most striking wildflowers. In addition to its beauty, it has other assets. The showy flowers, which open from the top of the stalk down, attract hummingbirds and butterflies, and they are long-lasting in cut arrangements. Natives of the Southwest called the plant chigger weed because it grows best in black soil where insects also thrive. The skyrocket is a similar species common in West Texas but not as densely flowered and more spindly in appearance. The name *Ipomopsis* means "resembling an impomoea," a small red-flowered morning glory, and *rubra* means red.

All parts of the phlox plant have been used in folk medicine. The petals have been used in infusions to treat childhood stomachache. Water from the boiled leaves was applied to boils, the scraped roots were soaked in water to make an eyewash, and boiled roots were used to treat venereal disease.[6]

In the language of flowers, phlox means unanimity or agreement. When sent by lovers in Victorian times, they signified a wish for sweet dreams or a proposal of love.

Pitcher Plant

Pitcher Plant Family (*Sarraceniaceae*)

*Common Names: Yellow Trumpet, Smallpox Plant,
Flytrap, Eve's Cup, Adam's Pitcher, Whippoorwill's Boots,
Huntsman's Cup, Sidesaddle Flower*

Thoreau called the pitcher plant the most "singular and remarkable" of all the plants he had ever seen. And Darwin, who considered the pitcher plant and its carnivorous cousins paradoxes in his evolutionary theory, made a lengthy study trying to work out where they fit into the food chain since they alone of all the plants seem to place themselves above the animals whose flesh they consume.

Of the five carnivorous or insectivorous plants found in the United States, four are native to Texas: pitcher plants, sundews, butterworts, and bladderworts. Only the venus flytrap is not found here. Each of the four types is found in nutrient-poor soil, and each has found its own way of trapping prey to supplement its diet. Although bladderworts are more widespread, pitcher plants are by far the largest and showiest of our flesh-eating wildflowers.

The pitcher plant family is a small one, and Texas has only one species, yellow trumpet (*Sarracenia alata*), which is found in acid bogs and flats or savannahs in eastern and southeastern Texas and along the Gulf Coastal Plain. Ranging in height from six inches to over two feet, the leaves and flowers appear at first glance to be two different plants because the underground connection cannot be seen. The large graceful yellow flowers hang face-downward at the tip of long naked stalks, and the funnel-shaped hollow leaves stand next to them like erect hooded sentinels with gaping mouths. The pitcher plant has a triple lure to entice insects into what is literally a pitfall: a strong odor, appealing colors including reddish stripes on the bronze-green leaves, and a sweet nectar. Enticed by the odor and color, an insect lands on the mouth of the hollow leaf and begins to enjoy the nectar exuded by the small glands around the mouth. As it crawls farther down hunting for more nectar, it finds itself on a slippery slope that ends in a pool of liquid, but when the insect tries to crawl out, it finds itself imprisoned by tiny, barbed, downward-pointing hairs. Repeated efforts to escape exhaust the prisoner, and eventually it drops into the liquid and drowns. The ingenious plant then uses the liquid, which consists of rain water plus digestive enzymes and acids, to break down the insect's body and absorbs the nitrogen and nutrients it needs. Obviously pitcher plants cannot be selective in choosing who will drop into their traps, and moths, ants, flies, beetles, grasshoppers, and the occasional lizard along with other skeletons, as many as forty-five, have been found in a single funnel leaf.

The *Sarracenia* genus is named for J. S. Sarrasin, a seventeenth-century physician and botanist who discovered the plant in America and sent it back to France. The name "alata" means winged, referring to the appearance of the hood. Such a strange-looking and -acting plant acquired many fanciful common names through the years. These include Indian dipper, Eve's cup, sidesaddle flower, whippoorwill's boots, devil's boots, huntsman's cup (perhaps referring to a powder horn), Adam's pitcher, water cup, flytrap, and fly-catcher. In some parts of Africa where monkeys have been observed breaking off the funnels and drinking the fluid, pitcher plants are called "monkey cups."[1]

Botanically, the New World *Sarracenia* and its counterpart the Old World *Nepenthes* are quite similar. *Nepenthe,* from the Greek "not" and "grief," was a magic potion mentioned by Greek and Roman poets and said to cause forgetfulness of sorrows and misfortunes. This pitcher plant, like those of the western world, has been employed medicinally as it yields a drug which has been used as a tonic and appetite stimulant. Reported to have been used by native North Americans with great success in saving lives and preventing unsightly pitting caused by smallpox, pitcher plant extracts, beginning about 1865, enjoyed a short-lived popularity in treating this dread disease in England. The Cherokees believed the pitcher plant had magical powers with the ability to attract game to hunters and fish to fishermen who carried it with them, and they also credited it with the ability to attract young women to young braves who kept it with them.[2]

The pitcher plant's method of trapping its prey is classified as passive, while the methods used by the sundew, butterworts, and bladderworts are considered active. It stretches the imagination to think of the petite, charming sundews (*Drosera*) as flesh eaters, but they are. The tiny flattened plants, less than two inches, are easy to overlook in the wet sands and bogs of East Texas. Dainty pinkish white flowers rising on long, slender spikes above the basal rosette of leaves add to the deceptively fragile look of the plants, but it is the dime-size roundish green leaves studded with reddish tentacles that do the dirty work. *Drosera* is from a Greek word meaning "dewy," and each tentacle is topped with jewel-like drops of clear, sticky fluid that glitter in the sunlight like drops of dew. The sparkling leaves attract gnats, mosquitoes, small spiders, ants, and other insects. Once the victim lands on a sticky leaf, it is stuck, and the leaf slowly folds over, forming a cup that entraps the victim completely. Enzymes secreted by the tentacles digest the insect in about four to six days, and then the leaf reopens, the skeleton blows away, and the trap is reset.

Darwin, who was fascinated by the sundew's trapping mechanism, studied it intensely, and in 1875 he discovered that the hairs on the plant respond when touched with a bit of meat or animal hair but do not respond to inorganic substances such as bits of gravel, sand, or glass. He concluded that while the pitcher plant attempts to break down whatever falls into its cup and the venus flytrap (in the same family as the sundew) will close on any moving object, the sundew is able to distinguish between insects and noninsects.[3]

As early as the thirteenth century, alchemists used the sap of the sundew in the treatment of tuberculosis. And in the sixteenth century John Gerard observed in his *Herball,* "Physicians have thought this herb to be a rare and singular remedy for all those that be in a consumption of the lungs." In European folk medicine sundew was used as an aphrodisiac, and because of their protein digesting enzymes, exudates from the leaves were used to treat warts. Today herbalists recommend sundew sap to sooth coughs due to irritation and ascribe to it antispasmodic properties that stop coughs.[4]

Texas has only one of the thirty-five known species of butterworts

(*Pinguicula*). These are found in the wet soils of savannahs and low pinelands on the Coastal Plain in southeastern Texas. Like the sundews, the butterworts have lovely pale flowers on slender stalks and depend on their leaves to provide sustenance. The genus name *Pinguicula* indicates a plant with oily or greasy leaves, as does the common name butterwort, which means "butter plant." The shiny leaves grow in a rosette at the base of the flower stalk, and when small organisms such as gnats and midges become stuck on a leaf, the trapping mechanism is stimulated by the struggle, and the edges of the leaf curl inward, enfolding the prey so that enzymes can do their work of digestion. Then the leaf unrolls again to await the next victim. In Sweden and Lapland the leaves of the butterwort have been used to curdle milk.

Butterworts are in the bladderwort family, and in the bladderwort genus of the family, *Utricularia,* we have in Texas ten known species occurring throughout the state. Perennial herbs that are either entirely aquatic or are found in wet soil, the bladderworts have the most complex method of all our insectivores of capturing prey. Bladders are utricles, and it is the numerous tiny bladders borne on the threadlike leaves that give the *Utricularia* both their scientific and common names. Our greatest concentration of bladderworts are in East Texas, floating on ponds, lakes, ditches, swamps, and slow streams.

Thoreau spoke disparagingly of the bladderwort, calling it "a dirty conditioned flower, like a sluttish woman with a gaudy yellow bonnet." But another naturalist, T. W. Higginson, characterized it more kindly: "The slender *Utricularia,* a dainty maiden whose light feet scarce touch the water."[5] This second description is a more accurate one of the plant that has pretty yellow flowers that look like sails moving the little structure along. Eight to ten floating hollow ribs or branches radiate from the bottom of the floral stem in a whorl, like spokes of a wagon wheel. From these spokelike ribs grow the masses of threadlike filaments that bear the numerous tiny bladders. Each bladder has two valves, a trapdoor that opens inward, and a mouth with waving tentacles or hairs to attract prey. When small water animals such as protozoa, water fleas, or minute crustaceans brush against these sensitive hairs, the walls of the bladder spring outward, creating a partial vacuum. The trapdoor opens, and a small volume of water rushes in to equalize the pressure, sucking the tiny aquatic animals in with it. The entire process takes less than 1/500th of a second.[6]

Trapped in the bladder, the victim is dissolved by enzymes into nutrients needed by the plant.

These curious meat-eating wildflowers—pitcher plants, sundews, butterworts, and bladderworts—are marvelous examples of the ability of plants to adapt in the struggle for survival. Their strange beauty combined with their efficient mechanisms for trapping their prey have fascinated scientists and laypeople from Darwin's time to the present day. If they can hold out against their chief enemies—humans—who are increasingly destroying their habitat, they will be here for future generations to marvel at.

Poinsettia

Spurge Family (*Euphorbiaceae*)

Common Names: Christmas Flower, Flame Leaf,
Parrot Plant, Flor de Navidad, Flor de la Noche Buena

Poinsettias, the handsomest members of the large *Euphorbia* genus of the enormous spurge family, grow abundantly in Mexico and Central America where in their native settings they become tree-like with crimson leaves measuring up to twenty inches long; and where they have moved across the border in South Texas, they rise to ten feet or more. In the wild, our Christmas poinsettia, *pulcherrima,* prefers sandy soil and is called fire-on-the-mountain, Mexican flame leaf, and parrot plant (because of its yellow, red and green coloration). Texas also has several less-spectacular species of poinsettias scattered throughout the state. The true flowers of the poinsettia are the greenish yellow knoblike structures in the center of the floral part, and the red "petals" are actually leaflike bracts. In addition to the familiar red-bracted plants, there are totally green poinsettias as well as double white and pink forms and a yellow variety that grows in Guatemala.

The poinsettia is named after Joel R. Poinsett of Charleston, South Carolina, an important U.S. diplomat in the first half of the nineteenth century. A fervent liberal, he always managed to become deeply involved in the internal politics of countries to which he was assigned. From 1825–29 he served as the first minister from the United States to Mexico, and the Mexicans coined the word "poinsettismo" to characterize his intrusive behavior. One of his unwelcome efforts was to try to buy Texas for the

United States. Poinsett, who had many interests including the fine arts, agriculture and botany, was charmed by the plant the Aztecs called "false flower" and the Mexicans called the "Christmas Eve flower" or "flame leaf." When he returned to his home in South Carolina Poinsett carried cuttings of the attractive plant with him, and after they thrived there, he sold cuttings to a nurseryman in Philadelphia. The plant, which was enthusiastically received by flower lovers all over the United States, soon became a popular symbol of Christmas and was christened "poinsettia" in his honor.[1]

The *pulcherrima* poinsettia with its deep green foliage and scarlet bracts well deserves its name as *pulchar* denotes beautiful or handsome in Latin. According to Pliny, the genus is named after an ancient king: "Iuba, king of Mauritanis, found out this herb *Euphorbia*, which he so called after the name of his own Physitian Euphorbus."[2]

The family name "spurge" refers to purge, as many of the family members have a gum resin that is still used medicinally as an emetic and purgative. Although many spurges have a milky sap that is caustic and sometimes poisonous and extremely irritating to the membranes of the eyes and mouth and also to the skin of some people, it has had its uses as the herbalist Culpeper says, "Spurges are mercurial plants, and abound with a hot and acrid juice, which, when applied outwardly, eats away warts and other excrescences."[3]

Important plants in the spurge family include the castor bean plant whose poisonous but oil-rich seeds yield the infamous castor oil. As an excellent lubricant for delicate machinery, it was in great demand during World War I. In tropical countries another family member, the manihot plant, yields cassava, an important food source as a vegetable, in tapioca and bread, and as a fodder.

Among the many *Euphorbias* in Texas probably the most useful has been candelilla or wax plant (*E. antisyphilitica*). Medicinally its juice has been used as a purgative and, as the species name indicates, it has been used in treating venereal disease. But its main importance in Mexico and formerly in the Big Bend area of Texas has been as a source of high grade wax, which is easily obtained by boiling the branches in water. This wax has been used in making candles, soaps, ointments, sealing wax, phonograph records, insulating material, shoe polish, floor polish, waterproofing and lubricants, and the fibrous stems can be used to make a high grade paper. Indiscriminate pulling up of the plants by their root instead of cutting the stems depleted the number of plants for a while, but now they grow alongside sotol and lechugilla in Big Bend National Park where they are protected.

In addition to castor bean plants, Texas also has several crotons and nettles, the most notorious being the bull nettle, which has clusters of fragrant waxy white flowers and large leaves covered with bristly stinging hairs. It has well earned its name of "tread softly" and *mala mujer* (bad woman) as its touch on bare skin causes a severe sting that is not soon forgotten. Bull nettle seeds, which explode violently from the seed pods, are said to have a nutlike flavor.

Next to the poinsettias, our most attractive *Euphorbias* are snow-on-the-mountain and snow-on-the-prairie. Both have showy green bracts trimmed in white, and from a distance they are similar in appearance, but close comparison reveals that the leaves of snow-on-the-prairie are much narrower than the leaves of snow-on-the-mountain. In late summer their snowy white masses provide a pleasant visual relief from the heat.

Nancy Ranson relates two origin legends connected with the poinsettia. The first is a pagan tale of heroism: Long ago, in a battle to defend the temple of their god, Quetzalcoatl, against Aztec tribes, every Toltec warrior was slain, leaving only the young boys of the tribe to carry on the fight. In an effort to disguise their youth, these children collected the feathered headdresses of their fallen elders and put them on in the darkness expecting to die fighting the next day for the temple of their god. Touched by their bravery and their spirit of self-sacrifice, Quetzalcoatl transformed the feather tips of their headdresses into tongues of living flame. At dawn the Aztec invaders, seeing the temple surrounded by leaping tongues of fire, became terrified and fled to their home. When they had gone, the boy warriors laid their flaming headdresses on the ground, and beautiful flame-tipped plants sprang up around the temple, commemorating forever the heroism of the young fighters.[4]

The second legend is a Christian tale of faith: Many years after the birth of the Christ Child, a small ragged child stood weeping outside the walls of a great cathedral because she had no gift for the Christ Child and could not join the joyous procession marching to His altar. Suddenly an angel appeared and told her to give whatever she could and to believe that in the giving it would become lovely. Finding nothing in the churchyard but a thick, coarse weed, she broke it off and carried it with faith in her heart to the altar, where she placed it reverently. As she knelt there the tips of the plant suddenly blazed out into glorious red stars, and the watchers, who believed it represented faith and love made beautiful, called the flower *Flor de Navidad* (flower of the nativity) and *Flor de la Noche Buena* (flower of the holy night).[5] Tomie DePaola has written a charming children's book based on this legend. In Christian symbolism the red Christmas poinsettia came to stand for the Virgin wife, the blood of Christ and everlasting life.

Today new varieties of poinsettias are constantly being created to decorate our homes and churches at Christmas time. And whether they are white, pink, speckled, or the traditional scarlet, it would be difficult to imagine the holiday season without them.

Poppy

Poppy Family (*Papaveraceae*)

*Common Names: Prickly Poppy, Golden Poppy,
Corn Poppy, Opium Poppy, Bloodroot, Red Puccoon*

Common characteristics of the some two hundred species of wild poppies are an acrid sap or latex, often yellow, orange or red in color (sometimes milky white) and showy flowers. The notorious opium poppy (*Papaver somniferum*), which grows wild and in cultivation over much of the world, is found in Texas as an escape. The crude opium from which the painkillers codeine and morphine or heroin are derived comes from the juice or sap of the unripe seed heads. The tiny poppy seeds, with their agreeable nutty taste, are popular ingredients in salad dressings and baked goods. These seeds contain a fine oil which is used in artists' paints and in soaps, and after the oil is expressed, the remaining pressed seed cakes furnish nutritious cattle feed.

Poppies have a long history both in myth and in reality. The ancient Minoan poppy goddess wore a tiara decorated with three pods of the poppy flower, and the goddess Isis is supposed to have prepared a headache medicine for Ra using a poppy seed pod. In Greek mythology the poppy is dedicated to Demeter, the goddess of vegetation, for whom it was supposedly created. After Pluto seized her daughter, Persephone, and carried her off to the underworld, Demeter was inconsolable and searched for her child day and night without resting. While she wandered in despair nothing on earth could grow. The Olympian gods decided she must sleep in order to restore the normal cycle of nature and caused a poppy, the first, to spring up in her path. Stooping to pick the lovely flower, Demeter fell asleep, and everything in nature was refreshed. It was said that Morpheus, the Greek god of dreams (for whom morphine is named), made crowns of poppies for those he wanted to sleep and that poppies decorated the portals of his temple. Also in Greek mythology, the twin brothers Hypnos and Thanatos (Sleep and Death) were pictured as crowned with poppies or carrying poppies in their hands.

The potential of the poppy plant for good and evil has been known for at least five thousand years, and its ability to bring sleep and erase pain made it susceptible to being used and abused in medical, religious and magic rituals. Ancient Egyptians and Assyrians understood its narcotic and soporific properties and used it to treat many diseases including foot ailments, stomach disorders, eye problems and impotence. The Sumerians, who called it the "joy plant," used it to induce sleep and end pain. Pliny carefully described how to collect raw opium, but warned: "Taken in too large quantities, it is productive of sleep unto death even."[1] Naturally it became a favorite ingredient in the nostrums sold by quacks, and since it lifted the spirits and gave relief from pain it became a popular drug.

As a tincture in the form of laudanum (a mixture of opium and alcohol) it was easily available and freely used in the nineteenth century in America. An 1896 Sears, Roebuck catalog offered medicine containing opium and morphine. Ironically, their 1899 catalog also offered (for seventy-five cents) a "Cure for the Opium and Morphia Habit." It wasn't until 1914 that morphine and opium along with cocaine and cannabis became controlled substances in the United States.[2]

It is curious that the poppy, the cause of the Opium Wars between Britain and China over trade rights, should have become the emblem of remembrance for those who have died in war since World War I. John McCrae, a Canadian physician and soldier, referred to the narcotic quality of the poppy in "In Flanders Fields":[3]

> If ye break faith with us who die
> We will not sleep, though poppies grow
> In Flanders fields.

After McCrae's poem was published anonymously in *Punch* in December, 1915, it became famous. An American woman, Moina Michael, who

was deeply touched by the poem, resolved to wear a poppy always, and she wrote a poem in reply which included these lines:

> We cherish, too, the Poppy red
> That grows on fields where valor led,
> It seems to signal to the skies
> That blood of heroes never dies.

A French woman, Madam Guerin, conceived the idea of making artificial poppies to be sold to help ex-servicemen and their dependents. In 1922 the Legion's poppy factory opened in London, providing work for disabled veterans and supplying huge quantities of scarlet paper poppies to be sold by veteran groups on Remembrance Day (Memorial Day in America), a custom that still continues.[4]

The poppies that grow in Flanders are corn or field poppies (*Papaver rhoeas*) having cup-shaped red flowers with six crinkled petals, three inner and three outer. They are slightly narcotic. In Texas, the corn poppy has escaped cultivation, as it did in Europe, where it became a pest to small grain farmers. John Ruskin, however, loved this particular species and wrote of it in *The Garden of Proserpina*. "It is an intensely simple, intensely floral flower," he said. "All silk and flame, a scarlet cup, perfect-edged all round, seen among the wild grass far away, like a burning coal fallen from Heaven's altars." Many of our cultivated garden poppies are descendants of the corn poppy.

Like many other wildflowers, poppies were thought to have powers to predict the future. Young men and women in both Greece and Rome tested the faithfulness of their loved ones with poppies. A petal was placed on the left hand and slapped smartly with the right; if it popped, the loved one was true, but if it failed to make a noise the outlook was not good. Theocritus (200s B.C.) alluded to this custom, complaining: "By a prophetic poppy leap, I found / Your changed affection, for it gave no sound."

In America before television, when children entertained themselves by using their imaginations, they made good use of flowers including the colorful and plentiful poppies. Bright skirts for dolls could be made from the crinkly, silky petals. Poppy shows or "pin-a-sights" (a pin being the fee for viewing) were popular: poppy leaves and flowers and stems were arranged to form colorful designs or pictures on a piece of glass, and over the design was pasted a paper cover with a moveable flap that could be lifted to display the hidden treasure.[5]

The soporific quality of poppies has been exploited in literature from the time of Virgil who referred to the "Lethean poppy." Shakespeare lumps poppies with "all the drowsy syrups of the world" in *Othello*. In "To Autumn" Keats pictures Autumn as a maiden lying "On a half-reap'd furrow sound asleep / Drows'd with the fume of poppies." In *Uncle Tom's Cabin* Harriet Beecher Stowe says "Whipping and abuse are like laudanum; you have to double the dose as the sensibilities decline." In *Tam O'Shanter* Robert Burns uses the fragility of the blossoms to make a point: "Pleasures are like poppies spread / You seize the flower, the bloom is shed." And several well-known writers including Samuel Taylor Coleridge, Thomas DeQuincey, and Edgar Allan Poe have stoked their muses with opium.

When Spanish explorers saw the brilliant golden poppies blanketing the mountains of coastal California, they called the region the "Land of

Fire," and ships off the coast used the huge, bright displays as beacons. Although recent development has eliminated much of this habitat, the golden poppy (*Eschscholzia californica*) still grows in great profusion in some parts of the state and is the state flower. Texas has a similar species in the look-alike Mexican gold poppy (*E. mexicana*) which has found a home in the Franklin Mountains in the far western part of the state. The Spanish name for this flower is *Amapola del campo,* "Poppy of the Countryside."

At least eight varieties of prickly poppies (*Argemone*) thrive in Texas, all of them beautiful to behold and all of them perilous to touch. Their papery, delicate blossoms—white, rose, pink, or yellow—are appealing, but the leaves, stems, and even the buds are covered with treacherous stickers. The genus name of the prickly poppies, *Argemone,* comes from the Greek *argema,* indicating a poppy used to treat cataracts. Although the tiny seeds are difficult to remove, the Comanches used an extract of the seeds to treat sore eyes, and folk healers used to treat warts with the juice of the prickly poppy.[6] As the thousands of tiny, black seeds ripen, mourning doves and whitewings time their migrations to take advantage of this bounty.

Bloodroot or red puccoon (*Sanguinaria canadensis*), found in the rich woods in East Texas, is a singular but handsome member of the poppy family. The blossoms are white, and *Sanguinaria* refers to the bloodlike color of the juice which readily stains everything it touches. Various Native American peoples made use of this characteristic, mixing the juice with animal fat to make a face and body paint and also to dye baskets and color clothing. In colonial days in America, bloodroot was recognized as a powerful herb and was used in powders and tinctures to treat a wide variety of ailments. Today it is being tried as a promising agent in fighting plaque and preventing gum disease as well as in treating skin diseases.[7]

In addition to being the emblem of Memorial Day, the poppy is the floral emblem of the month of August. In the language of flowers, the red poppy stands for consolation, and the white poppy stands for sleep and oblivion.

Prickly Pear

Cactus Family (*Cactaceae*)

*Common Names: Nopal, Pest Pear, Flap-jack Cactus,
Devil Cactus, Purple Prickly, Blind Prickly Pear*

The national flower emblem of Mexico is the prickly pear or nopal cactus. According to legend, the Aztecs (who called themselves *Mexica*) had been nomads for many years until the Great Spirit told the chiefs they should build a city where they would find an eagle perched on a cactus and holding a snake. After weary months of wandering they came to a lake where they found an eagle with a snake in its mouth standing on a cactus which was growing out of a rock. On this spot they built the city that we know today as Mexico City.[1] Both the Mexican coat of arms and the Mexican flag display this Aztec symbol of an eagle perched on a prickly pear cactus holding a snake.

Cacti are all-American plants, but when the prickly pear was introduced into Europe, sixteenth-century herbalists connected it with an odd prickly plant that the famous Greek philosopher and naturalist Theophrastus had described as growing near an African village called "Opuns." Consequently, the largest genus of the cactus family bears the inappropriate name *Opuntia*, derived from the name of an African town.[2] To add to the confusion, early herbalists, who thought the fruit of the prickly pear resembled figs, called it "Indian fig," a name that stuck. Del Weniger, who has studied the cacti of the Southwest intensively and published the most definitive works about them, has identified over ninety species and varieties of *Opuntias* in the area. He notes that the flat-stemmed varieties are generally called prickly pears while the large upright cylindrical-stemmed varieties are called chollas.

By any name the prickly pear is a sticky subject. In Kate Greenaway's *Language of Flowers* prickly pear means "satire," a good term to describe the character of a plant that attracts with its gorgeous flowers and tasty fruit and cruelly stings with its barbs, both large and small. The flat, oval stem joints or pads (sometimes mistakenly called leaves) are the most conspicuous feature of the prickly pear. The plants grow in sprawling clumps up to five feet high or even higher in some areas. Prickly pears produce seeds in quantities, but most new plants spring from fallen pads. When separated from the main plant and left in contact with any amount of soil, these pads or joints root and form a new plant, and as a result prickly pear can be found growing in crotches of trees, on decaying roofs of houses and in crannies of rock walls. In addition to the highly visible sharp stickers of many species, there are tiny, nearly invisible barbed needles, called glochids, on the areoles or eyes of both pads and fruit, eager to embed themselves into anything that touches them, such as cows' tongues or human fingers. The flowers, which may be translucent yellow, apricot, orange or reddish, are followed by urn-shaped fruit (tunas) in shades of purple or magenta.

A highly prized red dye source is found in the cochineal scale insects that live in white, cottony webs on the pads of the prickly pear. For this reason many countries import large numbers of prickly pear for use in the cochineal dye industry.

In the Southwest, American Pueblos called cactus "the plant that gives of itself," and Texas Indians made good use of the prickly pear as medicine. From the pads they made pulpy poultices to apply to wounds, boils and carbuncles. For painful rheumatic joints they applied the split pads. And from other parts of the plant they made tea to relieve headaches, eye problems and insomnia.

Early Native Americans enjoyed the delicious honey made by bees from the short-lived flowers, and they appreciated the fact that virtually every part of the prickly pear is edible at one time or another. South Texas Jumanos and Coahuiltecans relished the tuna of the prickly pear as a favorite food. They pounded the dried skins to make flour and preserved the fruit by roasting and storing it.[3]

Recently the prickly pear has come to be appreciated by our

health-conscious society as a flavorful addition to many dishes, with the added virtues of being low in calories, rich in vitamins and minerals, and containing no cholesterol. The pads are best when they are small, young and tender. In Mexico, where they are called *nopalitos,* they are sliced, breaded with cornmeal and fried. In Texas restaurants and homes they are frequently boiled and added to omelet-like dishes. Fresh nopalitos can be found in markets in San Antonio and other south Texas towns and canned in some large supermarkets.[4] Raw cactus pads need to be blanched before they are used in recipes unless they are very young. When the joints are cut into narrow strips and boiled, they are often compared to green beans as a vegetable, and they can also be used in soups, salads, and casseroles.

The ripe fruit, called tunas (or pear apples by old timers), have a flavor somewhat like that of kiwifruit. Contrary to the rule for harvesting the pads, the fruit should not be picked until it is fully mature and a deep purple color. A prickly pear should *never* be touched barehanded and since the long, sharp spines and nearly invisible glochids can penetrate even sturdy gloves, it's best to use tongs and a sharp knife for harvesting and skinning the pads and fruit. After the glochids have been rubbed or singed off, the tunas can be peeled and eaten raw, or the raw fruit may be used in salads, fruit drinks, and gelatin dishes. Delena Tull suggests making a candy-like treat by cutting the tunas in half, removing the seeds and rolling slices of the fruit in confectioners sugar.[5] Probably the favorite way to enjoy prickly pear fruit is in the delicious jelly that can be made from them. Cooks who want to try it themselves should remember that the tunas vary in sugar, acid and pectin content, so jellies and preserves made from them are not always consistent and should be prepared in small amounts at a time.

South Texas ranchers have a love/hate relationship with the prickly pear. Where poor farming practices and overgrazing by livestock have decimated the prairies of grasses and herbaceous plants, prickly pear have seized the opportunity to cover thousands of square miles of abused land in South Texas, and where the plants grow too densely they are a nuisance—although they can be valuable as windbreaks and soil stabilizers. As an emergency food, prickly pears have undoubtedly saved the lives of many wild animals, and early settlers in Southwest Texas fed their cattle in time of drought by chopping up prickly pear stems and burning off the thorns in brush fires. A more recent invention, the portable propane gas flame thrower, burns the spines off quickly allowing cattle to graze on the nutritious pads with impunity.

Arizona has chosen as its state flower the most impressive of all the cacti, the majestic saguaro, which may be fifty feet high and live as long as two hundred years. But no state has a wider range of odd and beautiful cacti than Texas. Not only do the flowers come in a variety of hues, they also range in size from thimble-sized to huge, showy saucer-size blooms. Common names attempt to describe the characteristics of particular plants. Jumping cholla has such extremely brittle joints with barbed spines that catch so easily in the hair of animals or on clothing that some people are convinced it lies in wait to jump out at them. Horse crippler or devil's head is an apt name for the low-growing species that hides in pasture grasses and punctures horses' flesh with its large, thick spines. Naturally, its lovely flowers are not enough to redeem it in the eyes of ranchers. Even cacti in the so-called spineless category may have nasty defenses. The blind prickly pear, which has eyespots formed by clusters of tiny, red-brown spinelets that fly in the air when disturbed, can blind cattle that attempt to eat its pads.

Other descriptive names for various Texas cacti are: hedgehog, claret cup, strawberry, rainbow, pin cushion, barrel, organ pipe, staghorn, eagle claws, lace, living rock, button, pineapple, pencil, spiny star, nipple, sea urchin, cowtongue, porcupine, grizzly bear, cylinder bells, long mama, and Glory of Texas. A most remarkable cactus is a scrawny plant that doesn't rate a second glance in daytime, but which after sunset unfolds its buds into large white flowers that make it one of the most beautiful of all the many beautiful cacti flowers. Texans know it as the night-blooming cereus, but Mexicans call it *reina-de-la-noche,* queen of the night.

Cacti continue to increase in popularity with home gardeners because they are not only striking in appearance but also are easy to care for. Insect and disease resistant and tolerant of heat and drought, about the only thing they cannot stand is wet feet, so well-drained soil is necessary. The chief threat to some of the slower growing or rare cacti is from predatory humans who uproot the plants from their native habitat to bring to market. Among the cacti on Texas' endangered or threatened list are: Tobusch fishhook, Sneed pincushion, mariposa, Davis green pitaya and black lace cactus—and the list is growing.[6] In order to preserve these unique plants, the only safe plan is to buy from established growers or reputable nurseries, leaving the wild cacti to be enjoyed in their natural habitat.

The prickly pear is frequently mentioned in literature about Texas. During the years that Cabeza de Vaca lived, more or less as a prisoner, with the coastal Indians of Texas, he noted in his journal that when the prickly pear tunas were ripe the Indians traveled upland to feed on them and enjoyed drinks made from them. Another chronicle of early life in Texas, A. J. Sowell's biography of Texas Ranger Captain Bigfoot Wallace, tells of an incident in which Wallace refused to allow an army surgeon to treat one of his wounded men because the surgeon would not use prickly pear poultices on the man's wound. And J. Frank Dobie says that nobody has written a better description of a prickly pear flat than O. Henry in his story "The Caballero's Way." In this story the Cisco Kid makes his way through a dense field of prickly pear where "uncanny and multiform shapes of cacti lift their twisted trunks and fat, bristly hands to encumber the way." As usual the Kid emerges unscathed, but O. Henry reminds his readers that to be lost in a prickly pear flat can be "to die almost the death of the thief on the cross, pierced by nails and with grotesque shapes of all the fiends hovering about."

Primrose/ Evening Primrose

Primrose Family (*Primulaceae*)
Evening Primrose Family (*Onagraceae*)

Common Names: Primula, Fairy Flower, Cowslip,
Flutter Mill, Wild Honeysuckle, Bee Blossom, Pimpernel

T he true primrose and the evening primrose are members of quite different families. Just how they came to have the same name is not clear, but it may have happened in the early 1600s when an European botanist, hearing a description of the American evening primrose, thought its sweet scent must be like that of wild European primroses and gave it the name that stuck. To add to the confusion, in Texas evening primroses are often called buttercups, which belong to another entirely different family. It's easy, however, to see why this common name persists, since both yellow and pink evening primroses have cupped petals and are abundantly supplied with a thready, powdery pollen that sticks to the nose and chin of anyone holding them up to sniff.

Both the primrose and the evening primrose families are quite large, with many subdivisions. The numerous varieties bloom worldwide from the Arctic to the Himalayas. The name "primrose" is from the Latin *primula* "little firstling," and it is the designated flower for the month of February.

According to a Greek myth, Paralisos, son of Flora and Priapus, died of grief because of the loss of his betrothed. His body was then transformed by his parents into the primrose. It is to this myth that Milton referred when he wrote in *Lycidas* of the "early primrose that forsaken dies." From Paralisos, the primrose was used in prescriptions as a specific for paralysis.[1]

The native primroses or cowslips are woven into English history. May Day festivals feature primroses tied to willow wands. Primrose Day is April 19, the anniversary of the death of Benjamin Disraeli, Earl of Beaconsfield. Queen Victoria had shown her gratitude to Disraeli for his support by having her ladies help her gather primroses in the woods when the court was at Osborne and shipping them to the Prime Minister in London. Disraeli called them "ambassadors of spring" and said they were his favorite flower. When Disraeli died, the Queen sent a wreath of primroses to his funeral with the inscription, "His favorite flowers from Osborne, a tribute of affection from Queen Victoria." In 1883, two years after Disraeli's death, the Primrose League, a political party, was named in his honor.[2]

In the language of flowers, the primrose is usually listed as a symbol of early youth and young love. The short life of the blossom, which only lasts for a day, has given poets an opportunity for imagery. In *The Winter's Tale* Shakespeare's Perdita regrets: "pale primroses / That die unmarried ere they can behold / Bright Phoebus in his strength." Milton compares the death of an infant to the early fading of the primrose: "O fairest flower, no sooner blown but blasted / Soft silken primrose fading timelessly." And Keats speaks of smiles "wan as primroses gathered at midnight / By chilly fingered Spring."[3] It was Shakespeare who linked forever the innocent flower to the peril of leading a life of ease and pleasure. In *Hamlet,* after Ophelia's brother Laertes gives her a full measure of brotherly advice, she tells him not to be like ungracious pastors who show their flock the "steep and thorny way to heaven" while they themselves tread "the Primrose path of dalliance." And in *Macbeth* the keeper of the castle gate speaks of the "primrose way to the everlasting bonfire."

Wordsworth used the primrose in his poem "Peter Bell" to illustrate what an insensitive clod his hero is: "A primrose by a river's brim / A yellow primrose was to him / And it was nothing more."

The primrose connection with fairy lore is reflected in its common names of fairy flower, fairy basin, and fairy cup, and fairies were supposed to take shelter in the blossoms. In *The Tempest* Ariel says: "Where the bee sucks, there suck I / In a cowslip's bell I lie; / There I couch when owls do cry." And in *A Midsummer Night's Dream,* Shakespeare says of the small crimson dots in the primrose blossoms "these be rubies, fairy favours."

In German folklore primroses were called "key flowers," and according to Bavarian legends they supposedly had the ability to open treasure chests. The name *himmelschlussel* (keys of Heaven) comes from the humorous folk tale in which St. Peter upon being informed that certain unworthy souls were trying to get into heaven by a back door instead of through the pearly gates, became so flustered he dropped his keys, and where they fell to earth a clump of primroses sprang up. Another popular German legend tells of an enchanted castle with a doorway overgrown with flowers. When a mortal is enticed to the castle, the key flower opens the door, and he or she passes into a room with vessels filled with gold and jewels and covered over with primroses. After the treasure is taken, the primroses must be replaced, otherwise the finder will be forever followed by a "black dog."[4]

Although Texas has no true primulas, among the members of the primrose family to be found in the state are the scarlet pimpernel and the common shooting star (American cowslip). The latter is easy to recognize because of the dart-like appearance of the blossoms with their swept back purplish-pink petals and fused stamens that form a beak.

In spite of its name, the scarlet pimpernel may be different colors in different parts of the state; e.g., it is salmon-colored in the Hill Country. Ancient Greeks believed the scarlet pimpernel to be a good medicine for liver problems and a promoter of cheerful spirits; hence its genus name *Anagallis* meaning delightful.[5] Among its common names are "shepherd's barometer" and "shepherd's weather-glass" because the sensitive flowers remain open only in bright sunlight and close when the sky becomes cloudy.

Around the turn of the century, Baroness Orczy became famous for her novel *The Scarlet Pimpernel* about a band of Englishmen pledged to rescue victims of the Reign of Terror in Paris. After it also became a highly successful play, people went around chanting: "Is he in heaven?—Is he in hell? / That demmed, elusive Pimpernel?" In Ireland the scarlet pimpernel acquired supernatural beliefs. Called the herb of Mary or the blessed herb, it was credited with the ability to move against the current when dropped into a stream and to give second sight to anyone holding it. It was also considered a protection against witchcraft.[6]

An old English proverb says: "No heart can think, no tongue can tell, / The virtues of the Pimpernel." In addition to its medical uses, apparently like the cowslip it was also used cosmetically. In the sixteenth century, William Turner, who helped lay the foundations for modern botany, mentions scathingly in *A New Herball:*

> Some weomen springkle yt floures of cowslip wt whyte wyne and after still it and wash their faces in that water to drive wrinkles away and to make them fayre in the eyes of the worlde rather than in the eyes of God whom they are not afrayd to offende with the scluttishness, filthines, and foulnes of the soule.[7]

The herbalist Culpeper also mentions using cowslip flower ointment as a beauty aid: "Our city dames know well enough the ointment or distilled water of it adds to beauty," and he adds "it taketh away spots and wrinkles of the skin, sunburnings and freckles." He also recommends using primroses to "strengthen the brain and the nerves."[8]

In old leech books primroses were often used in combination with other herbs to make ointments and tonics for burns or ulcers and for aches and pains of various illnesses. In folk medicine primrose tea was drunk to soothe upset stomachs, and drinking primrose tea twice a day was recommended to keep the mind clear. Cowslip recipes were widely used in England for hundreds of years. In Disraeli's novel *Lothair* Lord St. Jerome says, "They say primroses made a capital salad." Not only were the leaves and flowers eaten in salads, they were also used as potherbs and mixed with other herbs to stuff meats. The flowers were made into a conserve and also candied and pickled, and cowslip puddings, custards and tarts were favorite desserts. The popular cowslip wine was made from fermented flowers and widely enjoyed as a pleasant narcotic. In a letter to a friend, the poet Alexander Pope remarked, "I'll drown all high thoughts in the Lethe of Cowslip Wine."[9]

The evening primrose family, which includes neither primroses nor roses, has members scattered all over Texas. In colors varying from white to yellow to pink, depending on where they are growing and on the season of the year, many evening primroses open at dusk like small glowing lamps. They have the musky scent characteristic of night blooming plants, and often the plants cleverly open only one flower at a time on a stalk so the visiting moths will carry the pollen to another blossom on another plant. Only moths with long tongues such as the hawk moth can reach the deep nectar cup of the evening primrose.

The National Wildflower Center at Austin has chosen as its logo the common pink evening primrose (*Oenothera speciosa*), one of the most loved of Texas wildflowers. Its translucent petals belie its hardy, drought resistant nature. Colonizing large areas in fields and along highways it justifies its name "showy primrose," as it is more inclined to stay open in the daytime than other evening primroses. The young leaves of the pink evening primrose are sometimes added to salads or cooked as greens, and the plant yields an excellent yellow dye.

The flutter mill or Missouri primrose (*O. missouriensis*), which is also called a buttercup by Texans, is another drought resistant evening primrose that thrives on thin limestone soils from central Texas northwestward through the Panhandle. It has attractive large four-petaled yellow flowers and large, sturdy seedpods that are often used in dried arrangements.

Water primrose or primrose willows prefer wet habitats and bloom in wide bands and floating mats along the slow streams and ponds in South Texas, while the yellow beach evening primrose (*O. drummondii*) flourishes in the sandy soils of the Gulf Coast along beaches, bay shores and on sand dunes. In 1833 Thomas Drummond collected seeds of the beach evening primrose in South Texas and sent them back to Scotland, and the plants, which flourished outdoors at the Glasgow Botanic Garden in 1834, were christened *drummondii*.[10]

The *Gaura* branch of the evening primrose family grows on tall weedy spikes in colors varying from white to orchid to dark pink or red. Often called wild honeysuckle or bee blossom or kisses, it is a favorite of honeybees which are attracted by its delicate fragrance.

A yellow evening primrose (*O. biennis*) is as its name *biennis* implies a biennial, taking two years to complete its life cycle. The first year it forms a rosette of basal leaves and in the second year a tall flowering spike. *Oenothera* means wine-scenting, an allusion to the way the roots were used. The lemon scented yellow flowers are large with the four petals and cross-shaped stigma typical of the *Oenothera*. Like many other evening primroses its flowers open in the late afternoon in a series of starts and jerks until they are fully open in just a few minutes, and the next day they wilt. The first year taproots, which have a pungent taste like radishes, may be eaten raw or boiled like parsnips and served with butter, and the tender new leaves add a peppery taste to salads. In addition to humans other creatures who enjoy eating primroses include deer, rodents, birds and caterpillars.

Native Americans used the common evening primrose roots to treat obesity and stomach pains and made poultices from the roots for wounds. In modern herbal medicine the plant mucilage is used in cough remedies to inhibit coughing and in external preparations to soothe skin eruptions. Oil from the seeds is a rich natural source of gamma-linolenic acid (GLA), and evening primrose oil is being researched as a possible aid in treating burns and other skin wounds as well as eczemas, asthma, migraines, premenstrual syndrome, diabetes, heart disease, multiple sclerosis and alcoholism. At the University of Pennsylvania School of Medicine, ongoing studies support the use of GLA in treating arthritis.[11] If it proves to help in treating these ailments, the primrose will indeed be the "virtuous" plant it is called in an old English proverb.

In the meantime, the aesthetic appeal of primroses is unquestioned, for as Wordsworth says: "Long as there's a sun that sets / Primroses will have their glory."

Queen Anne's Lace

Parsley/Carrot Family
(*Umbelliferae*)/(*Apiaceae*)

Common Names: Wild Carrot, Bird's Nest,
Laceflower, Rantipole, Hemlock

Like the old puzzle that asks which came first—the chicken or the egg—there is a similar puzzle concerning Queen Anne's lace: which came first—the wild carrot or the cultivated carrot? Authorities disagree, some contending that our eating carrot was cultivated from the wild carrot, while others believe that Queen Anne's lace is a bastard offspring of cultivated carrots that escaped and went back to nature.[1]

At any rate, the name *carota* is mentioned in writings dating from the second century A.D., and it is also found listed as an ingredient in recipes in a cookbook dating from that time. The second century Greek physician Galen added the name *Daucus* (disk or dish-shaped) to distinguish the carrot from the parsnip, and when Linnaeus set up his botanical naming system in the eighteenth century, he kept these names and officially christened this wild carrot *Daucus carota*.[2]

Texas has two members of the *Daucus* genus, Queen Anne's lace and rattlesnake weed (*D. pusillus*). *Pusillus* implies that the plant is very small or insignificant, and although rattlesnake weed is more widespread throughout the state, it is smaller in most respects than Queen Anne's lace. As the common name implies, it was thought to be an antidote for rattlesnake bite by early settlers.

Queen Anne's lace is an attractive plant, at least in its youth, with tiny white flowers in intricately patterned clusters forming umbels. Each of these umbrella-shaped clusters consists of perhaps five hundred flowers and has at its center a single deep wine red or purple flower. In fruit the ribs of the umbels turn up to form a cup, giving the plant its popular names of "bird's nest" and "bee's nest." After the fruit ripens, the umbels reopen and release the prickly fruit that sticks to the fur of passing animals, or the dried nests may become tumbleweeds that distribute the fruit away from the mother plant. Because of its invasive capability, wild carrot has often been called a pesky weed, and in earlier times it acquired the nicknames of devil's plague or rantipole, a term designating a wild, unruly character.

According to tradition, the carrot was introduced into England during the reign of Elizabeth I by the Flemings who took refuge in England from persecution by Philip II of Spain. Since vegetables were rather scarce in England at that time, the carrot was enthusiastically received and cultivated, and during the reign of James I (1603–25), it became fashionable for ladies to wear frilly carrot leaves in their headdresses instead of feathers.[3] Sometime during the reign of Queen Anne (1702–14) the plant acquired its best known common name, Queen Anne's lace. Queen Anne was said to have been fond of wearing lace on her dresses and supposedly the deep red flower in the center of the plant symbolizes a drop of her blood that fell on a piece of lace she was making.

As Joseph Wood Krutch points out, the main difference between tame and wild carrots is in the size of the root, and the reason the resemblance is not more obvious is that since the cultivated carrot is a biennial, it needs a second year to flower and usually we dig it up at the end of its first season for the sake of the thick root. Krutch believed that carrot seeds brought to America by the first English colonists developed into plants that soon escaped from gardens and reverted to the wild state.[4]

As a wild plant the carrot has been used to treat many physical ailments, because as Culpeper noted, the wild plants were "more powerful in their operation" than the tame ones. In ancient times the seeds were used internally as a diuretic, to treat kidney stones, to increase menstrual flow and to hasten childbirth as well as to treat flatulence, colic, and hiccough. The seeds, leaves and roots were also used in poultices to treat serious tumors. Drunk with wine they were said to sooth spider bites. The Crow Indians used wild carrot for a multitude of healing and ceremonial purposes, and carrot fruit or wild carrotseed from Queen Anne's lace was official in *The Pharmacopoeia of the United States of America* from 1820 to 1882 as a "diuretic, stimulant and menstrual excitant."[5]

In folk medicine gout sufferers drank carrot tea, and today carrot juice is a popular tonic drink. Because both wild and cultivated carrot roots are rich in vitamin A, which among other virtues helps night vision, this is probably a good habit if it is not overdone, in which case the skin may acquire a yellow jaundiced look. Among other culinary uses, the British used carrots for making wine and bread and jelly and in dairies to give color and flavor to butter. In Europe carrots are grown in great quantities as fodder for livestock. In folk lore the flowers of wild carrot boiled in wine were used as a love potion and as a contraceptive.[6] A yellow dye can be made from Queen Anne's lace. Butterflies are attracted by the nectar of the flowers, and Geyata Ajilvsgi notes that black swallowtail lay their eggs on the foliage, which the larvae use as food.

In addition to carrots the *Umbelliferae* or *Apiaceae* family includes many other popular members including parsley, coriander, cumin, chervil, parsnip, caraway, celery, fennel, dill, anise and eryngo (described in the "Thistle" profile). It also includes some black sheep, the infamous water hemlock and poison hemlock, as well as bishop's weed, a harmless look alike—all found in Texas.

Our flowering hemlocks, which are not related to the forest trees of the same name, may be mistaken for Queen Anne's lace if not examined carefully. Water hemlock (*Cicuta maculata*), sometimes called cowbane and beaver poison, lacks the red or purple center flower of wild carrot. Also its umbels are more loosely clustered and it often has purple spots or blotches on its hairless stem. Delena Tull calls water hemlock "possibly the most violently poisonous and most deadly wild flowering plant in the United States," and adds that a single mouthful of the root can kill a cow or a man.[7] It has been reported that the Iroquois sometimes ate the root of water hemlock in order to commit suicide. Correll and Johnston, who note that it is found abundantly in wet places in Texas, label it "virulently poisonous." The similar species *C. mexicana* is also deadly poisonous.

The infamous poison hemlock of Greek history, *Conium maculatum*, is found in wet places in the south half of Texas. This is the hemlock that was in the death potion Socrates was condemned to drink, and it was a standard method of executing convicted criminals in classical times. Minute amounts of poison hemlock have been used in medicines, but overdoses produce paralysis with loss of speech and a depression of the respiratory function which finally ceases, resulting in death from asphyxia. Linnaeus assigned the plant its scientific name *C. maculatum* from *konas* meaning "to whirl about" because it causes vertigo preceding death and *maculatus* meaning spotted or blotched, referring to the stem markings. According to Christian legend, these purple marks on the stem represent the brand put on Cain's brow to show he was a murderer.

Such a virulent plant naturally became associated with witches, and hemlocks were dedicated to Hecate, the Queen of Darkness and protectress of witches. In *Macbeth* it is an ingredient in the evil brew described by one of the three witches in the opening scene in Act IV: "Root of hemlock digg'd i' the dark." Children have been poisoned from making whistles of the hollow stems of hemlock, and although quails seem to eat it with impunity, their flesh can become so impregnated with the poison that they become poisonous as food.

The carrot family is one that illustrates dramatically how different individual family members can be and also what extremes of potential good or harm may exist within individuals that appear on the surface to be so much alike.

Rose

Rose Family (*Rosaceae*)

Common Names: Macartney Rose, Cherokee Rose,
Pasture Rose, White Prairie Rose, Pink Prairie Rose,
Carolina Rose, Leafy Rose, Sunshine Rose, Arkansas Rose,
Woods Rose, Desert Rose, Sweet-Brier

Wild roses, ancestors of our elegant garden varieties, flourished on the earth long before humans made their appearance. As Walter de la Mare wrote in "All That's Past," "No one knows through what wild centuries / Roves back the Rose." From ancient times this evocative flower has cast its spell, luring people by its mystical beauty and perfume to attempt to create ever more perfect specimens.

One of the oldest flowers in cultivation, the rose was grown in China as early as the Shen Nung dynasty (about 2737–2697 B.C.). Confucius is said to have cultivated roses, and they are reported to have been favorites in the fabulous gardens of King Midas and in those of Alexander the Great as well as in the famous hanging gardens of Babylon. Paintings in the Palace of Knossos on the Island of Crete show that the rose was being cultivated there over four thousand years ago, and withered rose wreaths have been found in the tombs of Egyptian pharaohs.[1]

For as long as there has been writing, men and women have sung the praises of the rose and used it as a symbol of all that is lovely and as an illustration of the human condition with its paradox of beauty and pain. In his epic poems Homer described rosy-fingered dawns that perfumed the air, and other Greeks hailed the rose as the queen of flowers. Some six hundred years before Christ, the poet Sappho wrote: "If Zeus had willed it so, / That o'er the flowers one flower should reign a queen, / I know, ah well I know, / The rose, the rose, that royal flower had been."

Anacreon, the pleasure-loving Greek lyric poet of the sixth century, elaborated on this theme in "The Queen of the Garden," in which he calls the rose the "sweetest child of weeping morning" and "the boon of the earth." His account of the origin of the rose says that it sprang from Aphrodite's blushes when Zeus observed her bathing. In Greek mythology the rose was dedicated to Aphrodite (Venus), goddess of love, and in Botticelli's famous painting, "The Birth of Venus," she is seen rising from a sea shell, surrounded by pink roses.

Aphrodite presented the rose to her son Eros (Cupid), who in turn gave it to Harpocrates, the deity of silence, as a bribe to keep him from revealing the indiscretions of the gods and goddesses. Consequently, the rose became the symbol of silence and secrecy, and in Roman banqueting halls roses were hung over the tables to indicate that what was said there was to be kept *sub rosa* (under the rose), or confidential, a good idea in view of the quantities of rose and other wines consumed there. Eventually sculptured roses in the ceilings of banquet halls and dining rooms replaced the real thing and became a common architectural motif.

In the high days of the licentious emperors, Romans used roses so lavishly that they became linked with the extravagance and excess that led to the fall of the empire. Roman nobles strew rose petals over tables and floors, paths, and lakes. They bathed in rose water and wore garlands of roses around their necks and on their heads. Rose garlands festooned halls, and in dining rooms guests reclined on couches covered with rose petals and leaned on pillows stuffed with them. Wealthy Romans slept on mattresses stuffed with rose petals, and from this custom comes the expression "a bed of roses" to designate a situation of ease and pleasure. Wreaths of roses were given as prizes at public games, and rose wreaths crowned the heads of heros. Romans planted roses in cemeteries and often directed in their wills that roses be strewn and planted on their graves. Some shops in Rome sold nothing but roses.

The emperors set the example for lavishness. Fountains of rose water played in Nero's halls, and showers of rose petals rained down on his guests. At a single banquet Nero is said to have spent five million sesterces (a brass coin equal in value to four donkeys) for roses. The Emperor Caligula (who made his horse a consul) walked to bed over a carpet of red roses, and the Emperor Heliogabulus (who made his hair dresser commander-in-chief of his army) almost suffocated his guests with the scent of roses.[2] To honor her Roman lover, Mark Antony, Cleopatra had a carpet of rose petals a cubit (about twenty inches) deep spread over the floor of her banquet hall and covered with a fine net for her guests to walk upon.

In addition to wearing, walking upon, and lying on roses, Romans also ate and drank them and used them in medicines and cosmetics. A recipe from the time calls for pounded rose petals mixed with calf's brains, eggs, and wine and baked in a mold. Some Romans drank rose water with meals and again the morning after as a hangover cure. In his *Natural History* Pliny the Elder lists more than a dozen remedies using roses and comments that using the blossoms as decorations was the least important use made of them. And Anacreon wrote of the rose, "When pain afflicts and sickness grieves, / Its juice the drooping heart relieves."

Early Christians shunned the rose because to them it was the symbol of pagan debauchery. But such a beautiful and popular flower was difficult to ignore, and eventually, after it was consecrated to the Virgin Mary, it became woven into Christian legends. One of these says that after God created woman, he created the rose to please her, and another relates that when Eve kissed the white rose in the Garden of Eden, it blushed pink with pleasure. Still another Christian legend says that the roses that grew in the Garden were thornless, but after the Fall, they sprouted thorns to remind people of their sinful nature.

One of Mary's titles is "the mystical Rose," and a sacred legend says that the tomb of the Virgin was found filled with lilies and roses after her assumption. Paintings of the Madonna often picture her surrounded by roses or sitting in a rose garden. The word *rosary,* which means rose garden in Latin, came to represent the Virgin Mary's garden in a mystic sense, and the string of prayer beads called the rosary was originally made of compressed rose petals that were made into a pulp and formed into beads. A legend connects St. Dominic with the rosary: For many years he paid daily tribute to the Virgin Mary with an offering of roses. One day when evil was about to beset him, a heavenly light surrounded and protected him, and Mary appeared and wove the flowers into a garland, which she placed around his neck—the rosary. An old custom was for a bride to send her wedding bouquet to a convent to have the nuns make the flowers into a rosary.[3]

In the sixteenth century roses were placed over confessionals to indicate that what was said there was private. Even before that time the tradition began of having the Pope bless an intricately wrought golden rose on the fourth Sunday in Lent (Rose Sunday). The rose was then presented to sovereigns, cities, persons, or institutions of the Roman Catholic faith that the church wanted to honor. Queen Isabella of Spain, King Henry VIII of England, and Napoleon III of France were among famous recipients; in the twentieth century, the Queen of Italy in 1937 and the shrine of Our Lady of Fatima in 1964 have received the golden rose.[4] In the Middle Ages the rose became a popular motif for embellishing medieval tapestries and manuscript illustrations, and rose windows became one of the glories of European medieval churches.

In his masterpiece *The Divine Comedy,* Dante uses the rose in an effort to describe the Empyrean. As he enters this final heaven, he sees a huge white rose (the mystic rose of Paradise), whose petals are the thrones for the blessed souls who have reached this ultimate place of peace and light. Dante calls this celestial flower "the rose wherein the Word divine was made incarnate."

Scholars do not agree on what flowers are meant by references to roses in the Bible. The Moldenkes point out that wild roses are comparatively rare in Palestine but are widely distributed, and there is a thicket rose in Galilee with pure white flowers. The Rose of Jericho is often identified as the resurrection plant, a Syrian plant that rolls up when dry and expands again when moistened, and the Rose of Sharon is thought to be a species of narcissus by some and a meadow saffron or common St. John's wort by others.

Other religions and mythologies have adapted the rose to their purposes. In Norse mythology the rose was the flower of the goddess of love, Freyja, who was known for her ability to keep secrets. The Hindu goddess Lakshmi, bringer of love, beauty, and good fortune, was said to have been born from a rose. And in Islamic legend after the white rose sprang from the sweat of Mohammed on his journey to Heaven, it was stained red by his blood.

Ancient Persians regarded the rose as sacred and thought the song of the nightingale caused rosebuds to unfold even as its love for the rose caused the plaintive strain in the nightingale's song. This idea of a link between the rose and the nightingale spread to other countries. From

France came the legend that the rose is red because it is stained with the blood of the nightingale. English writers were particularly attracted by this theme. Lord Byron called the rose the "queen" of the nightingale; Thackeray attributed the music of the nightingale to its love for the rose; Elizabeth Barrett Browning refers to this idea in "Lay of the Early Rose"; Thomas Moore asks in "Lalla Rookh" of what significance is any spot to the nightingale "If there his darling rose is not?"; and Oscar Wilde wrote a touching children's story about a rose and a nightingale.

Since early Roman times, the rose has been a popular heraldic device. In the days of chivalry knights of the Order of the Rose wore roses embroidered on their sleeves to signify that gentleness accompanied courage. Ironically, although the crusaders wore emblematic roses, when the Moslem leader Saladin defeated the Christians in 1187, he ordered five hundred camel loads of Damascus roses distilled into rose water to cleanse the mosque of Omar in Jerusalem of the infidels' impurities. The crusaders brought hybrid roses back to Western Europe; in 1275 Edward I of England had in his garden at the Tower of London several hundred roses, and the Damask rose was listed in his "Bill of Medicines."

The rose, England's national flower, is closely woven into its history. In his *Herball* Gerard wrote: "The rose doth deserve the chief and prime place among all floures whatsoever; being esteemed for his beauty, vertues, and his fragrant and odoriferous smell; but also because it is the honor and ornament of our English scepter; as by the conjunction appeareath in the unity of those two most Royal Houses of Lancaster and Yorke."[5]

As Gerard indicates, the rose became an especially significant symbol in England in the fifteenth century during the civil wars known as the Wars of the Roses (1455–85) for possession of the throne. Although the rose-plucking scene depicted by Shakespeare in *Henry VI* between the Lancastrians (red rose) and the Yorkists (white rose) is essentially fictional, these roses did come to represent the two houses during the long and bloody struggle. After defeating Richard III at the Battle of Bosworth Field in 1485, the Lancastrian Henry Tudor (Henry VII) married the Princess Elizabeth of York, and their union gave rise to the Tudor rose, a superimposition of the white rose on the red, which Henry VIII had incorporated into his coat of arms.

In France roses were also entwined in politics and history. Until the seventeenth century it was the custom for all French nobles to present roses to the parliament at Paris during a huge breakfast feast, where every member of parliament received a garland and a large bouquet of roses.[6] While Napoleon was off creating his empire, his first wife, Josephine, set out to collect and cultivate every known variety of rose. The best gardeners of Europe were commandeered to turn 4,500 acres at Malmaison, near Paris, into a gigantic rose garden. Napoleon's armies collected roses wherever they found them, and the British Admiralty cooperated by issuing orders to its navy that if a ship carrying plants or seeds for Malmaison were seized, the botanical treasures were to be sent immediately to Malmaison. Realizing that her fabulous garden would not be maintained after her death, Josephine commissioned the artist Pierre-Joseph Redoute (who also had a passion for roses) to paint many of her best specimens. Redoute, who illustrated several books on roses, came to be known as the "Raphael de la Rose," and his rose paintings are still being reproduced as prints and on note cards and wrapping papers.

According to some accounts of the discovery of America, it was a rose branch bright with red hips that Columbus and his anxious crew picked out of the water on October 11, 1492, that gave them courage to continue their voyage. More than three hundred years later, the explorer Captain John Charles Fremont described the wild roses he had seen in America on virgin prairies, "Everywhere the Rose is met with . . . . It is scattered over the prairies in small bouquets, and, when glittering in the dew and swaying in the pleasant breeze of the early morning, is the most beautiful of the prairie flowers."[7] William Penn brought rose bushes in his luggage. George Washington planted roses at Mt. Vernon, and Thomas Jefferson grew them at Monticello. Practical John Adams planted a combined rose and vegetable garden at the White House in 1800, and Mrs. Woodrow Wilson redesigned the area outside the president's office into a formal rose garden in 1913. The Kennedys introduced other plants, but the area continues to be referred to as the "Rose Garden," and many important moments in our nation's history continue to occur in this beautiful setting. A new garden by the East Wing also featuring roses is named the Jacqueline Kennedy garden.

In 1986 Congress designated the rose the "national Floral Emblem of the United States of America." And four individual states—Georgia, New York, Iowa, and North Dakota—have officially adopted roses as their floral emblems.

The *Rosaceae* family is a huge one including many of our favorite orchard fruits such as apples, pears, cherries, quince, peaches, and plums as well as almonds, wild strawberries, blackberries, and raspberries and ornamentals such as spireas and pyracantha. The most important ornamentals are, of course, the *Rosas* of which Texas has fourteen species plus other subspecies and varieties, many of them having escaped from cultivation so long ago that they are thought of as natives. Some of Texas' wild roses have traveled great distances from their native lands. The Macartney rose (*Rosa bracteata*) is an example of such a traveler that has made itself at home in our state. In 1793 King George III sent Lord Macartney to China, where the ambassador found a white rose that he brought back to England, and eventually colonists brought it to North America, where it became completely naturalized from Virginia to Florida and East Texas. Early settlers in Texas planted windbreaks of this evergreen on the coastal plains to protect cattle from the vicious blue northers that seemed to come down straight from the North Pole. These living fences and soil binders readily escaped and ran wild in south Texas, where they can still be seen in white-blossomed tangled masses up to eight feet high.

The Cherokee rose (*R. laevigata*) is a similar white rose that made its way to the Southern United States from the Orient. Apparently it was originally taken overland from China to Persia, where it was picked up by Moslem Arabs and carried with them and eventually planted in their gardens in Spain. Spanish colonizers later brought the plant to Florida, and from there it escaped to become the celebrated "wild" rose of the South.[8] During the Civil War the Cherokee rose was often planted by soldiers as a memorial on the graves of their fallen comrades. Its fragrant blossoms open nearly flat amid the evergreen leaves, and like the Macartney rose, it easily spread in South Texas to form large bowers. After it was established in America, the Cherokee rose acquired its common name, and several Indian legends sprang up about it. According to one, an Indian girl who was captured by a hostile tribe was turned by magic into the Cherokee rose and given especially sharp thorns for protection. Another Indian legend says the rose received its name when a Cherokee maiden fell in love with a captured Seminole chieftain. They escaped together, but as they were leaving her home, she broke off a sprig from a rose bush and took it with her to her new home, where its milk white blossoms with bright golden centers reminded her of her childhood and her people, and from that time it has been called the Cherokee rose.[9]

Although there is no "yellow rose of Texas" except in song, a number of attractive pink and white wild roses (in addition to the Macartney and Cherokee) are widely distributed in the state. The beautiful pink prairie rose (*R. setigera*) with its long, climbing branches of pink flowers up to two inches across is found in open woods, thickets, and clearings in East Texas. A pink shrub rose also known as a prairie rose or sunshine rose (*R. arkansana*) grows in the Panhandle. And a smaller pink shrub rose called the Woods rose (*R. woodsii*), named for Joseph Woods, an Englishman who studied roses, is found in the Trans-Pecos, where it can form dense, thorny thickets. The spicy Carolina rose, which tolerates humidity, grows in the Big Thicket, and the leafy rose (*R. foliolosa*) with pure white flowers sometimes tinged with pink and dark green glossy leaves is native to North Central Texas. The desert rose (*R. stellata*) with its solitary deep rose-purple blossoms thrives in the Guadalupe Mountains, where it is heavily browsed by deer and elk. There are many beautiful rose gardens in Texas; the most famous ones are at Tyler, which is known worldwide for its production of field-grown rose bushes. Visitors come by the thousands each year to see the Tyler Municipal Rose Garden in bloom and to attend the autumn Rose Festival there.

Through the ages roses have been prized for their usefulness as well as for their beauty. In classical medicine they were among the herbs used by Hippocrates and Galen. Pliny recommended tinctures and infusions of fresh or dried rose petals steeped in wine to cure eye, ear, and mouth irritations, headaches, and toothache as well as diseases of the lung, stomach, and intestinal tract, sleeplessness, and excessive perspiration. The Medieval German abbess/herbalist Hildegard of Bingen (1098–1179) suggested using rose hip tea as the initial treatment for just about every known illness.[10]

Nicholas Culpeper, the herbalist who related everything to astrology, stated that red roses were under the sign of Jupiter, Damask roses under Venus, and white roses under the moon. He believed: "The distilled water of roses, vinegar of roses, ointment and oil of roses, and the rose leaves dried, are of very great use and effect." In addition to a long list of common diseases, he recommended using rose concoctions for memory loss, insomnia, swoonings, and to quicken faint spirits.[11]

Another popular herbalist, John Gerard, recommended the distilled water of roses for "strengthening of the heart, refreshing of the spirits, and likewise for all things that require a gentle cooling." He also suggested that rose water put into "junketting dishes, cakes, sauces and many other pleasant things, giveth a fine and delectable taste."[12]

Native Americans considered the wild rose important in their medical treatments, using the roots, inner bark, leaves, and petals as well as the hips to treat wounds and many other medical problems. They drank rose water and rose hip tea as sedatives and used oil of roses to soothe headache. A salve of ground rose petals combined with grease was used to treat mouth sores, and the ground petals were blown as a powder into the throat to relieve sore throat. Virginia Scully has passed along this Native American recipe for making an ointment to cure eczema: "Get a wildcat, extract his fat, mix it with ground rose petals and apply as ointment several times a day."[13]

Although rose hips may not live up to all of the extravagant claims made for the amount of vitamin C they contain, they are, for their size, quite rich in this important vitamin. During World War II, Britain turned to the roses growing in her hedgerows and in her gardens as a source of vitamin C when importing citrus fruit became difficult. Under government direction tons of rose hips were harvested and processed into syrup that was regularly given to children to prevent scurvy. In his 1966 book, *Stalking the Healthful Herbs,* Euell Gibbons offers numerous recipes using rose hips, and today health food stores sell rose hip pills, powders, and tonics as well as syrups as vitamin C supplements.

In the Middle Ages roses were used in making mead and also in preserves, chutneys, wine, syrups, and liqueurs. A 1744 cookbook published in London suggests making conserve of red roses by beating together in a marble mortar a pound of red rose buds and three pounds of powdered sifted loaf sugar.[14] During the eighteenth and nineteenth centuries, roses appeared on the table in many guises, including pickled rosebuds, rose butter, rose jelly, rose petal jam, rose hip jam, and rose petal sandwiches. Queen Victoria was fond of a sauce eglantine and a rose hip marmalade, and during her time rose water was an important flavoring in desserts and candies. Confectioners tucked pretty candied rose or violet petals among their nuts and chocolates. Many hostesses made their own crystallized rose petals for decorating cakes, although the process was tedious as it involved dissolving powdered gum arabic in rose water and painting it on each petal, dipping the petals individually in superfine sugar, and allowing them to dry before storing them in an airtight container.

In *The Forgotten Art of Flower Cookery* (1990), Leona Woodring Smith offers a recipe for a "liberated" cocktail called the Rosehattan, which calls for whiskey, dry and sweet vermouth, and rose water, as well as recipes for Lobster Salad a La Roses, Chicken a La Rose, Rosy Custard, Rose Souffle, Rose Crepes, and Rose Creams. The American Rose Society has a number of recipes using roses, including Rose Hip Jelly and Rose Hip Wine.

Animals and some humans eat raw rose hips, but their hairs can be irritating to the throat. A few years ago, before commercial "itching powder" was available, a popular childhood prank was to split open large rose hips and put the hairy seeds down the back of a shirt or dress to cause itching.

Ancient Persians, Egyptians, Greeks, and Romans used roses in cosmetics and perfumes, and attar of roses is still one of the most highly valued oils in the perfume industry. Histories of the Great Moguls of India tell of the romantic discovery of the oil or attar of roses. Between 1582 and 1612 for the wedding feast of the Emperor Djihanguyr and the princess Nour-Djihan, a canal circling the extensive palace gardens was filled with rose water. While the bridal pair was rowing on the fragrant water, they observed that the heat of the sun had caused the essential oil of the rose to settle out. After it was skimmed off, it was found to have an exquisite perfume.[15] The manufacture of attar of roses began almost immediately and has continued ever since, and it remains important in the making of fine perfume in many countries but especially in France, Bulgaria, and Western Asia. Since it takes sixty thousand roses to make one ounce of attar of roses, it has been well said that it is worth five times its weight in gold.

Like the ancients, more modern Europeans used roses to create air fresheners to cover up a host of evil odors. One method was to heat rose water with other herbs or spices such as cloves until a paste was formed. Then this was placed in a cassolette (a small metal box with a decorated perforated lid), which was placed near a fire to release the fragrance. Sachets and scented powders made with dried rose petals were sprinkled among clothing and linens, and every family had its own recipe for making potpourri, either moist or dry, which was kept in sweet jars or sweet bags. Sometimes the petals were mixed with gum benzoin and musk or ambergris and made into thin cakes that were dried in the sun and then burned to freshen the air.

As a cosmetic, rosaceum, an ointment of rose oil, honey, and rose water, was used lavishly in ancient Persia, Egypt, Greece, and Rome. Another recipe for a Roman beauty treatment calls for mixing dried roses with lion's fat. Rose water, not a perfume itself, is still used in cosmetics and perfumes.

Recently there has been a revival of interest in making rose petal bead necklaces. Made in the same way as the original rosary beads, they hold their fragrance for years.

In the language of flowers, roses have the most elaborate vocabulary of any flower. Although there is considerable difference in the various connotations listed according to the code maker, generally rose buds signify youth and beauty, red roses passion, white roses purity and innocence and yellow roses jealousy and/or infidelity.

Countless writers have used the rose symbolically, associating the buds and blossoms with love, beauty, youth, and perfection; the withering flowers with the ephemeral nature of beauty and youth; and the thorns with pain. In *The Rubaiyat of Omar Khayyam,* Edward FitzGerald uses the rose to express the mystery of time: "Each morn a thousand roses brings, you say: / Yes, but where leaves the Rose of Yesterday?" The *Romance of the Rose* was the most important literary influence on writing in English in the fourteenth century. This elaborate allegorical French poem set in the walled garden of the god of love comprised over twenty thousand lines. Chaucer translated it in part and used it in his *Canterbury Tales,* and many other writers have referred to it.

Shakespeare mentions the rose at least seventy times in his sonnets and plays, sometimes using the old mellifluous name "eglantine." Even people who have never read *Romeo and Juliet* are familiar with Juliet's question: "What's in a name? That which we call a rose / By any other name would smell as sweet."

Seventeenth-century British Cavalier poet Robert Herrick wrote a poem describing the funeral of a rose and another poem addressed "To the Virgins" advising them to "Gather Ye rosebuds while Ye may." But the English poet who used the *carpe diem* theme most effectively was Edmund Waller. In "Go, Lovely Rose," the poet sends a rose to tell his beloved how much he loves her, that her beauty is like that of the flower and what a shame it is if such beauty hides itself, and finally he commands the rose to die to remind her of the common fate of "all things rare. / How small a part of time they share / That are so wondrous sweet and fair."

Sir Walter Scott's "Lady of the Lake" is filled with wild roses and eglantine. In "A Red, Red Rose," Robert Burns says, "Oh, My luve is like a red red rose / That's newly sprung in June." John Keats calls the musk rose "mid-Mays eldest child." Tennyson personifies the rose in *Maud* as staying awake to watch for Maud whom he calls "Queen rose of the rosebud garden of girls." And in his prologue to *The Princess,* he describes his heroine as "A rosebud set with little willful thorns." Robert Browning in "The Patriot" gives us the enduring line, "It was roses, roses, all the way."

Like Oscar Wilde, William Thackeray used the rose in a fairy tale. "The Rose and the Ring" is a humorous story involving a magic rose and a magic ring that make the owner appear beautiful. Betsinda, one of the main characters, poses as a maid although she is actually the princess Rosalba.

The rose often appears in song. The old Scottish ballad "Fair Margaret and Sweet William" has a typical ballad ending in which the dead lovers are united symbolically: "Out of her breast there sprang a rose, / And out of his briar. / They grew till they grew unto the church's top, / And there they tied in a true love's knot." During World War I and afterward, the poignant lyrics of "The Roses are Flowering in Picardy" reminded generations of losses during that war. Thomas Moore, who often used roses in his songs, gave us the haunting "Last Rose of Summer." Among other enduring songs with rose themes are "Rose of Tralee," "Mexicali Rose," "Moonlight and Roses," and "One Dozen Roses."

Richard Strauss's much-loved opera *Der Rosenkavalier,* which was first performed in 1911, features a rose in its plot. And in *Le Spectre de la Rose,* a ballet written for the great Russian dancer Nijinsky, a rose is brought to life.

In the early twentieth century Gertrude Stein had her famous phrase "Rose is a rose is a rose is a rose" (*Sacred Emily*) printed in a circle conveying the shape of the flower and made it her enigmatic logo.

Someone has said that the history of the rose is the history of humanity, and in *The Poetry of the Earth* Florence Earle Coates writes:

> *There is always room for beauty: Memory*
> *A myriad lovely blossoms may enclose*
> *But, whatsoe'er hath been, there still must be*
> *Room for another rose.*

Sunflower

Sunflower Family (*Asteraceae*)

Common Names: Mirasol, Swamp Sunflower,
Common Sunflower, Maximilian Sunflower, Tickseed

Our common sunflower, *Helianthus annuus,* takes it genus name from the Greek words *helios* (sun) and *anthos* (flower). The poetic Spanish name *mirasol* means "looks at the sun," and botanists affirm that while it is developing the sunflower head actually does turn its face each day as it follows the sun from east to west. During the night it rests, but the next morning at sunrise it swings around to the east again to begin tracking its namesake. The Greeks, of course, had a myth to explain this striking physiological characteristic: Clytie, a water nymph, fell deeply in love with Apollo, the sun god. But he spurned her love, and gradually she pined away, sitting on the cold ground with her golden hair spread out over her shoulders. She neither ate nor drank and saw nothing but the sun, constantly turning her yearning eyes toward her beloved. At last her limbs rooted in the ground, and her face became the flower that turns on its stem to follow the passage of the sun across the sky.[1] In the nineteenth century's language of flowers, the sunflower symbolizes constancy, adoration, homage, and devotion. It might be noted however that the legend must have been adapted to fit the sunflower, which wasn't introduced into Europe until after explorers of the New World imported it.

When white men reached the New World, they found the Incas of Peru and the Indians of North America cultivating giant sunflowers. In *Joyfull Newes out of the Newe Found Worlde* (1577), Nicholas Monardes, a

Spanish botanist, wrote of the "Hearbe of the Sunne," describing it as "a straunge flower, for it casteth out the greatest flowers . . . greater than a greate Platter or Dishe."

In his *Herball* (1597) English herbalist John Gerard marveled that from seeds he sowed in his garden in April, sunflowers grew to be fourteen feet tall, with flowers weighing over three pounds each. By "triall" he discovered that the buds, boiled and eaten with butter and vinegar, were "exceedingly pleasant meat."[2]

The Incas revered the sunflower as a sacred symbol of their sun god. They placed golden sunflower images in their temples and adorned their priestesses (Maidens of the Sun) with large sunflower disks made of pure gold. These objects were also highly prized by the Spanish conquistadors, who venerated the gold if not the gods of the Incas.

In Christian religious symbolism the sunflower, representing light and sunshine, was dedicated to St. John the Evangelist. In the church of St. Remi at Rheims there is a window portraying the Virgin Mary and St. John on either side of the cross. An aureole of sunflowers encircles their heads, and each flower is turned toward the saviour as the true light of the world.

Native North Americans used the plant in religious ceremonies and placed ceremonial bowls filled with sunflower seeds by their dead so they would have food to sustain them on their long, difficult journey to the Happy Hunting Grounds. The Native Americans who cultivated sunflowers also taught white settlers many practical uses for the plant. They ate the seeds, parched or raw, ground them into meal and flour, and crushed them to obtain oil. They made thread and cordage from the fibers and used the leaves for fodder. From one variety they made a purple dye to decorate bodies and baskets, and from the pounded petals they extracted a yellow dye. Sometimes they smoked the dried leaves of sunflowers as a tobacco substitute. Among the medicinal uses they taught the pioneers were how to use various parts of the plant to treat snake bites and other wounds and cuts and how to make a tea from it to reduce fevers.

Nineteenth-century pioneers planted sunflowers near their houses to protect the family from malaria. Perhaps the strong scent of the flowers helped keep mosquitoes away. They also used infusions of sunflower blossoms in their bathwater to relieve arthritic pain.

In 1903 Kansas adopted the wild sunflower as its state flower, declar-

ing it to have "a historic symbolism which speaks of frontier days, winding trails, pathless prairies" and, as the legislators pointed out, it was a flower that "a child can draw on a slate, a woman can work in silk, or a man can carve on stone or fashion in clay . . . ."[3]

The cheery flower that gives Kansas its nickname of "Sunflower State" has gone forth into the world like a good ambassador. China uses its fiber as an adulterant of silk, Russia hybridizes it for larger seeds and higher oil content. Russians especially enjoy eating raw sunflower seeds, which are sold on the streets as peanuts are in America. In our diet-conscious world today, sunflower seeds, which are high in fiber, iron, and vitamins, are important as a source of polyunsaturated oils. And many countries use them to produce vegetable oil for salad dressing, cooking, and canning fish as well as in poultry feed and in paints. Parts of the plant are used in making paper, soap, and candles; the stalks are used for fuel and ashes are used as fertilizer. In the Panhandle and on the south plains of Texas, farmers grow hundreds of acres of large sunflowers for the seeds, which are sold as birdseed, or milled into low-fat oil, or shipped to Mexico or Spain for roasting and packaging as snack food. In 1994 more than eighteen thousand tons of sunflower seed were harvested in Texas.[4]

In Texas our common wild sunflowers (*Helianthus annuus*) may grow as high as ten feet, but in dry areas or dry seasons, they reach only a few feet in height. After a rain they blossom abundantly and line fences for miles or cover acres of fields. According to Jean Andrews they are territorial plants releasing toxins into the soil so that the growth of neighboring plants is inhibited. Maximilian sunflowers with tall stalks bearing numerous yellow flowers up to four inches across are found in many parts of Texas. They are named for naturalist Prince Maximilian of Wied Neuweid, who explored the western United States in the 1830s.[5] They are often sown on fallow fields as they are favorites of many game birds as well as of deer. Showy swamp sunflowers (*H. angustifolius*) form extensive colonies of brilliant yellow in moist soils. The name *angustifolius* is from the Latin, indicating that they have very narrow leaves. Plains or prairie sunflowers (*H. petiolaris*), smaller versions of the common sunflower, grow well in sandy ground, on open prairies or sandy plains. Tickseed sunflowers (*Bidens aristosa*), also known as sticktights and beggarticks, are probably the least popular members of the sunflower tribe in Texas because their barbed seeds cling to clothing and animal fur and are difficult to remove. *Bidens* indicates they are doubly toothed, and *aristosa* that they are bearded or fringed with hair. Sunflowers hybridize easily (to the dismay of sunflower farmers) and there are numerous wild varieties in Texas. New cultivars are constantly being produced in a rainbow of colors for gardeners.

Like the daisy at Vassar College graduations, the sunflower became a symbol attached to graduation ceremonies at the University of Texas School of Law. At the turn of the century, while the whole school was still contained in the old Main Building, the School of Law was in the basement. Inexplicably, when the graduates met and agreed to rent caps and gowns for commencement, the law students were not asked to participate in the decision. After some discussion, the law students agreed to wear white suits with sunflowers pinned to their lapels as a symbol that just as the sunflower keeps its face turned to the sun, the new lawyers would keep theirs turned to the light of justice. Today the graduates wear business suits, and a sunflower is pinned to each student's lapel as he or she crosses the stage.[6]

Victorian writers sometimes compared attractive women to sunflowers, but in *Vanity Fair* Thackeray says "Miss Sedley was *not* of the sunflower sort." In "Ah Sunflower" William Blake speaks of the sunflower as counting "the steps of the Sun." Of all the tributes paid to the devotion of the sunflower to its namesake, the most appealing was written by Thomas Moore in "Believe Me, If All Those Enduring Young Charms":

> *The heart that has truly loved never forgets,*
> *But as truly loves on to the close,*
> *As the sunflower turns on her god when he sets,*
> *The same look which she turn'd when he rose.*

Thistle

Sunflower Family (*Asteraceae*)

Common Names: Texas Thistle, Bull Thistle, Nodding Thistle, Wavyleaf Thistle, Star Thistle, Cotton Thistle

*A*fter Adam and Eve ate from the forbidden tree of knowledge in the Garden of Eden, God cursed the ground and promised Adam it would bring forth "thorns and thistles" (Genesis 3:18). And in the book of Hosea, among the curses the prophet rings down on Israel is one that says "the thorn and the thistle shall come up in their altars; and they shall say to the mountains, Cover us, and to the hills Fall on us" (Hosea 10:8). In other scriptural and rhetorical blasts, the term *thistles* is used to include similar prickly plants such as nettles. Man's enduring struggle with this thorny problem is shown by the fact that *thistle* has entered the dictionary as a verb meaning "to root up thistles."

There is, however, plenty of evidence showing that the virtues of various thistles were also known in ancient times. The thistle known as Carline in Europe is named for the Emperor Charlemagne. Legend says that after many of his soldiers died of the plague, he prayed for help. An angel appeared and told him to shoot an arrow at random and to make use of the herb it struck. When it landed on a thistle, Charlemagne had the plants boiled to prepare medicine for the plague victims. All recovered and the pestilence abated.[1] European peasants used the Carline thistle as a barometer because the flowers close when a storm threatens and open wide in bright weather.

The blessed thistle (*Carduus benedictus*) was a standard remedy for many ailments during the middle ages. It was also called Holy Ghost herb and holy thistle, and Monks grew it to cure smallpox. Early herbalists considered it a cure-all that could "both prevent and cure headache, provoke sweat, help memory, strengthen the heart and stomach, and cure external problems such as festering sores, boils and the itch."[2] Both Gerard's herbal (1597) and Turner's herbal (1568) mention its virtues. In the sixteenth and seventeenth centuries, it was widely recommended to relieve pain and inflammation of the heart. In Shakespeare's *Much Ado About Nothing,* one character advises another to "get you some of this distilled Carduus Benedictus and lay it to your heart; it is the only thing for a qualm . . . plain holy thistle" (act III, scene iv, line 80).

Although Culpeper—in the middle of the Reformation—says cynically, "It is called Blessed Thistle or Holy Thistle. I suppose the name put upon it by some that had little holiness themselves," he does acknowledge its medical properties, and as usual ties them into his beloved astrology: "It [blessed thistle] strengthens the attractive faculty of men and clarifies the blood, because [it is] ruled by Mars."[3] Herbalists in the nineteenth century prescribed a tea made from the plant tops to treat fevers. Today in herbal medicine it is used as a contraceptive and to treat cancer as well as heart and liver problems, fevers, and infections and as a digestive tonic.

According to Greek legend the thistle was created by the earth mother Gaea as an expression of her grief at the loss of Daphnis, the beautiful shepherd boy who is supposed to have originated pastoral poetry. The spines supposedly symbolize the pain in her heart at his loss. In Teutonic mythology the thistle was associated with magic and held sacred to Thor, god of thunder. If people carried or wore a piece of the plant, it was supposed to protect them from lightning. In some European countries thistles were placed on ripening corn stalks to keep evil spirits away from the fields.[4]

Every schoolchild in Scotland knows the story of how the thistle saved the country. In the year 1263 when the Scots and Danes were at war, the Danes managed to land unobserved on the coast of Scotland. Under cover of darkness the Danish invaders removed their boots and crept on bare feet toward the unsuspecting Scottish army. Victory seemed certain for the attackers when suddenly a sharp cry of pain shattered the stillness. A

Danish soldier had stepped on a thistle and ruined the surprise. The alerted Scots sprang into action and drove the invaders from the country's shores.

The thistle of Scotland, *Onopordum,* is similar to our cotton thistle, whose common name comes from the white cottony down that gives the plant a hoary appearance. Adopted as the Scottish national emblem in the fifteenth century, the prickly plant symbolizes the national motto: *Nemo me impune lacessit* (nobody provokes me with impunity). The institution of Scottish knighthood, The Order of the Thistle, was begun by James II in 1687. Sometimes called the Order of St. Andrew, its insignia include a collar of golden thistles and sprigs of rue. The Coat of Arms of the national bank of Scotland, granted in 1826, shows a figure of St. Andrew, the patron saint of Scotland, carrying his cross, surrounded by a border of thistles.

Mary, Queen of Scots, wanted to make the thistle called milk thistle or Our Lady's thistle *Silybum marianum* (which is also found naturalized in north central Texas) the official thistle of Scotland. The milk white veins on its striking leaves give the plant its name, and it is characterized by thick, prickly bracts which project in all directions around the purple flowers. Legend says the white veins were formed by milk that fell from the Virgin Mary's breast as she suckled the baby Jesus. Since ancient times the roots and seeds of the milk thistle have been used medicinally as a tonic and to treat complaints of the spleen, liver, and kidneys. At one time it was thought to increase the flow of milk in nursing mothers. Modern research has shown that this thistle contains silymarin, which stimulates the liver to regenerate itself, and therefore it is useful in treating hepatitis and cirrhosis.[5]

Their distinctive spiny characters make thistles easy to recognize as a family, but they can vary greatly in size. In legendary Tatary thistles were said to grow so tall that the natives built their huts under the foliage. Texas has none this size, but we do have an interesting variety of thistles and near-thistles with flowers ranging from lavender to deep purple and a few white or yellow specimens. Once established in an area, they multiply and spread readily as the blossoms become fluffy balls of winged seeds that are carried off by breezes to distant fields and roadsides. There is an old saying that first love floats from the memory like "thistledown in a breeze."

The common Texas thistle (*Cirsium texanum*) grows in all parts of the state except the Panhandle. Its rose-lavender blossoms are attractive to butterflies, especially the painted lady, whose larvae feed on the foliage.

Bull thistle (*C. horridulum*), the largest Texas thistle, can be a pest in pastures because it is difficult to eradicate and because its foliage is so very prickly, as indicated by its botanical name, from the Latin *horridus,* meaning bristly or very thorny. The flowers may be pink or purple or yellow.

Wavyleaf or plumed thistle (*C. undulatum*) has large pale flowers varying from pink and mauve to white. Common in the Trans-Pecos and Big Bend areas, it is browsed by deer while it is young. Turner thistle (*C. turneri*), also found in these areas, is a beautiful maroon-flowered thistle that was named by Dr. Barton Warnock for one of his outstanding botany students, Dr. Billie L. Turner. It is found growing on limestone overhangs or bluffs.

Nodding thistle (*Carduus nutans*), a very handsome, very thorny plant, thrives in the Panhandle and has been naturalized in central Texas. Its plump rose-purple disk flowers droop slightly over its bright green spiky body.

Although the so-called yellow-flowered sow thistles (*Sonchus*) have few admirers, rabbits, goats, and sheep as well as pigs relish them, and humans, too, have made use of the plant in salads and as cooked greens, in the same way dandelions are used. Fortunately for the gatherer, the sow thistle is not as prickly as true thistles. Carmine (Papa) Stahl recommends cooking sow thistle with sourdock, and Delena Tull suggests mixing it with dandelion greens and wild lettuce. Sow thistle yields a yellow dye, and its milky sap has been used to treat eye ailments and skin eruptions.

Eryngo or false purple thistle (*Eryngium leavenworthii*) is a spiny thistlelike plant that is actually a member of the parsley family. Its royal purple blossoms and purple bracts and stems brighten the Central Texas landscape in late summer and fall. The Greeks apparently thought of it as a thistle, as the name *Eryngium* means thistle. The botanical name *Leavenworthii* is in honor of Dr. M. Conkling Leavenworth, an American botanist, physician, and military man who traveled in the South collecting plants. Eryngo is excellent for dried arrangements, keeping its color for many weeks. Another attractive Texas *Eryngium*, Mexican thistle, is a silvery thistlelike plant. When it matures the small oval sky-blue heads are surrounded by a large whitish sunburst of spiny bracts.

Basket flowers (*Centaurea americana*) are not much like true thistles, but they are sometimes called star thistles. Like their relative the cornflower or bachelor's button, they have become great garden favorites. With their large lavender blossoms with creamy centers, picturesque buds, and pleasant fragrance, they are attractive additions to flower beds. Sometimes called powderpuff or shaving brush, the best-known common name of the basket flower derives from the woven basketlike appearance of the straw-colored bracts. The name *Centaurea* originated in a Greek myth that says that after Hercules killed the many-headed hydra, he visited Chiron, the famous Centaur. Hercules had with him an arrow that he had dipped in the poisonous blood of the monster, and when it accidentally touched Chiron's foot, Hercules plucked some leaves from a nearby plant and covered Chiron's wound. The Centaur recovered, and his name was given to the plant that saved his life.[6]

Another famous or infamous plant associated with thistles is the tumbleweed (*Salsola kali*), also known as Russian thistle, which has been immortalized in song. Introduced from Russia into the United States along with flaxseed in the nineteenth century, it soon became a serious pest to ranchers and farmers. Its many-branched, rounded form is dotted with numerous tiny flowers and may reach six feet across and three to four feet in height. West Texas winds blow clumps of dried tumbleweed across open lands and highways and into creekbeds and fences, where it collects in large masses. Aside from its symbolic connotations in song lyrics, a few other uses have been found for the pesky plant. The tender young shoots may be used in salads or soups, and the seeds can be roasted and ground into a coarse meal for bread. Recently it has been discovered that the dead plants can be pressed into logs for fuel, and because of its high alkali content, it may be used in glass.[7] Imaginative Texans spray paint the dried tumbleweed balls and make holiday decorations of them.

Because of the protective spines, only winged insects have access to the nectar of thistles, but bees make a delicious honey from certain species. The American goldfinch is known as the thistlebird because of its fondness for thistle seeds and its habit of using thistledown to line its nest. Pliny said of thistles that no four-footed animal except the ass would eat them, and it is true that mules appear to relish them as food after kicking and trampling the plants to subdue the prickles. The peeled stems and roots of young shoots of thistle used to be a common food for native people in many countries of the world including North America. The explorer Fremont praised a dish of thistle roots prepared by Native American women as being "sweet and well-flavored." When one of the early explorers of Yellowstone National Park became hurt and separated from his party, he escaped starvation for nearly a month by eating the fat roots of the thistles there.[8]

Delena Tull declares, "In spite of their spines, thistles provide one of the best wild salad greens and cooked vegetables in the state." Of the nine species of *Cirsium*, she recommends Texas thistle and bull thistle as the best for food.[9]

According to different lists, in the language of flowers thistles may represent austerity, retaliation, misanthropy, independence, or defiance and surliness. Perhaps the famous Scottish poet, James Hogg, expressed the meaning of the thorny emblem best in a patriotic ballad:

> *Up wi' the flowers o' Scotland,*
> *The emblem o' the free;*
> *Their guardians for a thousand years*
> *Their guardians still we'll be.*
> *A foe had better brave the de'il*
> *Within his reeky cell,*
> *Than our thistle's purple bonnet*
> *Or our bonny heather bell.*[10]

Verbena/ Vervain

Vervain Family (*Verbenaceae*)

Common Names: Texas Verbena, Prairie Verbena, Slender Vervain, Blue Vervain, Rose Vervain, Moss Vervain

Verbena is the genus name for a group of plants in the Vervain Family, but in popular usage trailing forms of the plants have come to be called verbenas and erect ones vervains.

In Roman antiquity "verbena" signified the leaves or twigs of certain sacred plants or shrubs such as olives, myrtles, or laurels used in religious ceremonies. Eventually the name became attached to particular plants— the verbenas or vervains used to decorate altars. Priests used them in their divinations, and the whole plant was soaked in water and used to cleanse the altar of Jupiter. By the time Horace (65–8 B.C.) was writing his odes, apparently vervain was the plant of choice to use in preparation for sacrifices, as he says: "The altar strew'd with vervain, / Hungers for the flow of lambkin's blood." (*Odes*, iv, xi, 7).

Although vervain was sacred to Mars, Roman god of war, one of its reputed powers was to reconcile the bitterest of enemies. Therefore Roman heralds wore crowns of verbena when they went to meet potential foes as ambassadors of peace or when they went to meet them to issue challenges to fight.

Ancient Persians also venerated verbena, and priests of temples carried branches of it as they approached the altar. It was harvested with great care on moonless nights, and honey was poured onto the place where the plant had grown to placate the earth for taking such a precious possession.[1]

In Egyptian mythology vervain was said to have sprung from the tears of Isis, goddess of nature, as she grieved for her murdered brother-husband, Osiris. A thousand years later vervain entered Christian folklore as the herb that grew at the foot of the cross on Mt. Calvary and that was said to have been pressed into Christ's wounds to stanch the bleeding. This plant is commonly described as *Verbena hastata* (known as blue vervain in Texas), but the Moldenkes say in *Plants of the Bible* that it is not possible that this plant was growing in that area of the world at the time of the crucifixion.[2] It was, nevertheless, a popular and persistent belief, and vervain acquired the common names of herb-of-the-cross and holy herb.

Long before the language of flowers was invented, Virgil spoke of vervain as the floral symbol of enchantment. Ancient priests in the Far East, as well as in Greece and Rome, used it in their divinations. In folklore witches used vervain in their spells and brews, but it was also supposed to have the power to keep them at bay, as the old English rhyme says: "Vervain and dill / Hinder witches of their will." The Druids of Britain used it in their rituals and regarded it as a magic plant, sacred to the priestesses as mistletoe was to the priests.

Many central European countries had superstitions connected with vervain. People wore the leaves to protect themselves from harm; it was said that those who bathed in its juice would be able to get whatever they wanted; and it was reputed to possess power in a love potion. Until recently German brides wore hats made of vervain to ensure lasting happiness in their marriages, and mothers commonly hung a piece of vervain around a child's neck to serve as a charm against sickness and evil. In Hungary criminals were suspected of making use of the belief that if a bit of verbena leaf were inserted into a small cut in the hand and the wound allowed to heal, they could open all kinds of locks and bars with the touch of their magic hands.[3]

Verbena was widely believed to promote merriment. In ancient Rome verbena water was sprinkled on banqueting couches before a feast to promote merriment, and Pliny suggested sprinkling verbena water in the dining chamber to make the guests merry. In the fourteenth century Albertus

Magnus wrote: "Infants bearing it [vervain] shall be very apte to learn and loving learnying and they shalbe glad and joyous."[4] And in the seventeenth century British dramatist John Fletcher had a character in *The Faithful Shepherdess* say, "And those light vervain, too, thou must go after / Provoking easy souls to mirth and laughter." Herbalist Gerard suggested that a host steep four leaves and four roots of verbena in the wine to make his party guests happy.

Because magic and medicine were closely related in earlier times, it is not surprising that vervain became known as a virtual panacea. During the Middle Ages when healing herbs were called simples and herbalists were known as simplers, vervain became known as "simpler's joy" because it was believed to cure so many ailments. Hippocrates had recommended vervain for fever and plague, but the simplers used it as a cure-all for at least thirty different ailments, including whooping cough, pneumonia, tuberculosis, asthma, ague, epilepsy, fits, scrofula, delirium, insanity, headache, insomnia, and appendicitis. Vervain baths were recommended to soothe rheumatic aches, and poultices of mashed leaves were applied to swellings and burns. Anglo Saxons called vervain "pigeon grass" because they thought pigeons ate it to improve their eyesight. They also believed it cured ulcers and tightened loose teeth and stopped hair from falling out. In the seventeenth century herbalist Nicholas Culpeper touted vervain as a treatment for many problems including acne and dandruff. Colonists found Native Americans using vervain to treat fever and gastrointestinal complaints. In American folk medicine vervain was called "fever-weed," and a popular use was to bruise the leaves in vinegar to clear the skin and eyes. Army surgeons made use of verbena during the Revolutionary War, and *Verbena hastata* appeared in the *National Formulary* until 1926.[5]

Correll and Johnston list fourteen genera of the vervain family in Texas, and *Verbena* is the largest, with some thirty-five species. One of our most abundant wildfowers is prairie verbena or Dakota vervain (*V. bipinnatifida*), often found growing in large patches. Its flat-topped clusters of small flowers in varying shades of purple, depending on soil conditions, are especially rich in nectar, and children for many generations have pulled off the corollas and sucked the sweet liquid from the tubular flowers. The whole plant may be used to make a yellow dye. Texas vervain (*V. halei*), also called slender vervain or blue vervain, is closely related to the famous Old World vervain (*V. officinalis*). Its upright square stems have a scattering of tiny pale blue or deep lavender flowers along their upper parts. Moss verbena (*V. tenuisecta*) is a sprawling native of South America that was introduced into the southern United States. Found growing along roadsides in Texas, it has richly colored violet purple flowers that form small bouquets. In cultivation it makes a long-lasting ground cover with attractive lacy evergreen leaves.

Rose vervain (*V. canadensis*) is one of the showiest and most aromatic of our *Verbenas,* and its fragrant rosy lavender blossoms are favorites of butterflies and rabbits. It may have been a cousin of this scented plant that Elizabeth Barrett Browning referred to in *Aurora Leigh:* "Sweet verbena! which being brushed against / Will hold you three hours after by the smell, / In spite of long walks on the windy hills."

Other interesting members of the vervain family in Texas are quite different from the *Verbenas.* The Big Bend area is famous for a delicious light-colored honey made from a plant appropriately called beebrush. Its fragrant white blossoms grow in profusion after a rain and attract numerous bees. Also called whitebrush, it may form impenetrable thickets known as chaparral west of the Pecos River. Texas frog-fruit, in spite of its funny name, is an attractive trailing perennial with dainty white flowers that might fit into a thimble vase. The leaves are a major food source for the larvae of the beautiful little phaon crescent butterfly.[6] Texas lantana (*Lantana horrida*) is also called calico bush. *Horrida* refers to its rough, prickly leaves that have a strong odor when crushed, but its parti-colored clusters of yellow and orange-red verbena-like flowers are colorful and tolerate hot, dry weather. The American beauty berry or French mulberry (*Callicarpa americana*) is valued more for its stunning clusters of reddish purple fruit than for its pale pink flowers. *Callicarpa* means "bearing beautiful fruit." Birds love the berries and will fight over territorial rights to nearby areas.

Although sand verbena looks like a verbena and has the verbena name, it is not a family member but belongs instead to the four o'clock family. Known as heart's delight, its vivid hot pink perfumed balls of flowers are especially attractive to butterflies. One of the most beautiful of Texas' endangered wildflowers is the large-fruited sand verbena (*Abronia macrocarpa*) found in East Texas. Like other four o'clocks, it begins to open in early evening, emitting a honeysuckle-like aroma that grows stronger as night deepens. In a midnight rendezvous the hawk moth visits the fragrant flowers and inserts its long tonguelike proboscis into the narrow throat of a blossom; pollen grains stick to the proboscis, and cross-pollination is achieved as the moth flits from flower to flower. The disappearance of this beautiful wildflower is attributed to the scarcity of hawk moths and to destruction of habitat caused by oil exploration and residential development.[7]

In the code of the language of flowers, verbena became the floral symbol for enchantment, an acknowledgment of its long history of magical powers.

Violet/Pansy

Violet Family (*Violaceae*)

Common Names: Violeta, Field Pansy, Heartsease,
Johnny-Jump-Up, Ladies' Delight

"What is charm? It is what the violet has and the camellia has not," wrote American novelist Francis Marion Crawford. In *North with the Spring* Edwin Way Teale called violets "the multitudinous footprints of spring," and John Greenleaf Whittier found in "the bloom of the apples / And the violets in the sward / A hint of the old, lost beauty / Of the Garden of the Lord!"[1] Even Dorothy Parker, not noted for sentimentality, was inspired to write a poem called "Sweet Violets," in which she called them "heaven's masterpieces."

American violets, with a few exceptions, belong to the genus *Viola*, which includes wild pansies and Johnny-jump-ups. In Texas the bird's-foot violet (*Viola pedata*), found in the eastern part of the state, is one of our largest and loveliest wild violets. Its name comes from the fact that the deeply segmented leaves suggest a bird's footprint. It reproduces only by seed from the showy flowers, unlike some of the smaller Texas violets such as Missouri violet (*V. missouriensis*), which have a back-up system of propagation. In addition to the open flowers that invite insects to visit, they produce inconspicuous cleistogamous (nonopening) flowers that are self-fertilizing and that are often mistaken for buds. The seeds ripen in the dark until the flower capsules open explosively to distribute them. Our wild pansies (*V. bicolor*) also have cleistogamous flowers that follow the conspicuous ones.

The violet is the flower for the month of March, and four states—Illinois, New Jersey, Rhode Island, and Wisconsin—have chosen it as their state flower emblem. In the language of flowers, the white violet is symbolic of innocence and the blue violet of faithful love. Modesty has always been associated with the plant, and in a famous painting Albrecht Durer captured the beautiful humility of the violet in watercolors.

It seems strange that the violet, a flower whose name is synonymous with shyness and modesty, should have acquired political fame as the symbol of Napoleon Bonaparte. As a child Napoleon loved the violets that bloomed on Corsica. After Josephine wore them on their wedding day, he gave her a bouquet of violets each year on their anniversary, and it was reported that when he died he was wearing a locket containing several faded violets from her grave. When Napoleon was exiled to Elba, he told his supporters he would "return with the violets," and during his absence the violet became the secret symbol of Bonapartists, who wore watch guards and rings of violet color. They asked strangers, "Do you love the violet?" If the answer was *"Oui"* (Yes), the questioner knew he was not talking to a confederate, but if the answer was *"Eh bien!"* (Well!), he knew he had found a fellow conspirator. When Napoleon did return on March 20, 1815, violets were in full season, and he was welcomed with showers of the blossoms. The violet remained the flower of the Empire until the Battle of Waterloo; after that it became a symbol of sedition, dangerous to wear or to mention, until the establishment of the Second Empire under Napoleon III, when it again became a popular political symbol.[2]

Many centuries earlier the violet was the flower of Athens, an emblem of that city as much as the rose is of England or the tulip is of Holland. The flowers were cultivated and on sale in marketplaces in Athens at all times of the year. Aristophanes called Athens "the City of the Violet Crown," and orators wishing to please crowds addressed them as "Athenians, crowned with Violets!" In Greek mythology the violet was dedicated to Orpheus, son of Apollo and Calliope, and under his special protection. One legend is that Orpheus, whose music charmed birds and beasts and even rocks and trees, played so sweetly that the flowers came and danced around him. Finally, exhausted, he sank down upon a green bank, dropping his lyre in the grass, and where it fell beautiful purple violets sprang up.[3]

A better-known origin myth for the violet has to do with Zeus and one of his many love affairs. Hera, with good reason, suspected him of dallying with Io, the daughter of a river god, and one day when he heard Hera approaching their trysting place, Zeus quickly changed Io into a milk white heifer. Still suspicious, Hera asked him to give her the animal as a gift, and he felt compelled to consent. Hera provided the poor creature a terrible life, causing a gadfly to chase her over much of the world. The only comfort Zeus could bring into Io's life was to cause violets to spring up for her to feed on instead of coarse grass wherever she wandered. Finally Mercury interceded, and Io was allowed to resume her own form and return to her parents, but the violets continued to grow.[4]

Another myth tells that all violets were once white until one day when Venus, seeking for Adonis, was wounded on her foot by a thorn. In sympathy the white violets bowed their heads and caught the drops of divine blood and became tinged with purple.

The reason violets seem to hide beneath their leaves is explained by the French poet Rapin: Midas, King of Phrygia, had a beautiful daughter, Ianthis, who was betrothed to Atys. Apollo saw Ianthis and was so charmed by her beauty that he demanded her in marriage. When her father refused, Apollo attempted to kidnap her. But the goddess Diana, hearing Ianthis's cries, changed her into a violet by the roadside, where hidden in her own green leaves she escaped capture.[5]

In Christian legend the violet is one of many flowers dedicated to the Virgin, and supposedly it droops because the shadow of the cross fell upon it. Mohammed is supposed to have preferred the violet to all other flowers, and in Persia the Mohammedans ate sherbet flavored with violets.

According to the doctrine of signatures, the heart-shaped leaves of violets recommended their use in treating heart problems. In his *Herball* Gerard says: "The floures are food for all inflammations, especially of the sides and lungs; they take away the hoarsenesse of the chest, the ruggednesse of the winde-pipe and jawes, and take away thirst."[6]

In Europe a syrup of violets was (and still is) given to children as a mild laxative and also used to treat several adult ailments, including epilepsy, pleurisy and jaundice. In North America the native Indians taught settlers to use essence of violet to treat pleurisy and to induce sleep. In folk medicine violets have persistently been touted as effective in curing growths including skin cancer, although there is not scientific proof that this is true.[7]

In Europe violets have long been prized as food. The young leaves are fried and eaten with lemon juice and sugar or used in salads or as greens. But their most popular use is to add color and flavor to candies and confections or as crystallized decorations on cakes and other sweets and as garnishes for canapes and cold soups. In the eighteenth century the English aristocracy enjoyed violet ices: They poured hot water over pounded blossoms and added sugar. After straining the mixture through a fine cloth, they placed it in an "icing pot" in the center of a tub filled with ice and salt and continually stirred until it froze. Before serving they placed it in elegant little moulds.[8] Queen Victoria is reported to have commanded her royal gardener always to have fresh violets available for her violet tea, syrup, jellies, and confections.

Euell Gibbons called violets "nature's vitamin pill" and had tests done proving that both blossoms and leaves are high in vitamins A and C. He made the point that pound for pound violet blossoms contain more vitamin C than oranges do.[9]

Before Rome was an empire, women there used to mix violets with goats's milk and apply it to their faces to improve their complexions. And before bathtubs gained popularity, violets were added to water for sponge baths. The perfume of violets has always intrigued men. In southern France there are large violet plantations, and at Grasse as many as 150 tons of the flowers have been used for perfume in a single season.[10] The chemical substance that gives violets their scent has a soporific effect on the sense of smell, so that after a short time the odor (temporarily) can no longer be perceived. That is why poets have called it fleeting. In *Hamlet* Laertes refers to this quality to persuade his sister Ophelia that Hamlet's feelings for her are not to be depended on, calling them "A violet in the youth of primey nature / Forward, not permanent, sweet or lasting / The perfume and suppliance of a minute / No more" (act II, scene iii, line 8).

Shakespeare would have been well acquainted with the violets that grow thickly in the woods around Stratford-on-Avon, and he refers to them in many plays. Ophelia tells Gertrude that the violets "withered all when my father died," and when Ophelia drowns herself and is refused the ritual church burial service, Laertes cries, "Lay her in the earth / And from her fair and unpolluted flesh / May violets spring!"(act V, scene i, line 260). In *A Midsummer Night's Dream* Oberon's bank is where "nodding, the violet grows," and in *The Winter's Tale* Perdita longs for "flowers o' the spring" including "violets dim / But sweeter than the lids of Juno's eyes / or Cytherea's breath" (act IV, scene iii, line 116). In *Henry V* the violet is used to illustrate the kinship of men whatever their rank: "I think the king is but a man, as I am / The violet smells to him as it doth to me"(act IV, scene i, line 101).

Countless other poets have been inspired by violets. Milton described a "violet-embroidered vale"; Keats wrote of "violet-beds nestling in sylvan bowers"; and the German poet Heinrich Heine called them "the deep, blue eyes of Springtime." Robert Browning exclaimed, "Such a starved bank of moss / Till, that May-morn, / Blue ran the flash across: / Violets were born!"[11] His wife, Elizabeth Barrett Browning, using the attribute of faithfulness, likened violets to the "kindest eyes that look on you / Without a thought disloyal." She may have been remembering that in the days of chivalry it was traditional in England for ladies to give violets to their knights to wear as a symbol of faithfulness.

Romans strewed violets on the graves of young children, and poets often used them in connection with death, as Wordsworth does in describing Lucy, the maid who "dwelt among the untrodden ways": "A Violet by a mossy stone / Half-hidden from the eye!" or Tennyson in "In Memorium" when he asks for his dead friend, "And from his ashes may be made / The violet of his native land."

The name pansy comes from the French *pensee* (thought), as Ophelia indicates when she says, "there's pansies, that's for thoughts." One of the most popular of garden plants, the pansy derived from the wild pansy of Europe and other species. Soon after 1800 British growers began to breed the familiar "faces" into pansies and to extend their usual purple and yellow colors into many shades and combinations. Numerous affectionate common names, some quite verbose, became attached to the pansy, including heartsease, three-faces-in-one-hood, cuddle me, herb trinity, call-me-to-you, and love-in-idleness. Johnny-jump-ups or kiss-me-quicks are cousins to the pansy, and like their larger relative, they are used in Europe as food garnishes and considered colorful, flavorful additions to salads and vegetable pates.

In the language of flowers the pansy colors—purple, yellow, and white—stand for memories, loving thoughts, and souvenirs, all helpful in easing lovers' hearts. In ancient tradition the pansy was an aphrodisiac, and its juice was used in love potions. In *A Midsummer Night's Dream*

Puck explains a superstition about pansy juice: "Yet mark'd I where the bolt of Cupid fell: It fell upon a little western flower / Before milk white, now purple with love's wound, / And maidens call it love-in-idleness . . . The Juice of it on sleeping eyelids laid / Will make a man or woman madly dote / Upon the next live creature that it sees" (act II, scene ii, line 106).

There are several European fables about pansies. One from Germany tells how the pansy lost its perfume: Originally pansies grew wild in fields and had such a wonderful fragrance that people trampled the grass to a pulp in their eagerness to pick them; consequently, the cattle were starving. The pansy then made a great sacrifice; she prayed that her sweet perfume be taken from her. When her prayer was granted, people lost interest in picking the flowers, and the cattle grew fat on the fresh green grass.[12]

In Scandinavia and Germany and also in Scotland, the pansy is known as the stepmother flower, and stories about the selfish stepmother are related to children in various versions as the storyteller pulls off appropriate parts of the blossoms.

Children of early settlers in America made pansy dolls by lining up the flower faces and pasting on leaf skirts and twig arms. With violets they played a game called "violet war" by intertwining the hooks where the violet blossom meets the stem and trying to pull them apart like wishbones; the one who pulled off the most blossoms from the stems held by another was the winner.[13] A superstition among pioneers was that a handful of violets taken into the farmhouse in the spring ensured prosperity, and to neglect this ceremony brought harm to baby chicks and ducklings.

The lore and legends connected with these much-loved wildflowers is endless, for as Wordsworth reminds us: "long as there are violets / They will have a place in story."

Water Lily

Water Lily Family (*Nymphaeaceae*)

Common Names: Water Nymph,
Fragrant Water Lily, Blue Water Lily, Yellow Water Lily,
Spatterdock, Yellow Cow Lily, Egyptian Lotus,
Chinquapin, Yellow Lotus

I n Greek myths nymphs were beautiful young maidens with the status of minor divinities who lived in natural places such as streams, rivers, and lakes. The *Nymphaeaceae* family includes the aquatic lilies and the lotus plants whose stems reach down to the muddy soil under the water while their long-stalked leaves or pads and elegant flowers float on the surface or stand above it. Water lilies, especially white-flowered ones, have long been associated with virginal aloofness and reputed to have antiaphrodisiac properties.[1] In the language of flowers the water lily speaks of purity and majesty, and it is the flower emblem for the month of July.

In Central America and Mexico, the Mayas revered the water lily as the sacred symbol of the earth. In Texas even the fierce Comanches were said to admire its regal beauty, and there is a Native American legend about the origin of the white water lily: One night a little boy had a dream that a star came to earth seeking a new home. It first went to live on a mountaintop but felt too lonely there. Then it settled in the heart of a prairie rose, but the buffalo and people on horses trampled it underfoot. As the star sadly started to return to its home in the sky, it saw its reflection in a lake and decided to settle there. At first the people laughed at the little boy's dream, but when they visited the lake the next morning, they found the water dotted with large white water lilies. Taking this beautiful sight as a sign of blessing from the Great Spirit, the Native Americans called it "white star flower."[2]

The fragrant water lily (*Nymphaea odorata*) that grows in the bogs and baygalls of the Big Thicket is sometimes called "alligator bonnet." The solitary, very fragrant white blossoms with purplish backs usually float on the water, opening at dawn and closing at noon for three or four days. The roots of the fragrant water lily are rich in tannins and mucilage and have been used as an astringent and as a source of black dye. The leaves and roots have been used to make poultices to treat boils, tumors, and ulcers, and an infusion has been made from them to use as a gargle for ulcers in the mouth and throat.[3] The blue water lily (*N. elegans*) found in ponds, pools, and ditches in South Texas has blue or pale violet flowers that are usually raised on long peduncles up to ten inches above the water.

Yellow water lily (*N. mexicana*), a Texas species with bright yellow petals rising above bright green pads, has a romantic history. As the name indicates, it was first named for plants collected in Mexico, but only a few years later it was discovered in Florida by Edward F. Leitner, and Audubon included it in one of his paintings. After Leitner died the yellow water lily apparently remained unseen for nearly a century, and Audubon's rendering of it was considered a bit of artistic imagination until the plant was rediscovered at the beginning of the twentieth century.[4]

The most common of the Texas yellow pond lilies (*Nuphar*) is spatterdock or yellow cow lily, which has attractive blossoms rising like waxy golden cups above its heart-shaped leaves. The flowers, which never fully open, are called brandy bottle in England. Like the white water lily, the yellow pond lily contains tannin and mucilage and has been used as an astringent and demulcent. Its roots, steeped in milk, are said to kill beetles and cockroaches.[5]

Water lily leaves, flower buds, seeds, and tubers have been used as food, cooked like green vegetables, made into flour, or eaten as potato substitutes. The seeds are rich in starch, oil, and protein, and the large seeds of yellow pond lilies may be fried or parched or the kernels winnowed and ground into flour or creamed like corn.

The most famous member of the water lily family is the lotus. Native to many parts of the world, it was held sacred by the ancients in the near and far East and has a symbolic history going back over five thousand years.

Along the Nile River the white or rose-purple flowers of the Egyptian lotus may measure a foot across. Horus, the god of light and heaven, is represented in Egyptian mythology issuing from the cup of the lotus blossom, and the flower was dedicated to him. The sacred lotus of the Hindus is white or delicately pink, and according to some sectarian Hindu myths, Brahma sprang from the bosom of the flower. He is often depicted in Hindu art either seated or standing on a lotus throne. Buddhists revere the lotus as the symbol of Buddha, who they represent seated on a majestic lotus blossom. Some sects of Buddhists believe in the Western Heaven with its sacred Lake of Lotuses. The state of *samadhi,* or spiritual ecstasy, in yoga is represented by a lotus flower of a thousand petals, and various texts concerned with the Buddhistic faith are called "The Lotus of the Good Law" and "The White Lotus of Compassion." Because some lotus plants display buds and blossoms and seed pods at the same time, ancient people considered it an emblem of the past, present, and future.

Texas' lotus (*Nelumbo lutea*) is called yellow lotus and water chinquapin. In quiet ponds and sluggish streams in the eastern third of the state in early summer, its large pale yellow flowers rise two or three feet above the water on stout stalks. The nutlike fruits are embedded in separate pockets of the seed case, which resembles a wasp's nest. In pioneer days the seeds were an important food for the Native Americans and early settlers who gathered sacks of them to store for the winter.[6]

In *The Odyssey* Homer tells of Ulysses's encounter with the lotus eaters, when he of all his company refused to eat the narcotic fruit, and Tennyson in "The Lotos-Eaters" retells the story of the "mild-eyed, melancholy lotos eaters" who gave the mariners the "enchanted" plant that made them willing to forsake their wives and children to live like sleepwalkers, believing "slumber is more sweet than toil." Many plants are called lotus, and although scholars agree that Homer's plant was not a water lily, since none of them could have produced such extreme languor, there is disagreement over what plant it was. A number of writers have come down in favor of the jujube tree, but orientalist Sir Richard Burton thought it was hashish, known today by its Mexican name "marijuana."[7]

Since ancient times lotus designs have been used to enhance architecture. The "bell" capitals of Egyptian buildings were modeled on the expanded flowers and often called "lotus-blossom capitals," and Chinese temples and buildings in India also featured lotus decorations. When Joseph Paxton was commissioned to design the great Crystal Palace for the World Exhibition of 1851 in London, he studied the intricate plan of the spectacular Queen Victoria water lily (*Victoria amazonia*) and gave the flower credit for his ingenious design, which included longitudinal and transverse girders and supports like those of the flower.

Like artists of ancient Egypt, Greece, Rome, China, and Japan, modern artists have been inspired by the beauty of water lilies. Edward Alexander MacDowell (1861–1908), a famous American composer best known for his descriptive piano pieces, wrote "To a Water Lily." The French artist Claude Monet, a founder of impressionism, devoted the last years of his life to studying and painting a great lyrical series of pictures of the water lilies in the pond in his garden at Giverny. In his poetry Tennyson often mentions the water lily, and in "Paradise and the Peri," Thomas Moore wrote of:

> *Those virgin lilies all the night*
> *Bathing their beauties in the lake,*
> *That they might rise more fresh and bright,*
> *When their beloved sun's awake.*

Yarrow/Milfoil

Sunflower Family (*Asteraceae*)

*Common Names: Allheal, Woundwort, Knight's Milfoil,
Staunchweed, Devil's Nettle, Thousand Seal*

Yarrow or milfoil, a common wildflower in Texas, has a long history. The scientific name (*Achillea millefolium*) indicates that it is a plant of a thousand leaves connected with Achilles. In his *Herball* John Gerard says, "This plant is thought to be the very same wherewith Achilles cured the wounds of his soldiers." In Greek mythology Chiron, the wise centaur, taught Achilles the virtues of yarrow, and during the battle for Troy after Achilles wounded Telephus, son-in-law of the king of Troy, with his spear and the wound became infected, Telephus promised to conduct Achilles to the city if he would heal the wound. Achilles agreed and scraped rust off his spear, and from the filings arose a yarrow plant with which he cured Telephus's wound.[1] During the American Civil War yarrow was still being used to treat battle wounds.

"Yarrow" is said to be a corruption of *gaerwe*, the Anglo-Saxon name for the plant, which means "ready to heal." The English call yarrow allheal and the Native Americans called it life medicine. In France it is called carpenter's weed because carpenters used it frequently to stop bleeding when they injured themselves.

In recent times more than 120 biologically active compounds have been identified from the plant, which explains why it may be used both to stop and to cause a nosebleed: it contains both achilleine, an alkaloid that is a hemostatic agent (used to promote clotting) and coumarin (used to promote blood flow).[2] Monks used yarrow extensively in their medicinal concoctions. Most of the old herbalists recommended drinking yarrow infusions at the commencement of colds and fevers and also to purify the blood.

The Navajos used it as a spring tonic. Rodale's *Encyclopedia of Herbs* lists twenty-eight separate medicinal uses of yarrow by forty-six different Native American tribes. The leaves were chewed, fresh or dry, with a little salt as an aid to digestion. A leaf decoction was used to relieve headache. Dry flowers were swallowed with water twice daily to dissipate a cough. Yarrow tonic was given to new mothers as a blood builder after childbirth. The root was chewed to relieve colds, and the greens were chewed for toothache.[3]

Virginia Scully calls yarrow "one of the most valuable medicinal plants for Indians," and among the many herbal remedies she lists are a warm infusion as an anti-hysteric and stimulant; oil of yarrow as an abortion agent; leaves steeped in water to make styptic to stop flow of blood; poultice of entire plant for rashes, itches, sprains, and to treat rheumatism; leaves crushed and applied to fresh wounds.[4]

From 1836 to 1882 *The Pharmacopoeia of the United States of America* listed yarrow as an official drug for use as a stimulant and as an agent to promote menstrual flow. Rural people in England still use it to treat rheumatism. Scottish Highlanders still make an ointment from it to treat wounds in both humans and beasts. And the old women of the Orkneys are said to brew milfoil tea to dispel melancholy.[5]

The common names bloodwort, nosebleed, soldier's woundwort, knight's milfoil, and staunchweed reflect yarrow's widespread medicinal usefulness. Other common names come from other characteristics. The botanical name *millefolium* (of a thousand leaves) and the common names thousand seal or thousand weed or thousand leaf refer to its fine, feathery, fernlike leaves. Old man's pepper refers to its distinctive spicy odor and mildly pungent taste.

Both the English and Native Americans enjoyed the very young tender yarrow flowers as food. Swedes called yarrow field hops and made a beer from it that the Swedish botanist Linnaeus pronounced more potent than brew made with hops. Many people still enjoy yarrow tea made by pouring boiling water over the blossoms. The nectar is obviously popular among insects. A watched plant was reported to have been visited by more than 120 species of bees and butterflies in a single day.[6] Farmers, however,

are not fond of yarrow when it invades their fields and they discover (as an old saying goes) they cannot "make hay" without "making yarrow."

In addition to medicine and food, a number of other uses have been found for yarrow. These include making it into a powder to use as snuff and smoking the leaves. The Chinese traditionally believed that yarrow brightened the eyes and promoted intelligence, and they used dried yarrow stems in the *I, Ching* ritual to predict the future. Cosmetically, the leaves, dried and made into a liquid, were applied to the head to improve the condition of the scalp and hair, and a decoction was used to brighten blond hair. In dyeing wool the entire plant yields an olive color, while the flowers alone give a yellow to gold color.[7] Today the dried plant, which keeps its shape and color, is used in crafts and in dried arrangements.

Much folklore naturally attaches to such a versatile plant. Timid people used to carry yarrow leaves on their persons to drive away fear. Both witches and their master, Satan, supposedly made use of it in incantations, in casting spells, and in divinations. Its nicknames of devil's nettle, devil's plaything, and bad man's plaything support the idea that it is one of the herbs dedicated to Satan.

On the other hand, it was a plant connected with love and love charms. In some countries it was brought to weddings to ensure seven years of love, and bridal wreaths woven of yarrow supposedly guaranteed happiness and health to the wearer. A lovesick maiden placed an ounce of yarrow sewed up in flannel under her pillow and repeated this formula:

> *Thou pretty herb of Venus' tree,*
> *Thy true name it is yarrow;*
> *Now who my bosom friend must be,*
> *Pray tell thou me to-morrow.*[8]

The next day she put the yarrow in her shoe and asked it to guide her to her future husband; the first single man she met was "it."

Laura Martin relates this Native American legend about the origin of the yarrow flowers:

Once there was a happy and peaceful tribe who were so healthy that the medicine man had little to do, so he spent much of his time teaching his young grandson about the healing herbs. Then all of the tribe members fell victims to a strange illness. When the medicine man realized he was too weak to climb the mountain to collect the plant he needed to cure his people, he sent his grandson to find it. Although the boy was ill and weak, he struggled slowly up the mountain, but by the time he reached the area where the plant grew, the sun had set. In the darkness he searched and searched, but he could not find the plant. In despair, he knelt and asked the Great Spirit for help. As he rose to his feet, the stars seemed to become brighter and brighter until they exploded, and as the tiny light fragments fell, they landed on the ferny-leaved plant he was searching for. The medicine man was pleased that his grandson had found the right plant, but he was amazed at the tiny lights clinging to it. From that time the yarrow plant has had clusters of soft white blossoms.[9]

In the language of flowers of the nineteenth century, yarrow or milfoil represents war, and in the language of contemporary herbalists, it is called an "herbal band-aid" and prescribed for fevers and infections as well as for treating wounds, just as it was in the days of Achilles.[10]

Yucca

Agave Family (*Agavaceae*)
Common Names: Spanish Dagger, Spanish Bayonet, Adam's Needle, Beargrass, Soapweed, Our Lord's Candle, Lamp of Our Lord

Whether growing in its native desert setting or as an invited guest in flower beds, the yucca is an impressive plant, both formidable and beautiful in appearance. On its tall, sometimes branched stem, sharp-pointed leaves radiate in a cluster, and out of this daunting green arsenal arises the showy flower stalk with its masses of creamy white bell-shaped blossoms.

Like its fellow desert dwellers, agave and sotol, yucca is sometimes mistakenly called a cactus. It traditionally has been classified as a member of the lily family, but today is more often found listed as a member of the agave family, which includes sotol and agave. Common names reflect the yucca's lethal potential: Spanish dagger, Spanish bayonet; its usefulness: Adam's needle, soapweed; and its mystical beauty: our Lord's candle, lamp of our Lord. Characteristically as a yucca plant adds new growth at the top, the dead leaves drop down like a grass skirt. Perhaps this is why it is sometimes referred to as "old shag."

There are some twenty native species of yucca in Texas, plus some introduced ornamental varieties, and since they have a habit of hybridizing with each other, it can be difficult to distinguish among them. They come in many heights, from the tall treelike giant daggers of the Guadalupe Mountains and Big Bend area to smaller shrub-like plants only a few feet

high such as *Yucca angustifolia* found on the Llano Estacado. Many species have a slight, delicate scent, but the twisted-leaf yucca, found in the
Hill Country, is noted for it pungent aroma. Plains yucca helps stabilize
the sandy soil of West Texas and provides forage for livestock in the spring.
Torrey yucca, which furnishes food for deer, may be observed in flower
almost all year round in the Big Bend. Barton Warnock says the ripened
fruits taste like applesauce. The stately *Y. elata,* New Mexico's state flower,
is common in West Texas. It is sometimes called palmella or soaptree,
because its roots contain saponin. Datil yucca or banana yucca yields fruits
up to six or eight inches long that are considered a delicacy—when deer
and livestock leave enough of the flower clusters to ripen.[1]

The strangest thing about the yucca plant is its unique method of
pollination, for which it depends upon a small white moth. In turn, the
moth is dependent on the yucca plant for continuing its species, and neither would survive in the wild without the other. Generally referred to as
the yucca moth, its scientific name is *Pronuba,* an apt designation as in
Roman mythology Juno as Pronuba is the foundress of marriage, and
subsequently a woman who arranged a marriage came to be called a
pronuba.[2]

After being fertilized by the male, the female yucca moth eats nothing herself but devotes her life to making sure there will be food for her
offspring. When the yucca flowers open in the evening, she gathers pollen from the anthers and rolls it into a ball, which she tucks into a depression behind her head. She lays her eggs on the pistil (ovaries) of another
flower and vigorously rubs the pollen onto the stigma, thus ensuring there
will be seeds for the larvae to feed on. After repeating this procedure several times, she dies without seeing the offspring for which she has provided. The moth eggs and the seeds develop together in the yucca ovary,
and the tiny caterpillars eat the developing seeds. But since there are only
two or three larvae in each blossom and hundreds of seeds in each ovary,
the plant is not harmed. When it is ready for the pupa stage, the larva
chews a hole in the seed pod and spins a thread by which it lowers itself to
the ground. Burrowing a few inches into the soil, it slowly completes its
metamorphosis and emerges as an adult moth the following year just as
the yucca is in bloom—and the cycle begins again.[3]

Native Americans discovered how to make medicinal use of various
parts of the yucca. Juices were used as diuretics and as laxatives, and the

roots, mashed and boiled, were used in treating diabetes. A tea was made from the roots and bark to alleviate the pain of arthritis, and today yucca tablets for arthritis are available at health food stores. Early Texas ranchers learned to use the yucca's daggerlike leaves to save the lives of men and beasts who were bitten by rattlesnakes. The leaf lance was driven deeply into the site of the wound, causing the blood to flow freely and carrying off the deadly venom.

Like the agave, yucca provides a satisfactory substitute for soap. For thousands of years Native American tribes in the Southwest used yucca soap ceremonially in shampooing their hair and washing their bodies as well as for washing their clothing. The rootstock is dug up, broken into convenient size pieces and washed free of dirt. When needed, a piece is mashed with a stone or hammer and dropped into water, cold or warm. As it is rubbed a lather forms and after the fiber is dipped out, the sudsy mixture is ready to use. It is soft and effective for bathing, shampooing, and washing anything that can be washed with soap.[4]

Yucca is an important fiber plant. Evidence has been found that prehistoric cliff dwellers of the Southwest used yucca fibers in making rope, sandals, and cloth.[5] *Yucca baccata* is referred to in the folklore of the Navajos, who made ceremonial masks for religious rites from its leaves. Early Mexican settlers in West Texas used yucca for fencing and for fuel, and for making thatch and other building materials as well as for making baskets, nets, mats, and rough cloth. They found a crude twine could be made from the green leaves to tie bundles of oats, cornstalks, and other fodder. The common name Adam's Needle testifies to the use of the crude needle and fiber threads found at the tips of the leaves, which were useful in sewing clothing, sacks, and other objects. During WWI when imported jute became scarce, yucca fibers were used in making burlap bags. And in WWII the United States Navy manufactured rope, twine, and heavy paper from yucca fibers.[6] Today baskets made from yucca leaves are popular with tourists in the Southwest.

Early dwellers in West Texas ate the buds, flowers, fruit, and young stalks of the yucca raw, boiled, roasted, and ground into meal. Native Americans and Mexicans introduced Anglo travelers to the treat of yucca pods roasted in the hot ashes of campfires. After the blackened rind is removed, they are said to be pleasantly suggestive of sweet potatoes. These early travelers also found the leaves of the tall yuccas handy for hanging bacon, fish, and game. They used the hot sun to their advantage in pre-serving food to be eaten at a time when it was less plentiful.

In his book on edible wild plants, Charles Saunders describes the Native American method of conserving yucca fruit. After it was baked and peeled and the fiber removed, the remaining pulp was boiled down to a firm paste. This was rolled out in sheets one inch thick and carefully dried. These were stored and pieces could be broken off to eat as sweetmeats or dissolved in water to be used like molasses on bread or tortillas.[7] Native Americans and Mexicans also made a fermented beverage from the fruits. Cattle and deer browse the tender blossoms in the spring, and some ranch-ers along the Texas-Mexico border harvest yucca flowers and feed them to their livestock.

The petals of the yucca blossom, which are high in vitamin C, may be eaten raw or cooked, pickled, fried, or sauteed. Some species are more palatable than others, and yucca fanciers chop the blossoms and add them to salads and soups or serve them as a creamed vegetable.

Since Native Americans of the Southwest discovered the yucca plant some twelve thousand years ago, it has been a faithful friend to man and beast. In flower language yucca means, "Yours until death."

Afterword

Emerson said, "What is a weed but a plant whose use has not yet been discovered?" And in laboratories all over the world, scientists are at work trying to unlock the secrets wildflowers may hold that will help in preventing, treating, and curing numerous illnesses. In other laboratories cosmetologists, nutritionists, and industrial engineers are uncovering new ways in which wildflowers can help us. Their work is complicated by the fact that simply extracting a substance from a plant and using it alone without the interaction that might occur in company with other substances found in the plant does not always work. In addition, extracts from the same type of plant growing in different habitats may have different effects. Nevertheless, scientists are constantly making important discoveries connected with old and new uses of plants.

In ancient times when people were more aware of their dependence on plants to provide food, medicine, fuel, and materials for clothing, there grew up a vast amount of superstition and folklore and even plant worship, some of which has been described in these profiles. Over the years much of the folk wisdom about plants was forgotten or ignored as more sophisticated scientific technology ruled the world. Only recently have we become aware that the lowliest wildflower may harbor some important secret, and only *very* recently have we become aware of how profligate we have been in destroying these potential sources of life and well-being. If we and our planet are to survive, this awareness must increase quickly as more and more plants enter the endangered or threatened lists.

Wildflowers are important not only to the well-being of our bodies but also to the well-being of our spirits. The more we learn about wildflowers—their astounding variety, their tricks and ways of attracting propagators, their histories, their clever survival tactics, and their many forms of beauty—the more we will enjoy them.

Every trip to a new environment and every walk in the country will become a journey of discovery. We can enliven our gardens and our lives by planting wildflowers that will attract birds and butterflies. Like grace notes in our lives, these gifts of nature soften the effects of living in a world that is often violent and callous. Long before there were cultivated flowers, there was the custom of giving flowers as symbols of peace and love.

Keats wrote, "A thing of beauty is a joy forever." As we look at fields of wildflowers enameled by nature's color palette, we might remember the old Shoshone legend that says, "Wild blooms are the footprints of little children who have died and come back to gladden us." If we welcome them into our lives, wildflowers can indeed bring us joy and gladness and endless pleasure.

Notes

AGARITA

1. Nicholas Culpeper, *Culpeper's Complete Herbal*, p. 33.
2. *Texas Wildflower Newsletter*, spring, 1979.
3. Culpeper, *Complete Herbal*, p. 33.
4. *Reader's Digest*, "Magic and Medicine of Plants," p. 148.
5. Ibid., p. 246.
6. Jack Sanders, *Hedgemaids and Fairy Candles*, pp. 73–74.
7. *Encyclopaedia Britannica; Micropaedia*, 15th ed., s.v. "barberry."
8. San Antonio Botanical Center, *Native Plant Key*, B-29.

AGAVE

1. Michael Moore, *Medicinal Plants of the Mountain West*, p. 19.
2. Delena Tull, *A Practical Guide to Edible and Useful Plants*, p. 22.
3. Some scholars believe that the Native Americans had a rudimentary knowledge of distillation before the coming of the Europeans. (Virgil J. Vogel, *American Indian Medicine*, pp. 170–71)
4. P. Mick Richardson, *The Encyclopedia of Psychoactive Drugs: Flowering Plants*, p. 49.
5. Tull, *Practical Guide*, p. 22.
6. Barton H. Warnock, *Wildflowers of the Big Bend Country, Texas*, p. 25.

ANEMONE

1. Culpeper, *Complete Herbal*, 21; Virginia Scully, *A Treasury of American Indian Herbs: Their Lore and Their Use for Food, Drugs and Medicine*, pp. 6, 108.
2. Ernst Lehner and Johanna Lehner, *Folklore and Symbolism of Flowers, Plants and Trees*, p. 54.
3. Edith Hamilton, *Mythology*, pp. 90–91; John Addington Symonds, *Greek Poets*, vii, 403.

4. John Gerard, *Leaves from Gerard's Herball,* p. 9.
5. Harold N. Moldenke and Alma L. Moldenke, *Plants of the Bible,* p. 45.
6. Vogel, *Medicine,* pp. 271–272.
7. Alice M. Coats, *Flowers and Their Histories,* p. 22.

ASTER

1. For an Indian legend of the creation of the aster, see the goldenrod profile.
2. Coats, *Flowers,* p. 32.
3. Donovan Stewart Correll and Marshall Conring Johnston, *Manual of the Vascular Plants of Texas,* p. 1593.
4. Tull, *Practical Guide,* p. 398.
5. Geraldine Nicholson, *Flower Fables,* p. 8.
6. Scully, *Treasury,* pp. 10, 114, 279.
7. William A. Quayle, *God's Calendar,* n.p.

BLUEBELL

1. Mary Durant, *Who Named the Daisy? Who Named the Rose?,* p. 72; Coats, *Flowers,* p. 102.
2. Quoted in Coats, *Flowers,* p. 102.
3. Kathryn G. March and Andrew L. March, *Wild Plant Companion,* pp. 40–41; Michael Castleman, *The Healing Herbs,* p. 184.
4. Durant, *Who Named the Daisy?,* p. 73.
5. Castleman, *Healing Herbs,* pp. 183–84.

BLUEBONNET

1. Fred B. Manchee, "Texas Dons Her Blue Bonnet," *Our Heritage of Flowers,* pp. 94–95.
2. Jean Andrews, *The Texas Bluebonnet,* pp. 15–16.
3. J. Frank Dobie, *Tales of Old-Time Texas,* p. 141.
4. Publications of the Texas Folklore Society, *Legends of Texas,* pp. 198–200.
5. Dobie, *Tales,* pp. 142–46.
6. Andrews, *Bluebonnet,* pp. 18–19.

BROOMWEED

1. Ellen D. Schulz, *Texas Wild Flowers: A Popular Account of the Common Wild Flowers of Texas,* p. 410.
2. Zoe Merriman Kirkpatrick, *Wildflowers of the Western Plains,* p. 69.
3. *Reader's Digest,* "Magic and Medicine of Plants," p. 121.
4. Tull, *Practical Guide,* pp. 348, 396.
5. *Reader's Digest,* "Magic and Medicine of Plants," p. 121.

BUTTERCUP

1. Katherine M. Beals, *Flower Lore and Legend*, pp. 66–67.
2. The National Geographic Society, *The Book of Wildflowers*, p. 89.
3. Joseph Wood Krutch, *Joseph Wood Krutch Herbal*, pp. 126, 156.
4. Edward Lear, "The Pobble Who Has No Toes"; Robert Browning, "Home Thoughts, From Abroad"; Wilfred Owen, "Spring Offensive."
5. Beals, *Flower Lore*, pp. 68–70.

CLOVER

1. Emily Dickinson, "The Pedigree of Honey," version 2, *c.* 1884.
2. Beals, *Flower Lore*, p. 102.
3. *Reader's Digest*, "Magic and Medicine of Plants," pp. 281, 312.
4. Leona Woodring Smith, *The Forgotten Art of Flower Cookery*, p. 43.
5. Harold William Rickett, *Wildflowers of the United States (Texas)*, pt. one, p. 250; Geyata Ajilvsgi, *Wildflowers of Texas*, pp. 57, 183; Campbell and Lynn Loughmiller, *Texas Wildflowers*, p. 132.
6. Gregory C. Aaron, ed., *The Language of Flowers*, n.p.
7. Quoted in Sanders, *Hedgemaids*, p. 124.

CORAL BEAD

1. Schulz, *Texas Wild Flowers*, p. 95; Tull, *Practical Guide*, p. 189; Eula Whitehouse, *Texas Flowers in Natural Color*, p. 31.
2. *Reader's Digest*, "Magic and Medicine of Plants," p. 253.
3. Elizabeth Silverthorne, *Christmas in Texas*, pp. 21–22.

DAISY

1. Rev. Hilderic Friend, *Flowers and Flower Lore*, p. 392.
2. Beals, *Flower Lore*, p. 85.
3. William Shakespeare, *Cymbeline*, act IV, scene ii, line 398.
4. Joseph Severn, letter to John Taylor, Mar. 6, 1821. Quoted in *The Oxford Dictionary of Quotations*, 3rd ed., p. 295.
5. Beals, *Flower Lore*, pp. 87–88.
6. Scully, *Treasury*, p. 153.
7. Jean Andrews, *American Wildflower Florilegium*, p. 52.
8. Ajilvsgi, *Wildflowers of Texas*, p. 25.
9. Buckner Hollingsworth, *Flower Chronicles*, pp. 157–158.

DANDELION

1. Moldenke and Moldenke, *Plants*, p. 75.
2. Culpeper, *Complete Herbal*, pp. 106–107.

3. Mrs M. Grieve, *A Modern Herbal*, vol. I, pp. 252–255.
4. "Enduring Weeds are Endearing Dandelions in Diet,"*Austin American-Statesman*, May 9, 1992.
5. Tull, *Practical Guide*, pp. 40–41.
6. Grieve, *Modern Herbal*, p. 251.
7. J. Ward-Harris, *More Than Meets the Eye: The Life and Lore of Western Wildflowers*, p. 86.
8. Moldenke and Moldenke, *Plants*, p. 75.
9. Quoted in Beals, *Flower Lore*, p. 40.

DOGWOOD

1. National Geographic Society, *Book of Wildflowers*, p. 93; Manchee, *Our Heritage*, pp. 102–103.
2. Schulz, *Texas Wild Flowers*, p. 269.
3. Vogel, *Medicine*, p. 299; *Reader's Digest*, "Magic and Medicine of Plants," p. 165.
4. Vogel, *Medicine*, p. 301.
5. Tull, *Practical Guide*, p. 353.
6. Manchee, *Our Heritage*, pp. 74–75, 102–3.
7. Schulz, *Texas Wild Flowers*, pp. 270–71.
8. Moldenke and Moldenke, *Plants*, p. 2.

FOXGLOVE/PENSTEMON

1. Ludwig W. Eichna, *The Pharos*, winter, 1994, pp. 14–17. *Encyclopaedia Britannica; Micropaedia*, 15th ed., s.v. "foxglove"; *Reader's Digest*, "Magic and Medicine of Plants," pp. 66–77, 188.
2. Vogel, *Medicine*, pp. 10–11.
3. Tull, *Practical Guide*, p. 280.
4. Scully, *Treasury*, pp. 141, 161–62, 192, 224.
5. Schulz, *Texas Wild Flowers*, p. 359.
6. Bob Parvin, "The Barometer Bush," *Texas Highways*, Aug., 1981, pp. 12–13; Barton H. Warnock, *Wildflowers of the Davis Mountains and the Marathon Basin, Texas*, p. 203; Benny J. Simpson and James C. Read, "Cenizo," *Texas Parks and Wildlife*, Oct., 1976, pp. 24–27.
7. Nancy Richey Ranson, *Texas Wild Flower Legends*, p. 18.
8. Nicholson, *Flower Fables*, p. 29; Jeanne R. Chesanow, *Honeysuckle Sipping*, p. 93.

GAILLARDIA/INDIAN BLANKET

1. Helen Shields, *Desert Plants: Recipes and Remedies*, p. 29.
2. Eliza Griffin Johnston, *Texas Wild Flowers*, p. 72.

3. Schulz, *Texas Wild Flowers*, pp. 459–460.
4. Kirkpatrick, *Wildflowers*, p. 65.

GOLDENROD

1. Nicholson, *Flower Fables*, p. 31.
2. Laura C. Martin, *Wildflower Folklore*, p. 177.
3. Gerard, *Leaves*, p. 210; Beals, *Flower Lore*, p. 214.
4. Martin, *Folklore*, p. 175.
5. *Reader's Digest*, "Magic and Medicine of Plants," pp. 106, 198.
6. Tull, *Practical Guide*, p. 42.
7. Manchee, *Our Heritage*, p. 63.
8. Beals, *Flower Lore*, pp. 215–217.

HOLLY

1. National Geographic Society, *Book of Wildflowers*, p. 116.
2. *Reader's Digest*, "Magic and Medicine of Plants," p. 168.
3. Moldenke and Moldenke, *Plants*, p. 111.
4. Gerard, *Leaves*, p. 279.
5. Quoted in Peter Loewer, *The Wild Gardener*, p. 217.
6. Jill Senior Nokes, "Hollies of Texas," *Texas Wildflower Newsletter*, winter, 1978, p. 8.
7. Steven Foster and James A. Duke, *Eastern/Central Medicinal Plants*, p. 286.
8. Grieve, *Modern Herbal*, vol. I, pp. 406, 407.

HONEYSUCKLE

1. Correll and Johnston, *Vascular Plants*, p. 1, 500.
2. Culpeper, *Complete Herbal*, pp. 306–307.
3. Foster and Duke, *Medicinal Plants*, p. 298.
4. Edith S. Clements, "Wildflowers of the West," *National Geographic*, May, 1927, p. 610.
5. *Reader's Digest*, "Magic and Medicine of Plants," p. 106.
6. Schulz, *Texas Wild Flowers*, p. 381.
7. Grieve, *Modern Herbal*, vol. I, pp. 266, 267.
8. Ibid., pp. 266–267.
9. Scully, *Treasury*, p. 40.
10. *Reader's Digest*, "Magic and Medicine of Plants," p. 166.
11. Foster and Duke, *Medicinal Plants*, p. 240. Cited in Grieve, *Modern Herbal*, vol. I, p. 269.
12. Grieve, *Modern Herbal*, vol. I, p. 272.
13. Scully, *Treasury*, p. 40.
14. Grieve, *Modern Herbal*, vol. I, p. 268.

15. William Shakespeare, *A Midsummer Night's Dream,* act IV, scene i, line 44.

IRIS

1. Hollingsworth, *Chronicles,* pp. 58–59.
2. Beals, *Flower Lore,* p. 194.
3. Michael Moore, *Medicinal Plants,* pp. 39–40; *Reader's Digest,* "Magic and Medicine of Plants," p. 115.
4. Johnston, *Wild Flowers,* pp. 150–51.
5. Beals, *Flower Lore,* p. 18.
6. Moldenke and Moldenke, *Plants,* p. 87.
7. Coats, *Flowers,* pp. 126–34
8. Hollingsworth, *Chronicles,* pp. 66–67.
9. Manchee, *Our Heritage,* pp. 92–93.

LILY

1. Gerard, *Leaves,* pp. 57–58.
2. David M. Robb and J. J. Garrison, *Art in the Western World,* pp. 864–865; Moldenke and Moldenke, *Plants,* p. 44; Coats, *Flowers,* p. 142.
3. Moldenke and Moldenke, *Plants,* pp. 41–44, 114–16.
4. Culpeper, *Complete Herbal,* pp. 172–173.
5. Grieve, *Modern Herbal,* vol. II, pp. 481–482.
6. Bill Neal, *Gardener's Latin,* p. 33.
7. Ghillean T. Prance, *Wildflowers for All Seasons,* p. 126.
8. Krutch, *Herbal,* p. 82.
9. *Reader's Digest,* "Magic and Medicine of Plants," p. 100.
10. Moldenke and Moldenke, *Plants,* p. 114.
11. Edith Hamilton, *Mythology,* pp. 88–89.
12. Grieve, *Modern Herbal,* vol. I, p. 424.
13. *Reader's Digest,* "Magic and Medicine of Plants," pp. 194, 261.
14. John B. Lust, *The Herb Book,* p. 620.
15. Gerard, *Leaves,* p. 89.
16. Quoted in Krutch, *Herbal,* p. 82.

MALLOW/ WINECUP

1. Krutch, *Herbal,* p. 236.
2. Martin, *Folklore,* p. 214.
3. *Reader's Digest,* "Magic and Medicine of Plants," p. 216.
4. Andrews, *Wildflower Florilegium,* p. 96.
5. Tull, *Practical Guide,* p. 119.
6. Schulz, *Texas Wild Flowers,* pp. 228–229.

MILKWEED

1. National Geographic Society, *Book of Wildflowers*, p. 153.
2. Schulz, *Texas Wild Flowers*, p. 299.
3. The fact that all milkweeds contain asclepain (a proteolytic enzyme) supports the folk remedy of applying milkweed sap daily to eliminate warts. (Kirkpatrick, *Wildflowers*, p. 6.)
4. Vogel, *Medicine*, pp. 243, 336–337; *Reader's Digest*, "Magic and Medicine of Plants," p. 249.
5. Quoted in Vogel, *Medicine*, p. 287.
6. Lee Allen Peterson, *Edible Wild Plants: Eastern and Central North America*, p. 112; Howard Peacock, "Orange Milkweed," *Texas Highways*, May, 1987, p. 48.
7. Tull, *Practical Guide*, p. 249.
8. Tull, *Practical Guide*, p. 250; Chesanow, *Honeysuckle*, p. 138.

MISTLETOE

1. Thomas Bulfinch, *Bulfinch's Mythology*, pp. 343–46.
2. Lust, *Herb Book*, p. 603.
3. Ranson, *Wild Flower Legends*, p. 79.
4. Charles Dickens, *The Pickwick Papers*, pp. 350–51.
5. Washington Irving, "Christmas Eve," *Sketch Book*, III, 32.
6. *Reader's Digest*, "Magic and Medicine of Plants," p. 85.
7. Moore, *Medicinal Plants*, pp. 107–9.

MORNING GLORY

1. Nancy Richey Ranson, *Wildflowers: Legends, Poems, and Paintings*, p. 64.
2. Ibid., p. 64–66; Schulz, *Texas Wild Flowers*, pp. 306–9.
3. Richardson, *Encyclopedia of Psychoactive Drugs*, pp. 67–68.
4. Foster and Duke, *Medicinal Plants*, p. 20.
5. Schulz, *Texas Wild Flowers*, p. 311.
6. Thomas Hardy, *The Return of the Native*, p. 106.
7. Laura C. Martin, *Southern Wildflowers*, p. 189.

MULLEIN

1. Sanders, *Hedgemaids*, p. 172.
2. Vogel, *Medicine*, p. 44.
3. Moore, *Medicinal Plants*, p. 112.
4. Barton H. Warnock, *Wildflowers of the Guadalupe Mountains and the Sand Dune Country, Texas*, p. 125.

MUSTARD

1. Durant, *Who Named the Daisy?*, p. 136.
2. Matt. 13:31–32, 17:20; Mark 4:31–32; Luke 13:19, 17:6; Moldenke and Moldenke, *Plants*, pp. 59–60.
3. Quoted in Grieve, *Modern Herbal*, vol. II, p. 568.
4. Nelson Coon, *Using Wayside Plants*, p. 214.
5. *Reader's Digest*, "Magic and Medicine of Plants," p. 330.
6. Krutch, *Herbal*, p. 88.
7. Culpeper, *Complete Herbal*, p. 201.
8. *Oxford English Dictionary*, compact vol. I, p. 1883.
9. Gerard, *Plants*, p. 45.
10. Phillips Petroleum Company, *Pasture and Range Plants*, p. 157.
11. Gerard, *Plants*, p. 11.
12. *Reader's Digest*, "Magic and Medicine of Plants," p. 326.
13. Quoted in William Morris and Mary Morris, *Morris Dictionary of Word and Phrase Origin*, p. 165.

ORCHID

1. Quoted in Durant, *Who Named the Daisy?*, p. 141.
2. National Geographic Society, *Book of Wildflowers*, p. 164.
3. Culpeper, *Complete Herbal*, pp. 207–8.
4. Gerard, *Leaves*, pp. 132–33.
5. Brian Williams, *Orchids for Everyone*, pp. 29–30.
6. Ibid., pp 32–33.
7. Grieve, *Modern Herbal*, vol. II, pp. 602–5.
8. Martin, *Wildflowers*, p. 76.
9. Luis Marden, "The Exquisite Orchids," *National Geographic*, Apr., 1971, p. 499.
10. *Temple Daily Telegram*, Feb. 28, 1994.

PAINTBRUSH

1. Elinor Clark, "Castilleja Growth With and Without HostSpecies," *Journal of the National Wildflower Research Center* (spring/summer, 1990): pp. 6–9.
2. Foster and Duke, *Medicinal Plants*, p. 138; Martin, *Folklore*, p. 237; Scully, *Treasury*, p. 222.
3. Tull, *Practical Guide*, p. 310.
4. Nancy Richey Ranson, *Wildflowers*, pp. 75–76.

PASSIONFLOWER

1. Beals, *Flower Lore*, p. 144.
2. Durant, *Who Named the Daisy?*, p. 145.

3. Charles Francis Saunders, *Edible and Useful Wild Plants of the United States and Canada,* pp. 101–2.
4. Marjorie Kinnan Rawlings, *Cross Creek,* pp. 167–68
5. *Reader's Digest,* "Magic and Medicine of Plants," p. 266; Moore, *Medicinal Plants,* p. 84.
6. Beals, *Flower Lore,* pp. 144–45.

PHLOX
1. Richard Phelan, *Texas Wild,* pp. 182–83.
2. Bob Flagg, "Flocks of Phlox," *Texas Highways,* Mar., 1992, pp. 42–45.
3. Ibid.
4. Coats, *Flowers,* p. 205.
5. Carroll Abbott, *How to Know and Grow Texas Wildflowers,* p. 27.
6. Scully, *Treasury,* pp. 225, 281.

PITCHER PLANT
1. Terrie Whitehead, "Predatory Plants of Texas," *Texas Parks and Wildlife,* May, 1975, p. 18.
2. Grieve, *Modern Herbal,* vol. II, p. 640; *Encyclopaedia Britannica, Micropaedia,* 15th ed., s.v. "Sarracenioles"; Martin, *Wildflowers,* p. 200.
3. Whitehead, "Predatory Plants of Texas," p. 18.
4. *Reader's Digest,* "Magic and Medicine of Plants," p. 311.
5. Quoted in Mrs. William S. Dana, *How to Know the Wild Flowers,* p. 189; T. W. Higginson, *Out-Door Papers* (1883); Quoted in Neal, *Gardener's Latin,* p. 129.
6. Steve Bender, "Carnivorous Plants Even the Score," *Southern Living,* June, 1984, p. 74.

POINSETTIA
1. *Encyclopaedia Britannica, Micropaedia,* 15th ed., s.v. "poinsettia."
2. Quoted in Neal, *Gardener's Latin,* p. 49.
3. Ibid.
4. Schulz, *Texas Wild Flowers,* p. 195.
5. Ranson, *Wildflowers,* pp. 79–80. Nancy Ranson, "Christmas Flowers Symbolize Giving," *Dallas Morning News,* Dec. 25, 1975.

POPPY
1. Hollingsworth, *Chronicles,* pp. 170–71.
2. Peter T. White, "The Poppy," *National Geographic,* Feb., 1985, p. 141.
3. Col. John McCrae died of pneumonia a few months before the Armistice in 1918.
4. Peter Coats, *Flowers in History,* pp. 133–37.

5. Chesanow, *Honeysuckle,* pp. 87–88.
6. *Reader's Digest,* "Magic and Medicine of Plants," p. 272.
7. Ibid., p. 113; Sanders, *Hedgemaids,* pp. 18–19.

PRICKLY PEAR

1. Elizabeth Silverthorne, *Fiesta! Mexico's Great Celebrations,* p. 12.
2. Krutch, *Herbal,* p. 92.
3. W. W. Newcombe, Jr., *The Indians of Texas,* pp. 41, 44.
4. Del Wenigar, *Cacti of Texas and Neighboring States,* p. 230.
5. Tull, *Practical Guide,* p. 57.
6. Jackie M. Poole and David H. Riskind, "Cacti," *Endangered, Threatened or Protected Native Plants of Texas.*

PRIMROSE

1. Hollingsworth, *Chronicles,* p. 196.
2. Alice M. Coats, *Flowers,* p. 218.
3. John Milton, "On the Death of a Fair Infant"; John Keats, "Endymion," IV, 969.
4. T. F. Thiselton-Dyer, *The Folk-Lore of Plants,* pp. 81–82.
5. Schulz, *Texas Wild Flowers,* p. 284.
6. Nicholson, *Flower Fables,* p. 46.
7. Quoted in Hollingsworth, *Chronicles,* p. 199.
8. Culpeper, *Complete Herbal,* pp. 97–98.
9. Grieve, *Modern Herbal,* vol. I, p. 231.
10. Eula Whitehouse, *Common Fall Flowers of the Coastal Bend,* p. 50.
11. Foster and Duke, *Medicinal Plants,* p. 92; Sanders, *Hedgemaids,* p. 177; Leonard Hansen, "New Ways Offered to Good Health," *Temple Daily Telegram,* May 22, 1994.

QUEEN ANNE'S LACE

1. Sanders, *Hedgemaids,* p. 140.
2. Grieve, *Modern Herbal,* vol. I, p. 161.
3. *Reader's Digest,* "Magic and Medicine of Plants," p. 278.
4. Krutch, *Herbal,* p. 192.
5. Vogel, *Medicine,* p. 388.
6. Sanders, *Hedgemaids,* p. 142.
7. Tull, *Practical Guide,* p. 242.

ROSE

1. Matthew A. R. Bassity, *The Magic World of Roses,* pp. 19–20.
2. Peter Coats, *Flowers in History,* pp. 162–63.

3. Smith, *Flower Cookery*, p. 110.
4. J. Ward-Harris, *More Than Meets the Eye*, p. 148.
5. Gerard, *Leaves*, p. 94.
6. Beals, *Flower Lore*, pp. 125–26.
7. Quoted in Bassity, *World of Roses*, p. 27.
8. Wendall H. Camp, *The World in Your Garden*, p. 30.
9. Manchee, *Our Heritage*, p. 29.
10. Castleman, *Healing Herbs*, pp. 308–9
11. Culpeper, *Complete Herbal*, pp. 242–44.
12. Gerard, *Leaves*, p. 97.
13. Scully, *Treasury*, pp. 242–43.
14. Camp, *World in Your Garden*, p. 26.
15. Grieve, *Modern Herbal*, vol. II, pp. 684–85.

SUNFLOWER

1. Hamilton, *Mythology*, p. 291.
2. Gerard, *Leaves*, pp. 214–16.
3. Kansas State Bill #444, signed by Gov. W. J. Bailey, Mar. 13, 1903.
4. Vince Brach, "Seeds of Plenty," *Texas Highways*, Aug., 1995, p. 42.
5. Ajilvsgi, *Wildflowers of Texas*, p. 123.
6. Brach, "Seeds of Plenty," p. 40.

THISTLE

1. Ranson, *Wild Flower Legends*, p. 111.
2. *Reader's Digest*, "Magic and Medicine of Plants," p. 112.
3. Culpeper, *Complete Herbal*, pp. 285–86.
4. Schulz, *Texas Wild Flowers*, p. 470.
5. *Reader's Digest*, "Magic and Medicine of Plants," p. 248.
6. Ranson, *Wildflowers*, p. 63.
7. Tull, *Practical Guide*, p. 68.
8. Scully, *Treasury*, pp. 94–95.
9. Tull, *Practical Guide*, pp. 51–52.
10. Quoted in Beals, *Flower Lore*, p. 202.

VERBENA

1. Beals, *Flower Lore*, p. 167.
2. Moldenke and Moldenke, *Plants*, p. 5.
3. Alice M. Coats, *Flowers*, p. 261.
4. Scully, *Treasury*, p. 142.
5. Vogel, *Medicine*, p. 386.
6. Ajilvsgi, *Wildflowers of Texas*, p. 93.

7. Texas Parks and Wildlife Department, "Threatened or Protected Plants of Texas," Bulletin, Apr. 12, 1991.

VIOLET

1. Francis Marion Crawford, chap. 5 in *Children of the King;* John Greenleaf Whittier, *The Minister's Daughter,* st. 7.
2. Friend, *Flowers and Flower Lore,* pp. 394–95.
3. Beals, *Flower Lore,* p. 46.
4. Bulfinch, *Mythology,* pp. 29–31.
5. Beals, *Flower Lore,* p. 47–48.
6. Gerard, *Leaves,* p. 3.
7. Scully, *Treasury,* pp. 228, 284; *Reader's Digest,* "Magic and Medicine of Plants," p. 316.
8. Camp, *World in Your Garden,* pp. 26–27.
9. Martin, *Wildflowers,* p. 119.
10. Coats, *Flowers,* pp. 268–70.
11. Robert Browning, *The Two Poets of Croisic,* intro. I.
12. Nicholson, *Flower Fables,* p. 44.
13. Chesanow, *Honeysuckle,* pp. 30–31.

WATER LILY

1. Lust, *Herb Book,* pp. 392–93.
2. Schulz, *Texas Wild Flowers,* pp. 99–101.
3. Prance, *Wildflowers,* p. 132.
4. Grieve, *Modern Herbal,* vol. II, p. 484.
5. *Reader's Digest,* "Magic and Medicine of Plants," p. 328.
6. Schulz, *Texas Wild Flowers,* pp. 97–98.
7. Krutch, *Herbal,* p. 60.

YARROW

1. Sanders, *Hedgemaids,* pp. 136–37.
2. Tull, *Practical Guide,* p. 8.
3. Scully, *Treasury,* p. 294.
4. Ibid., p. 120, 124, 191–92, 293–94.
5. Dana, *How to Know the Wildflowers,* p. 104.
6. National Geographic Society, *Book of Wildflowers,* p. 52.
7. Tull, *Practical Guide,* p. 373.
8. Grieve, *Modern Herbal,* vol. II, p. 864.
9. Martin, *Wildflowers,* pp. 224–25.
10. Castleman, *Healing Herbs,* pp. 378–79.

YUCCA

1. Warnock, *Guadalupe Mountains*, pp. 43–45.
2. *Oxford English Dictionary*, s.v. "Pronuba."
3. Zoe Merriman Kirkpatrick, "Bear Grass and the Yucca Moth," *Native Plant Society of Texas News*, Sept./Oct., 1993, pp. 1–2.
4. Saunders, *Edible and Useful Wild Plants*, pp. 168–69.
5. Ibid., p. 216.
6. Tull, *Practical Guide*, p. 28.
7. Saunders, *Edible and Useful Wild Plants*, pp. 105–6.

Bibliography

Aaron, Gregory C. *The Language of Flowers.* Philadelphia: Running Press, 1991.

Abbott, Carroll. *How to Know and Grow Texas Wildflowers.* Kerrville, Tex.: Green Horizons Press, 1979.

Ajilvsgi, Geyata. *Wildflowers of the Big Thicket, East Texas and Western Louisiana.* College Station: Texas A&M University Press, 1979.

———— *Wildflowers of Texas.* Bryan, Tex.: Shearer, 1984.

Andrews, Jean. *American Wildflower Florilegium.* Denton: North Texas Press, 1992.

————. *The Texas Bluebonnet.* Austin: University of Texas Press, 1986.

Bassity, Matthew A. R. *The Magic World of Roses.* New York: Hearthside Press, 1966.

Beals, Katherine M. *Flower Lore and Legend.* New York: Henry Holt and Company, 1917.

Bender, Steve. "Carnivorous Plants Even the Score." *Southern Living,* June, 1984, p. 74.

Birdsong, Gussie Mae. *Texas Wild Flowers.* San Antonio: Naylor Company, 1957.

Bonta, Marcia Myers. *Women in the Field: America's Pioneering Women Naturalists.* College Station: Texas A&M University Press, 1991.

Brach, Vince. "Seeds of Plenty." *Texas Highways,* Aug., 1995, pp. 39–43.

Bulfinch, Thomas. *Bulfinch's Mythology.* New York: Avenel Books, 1978.

Busch, Phyllis S. *Wildflowers and the Stories behind Their Names.* New York: Charles Scribner's Sons, 1977.

Camp, Wendell H. *The World in Your Garden.* Washington, D.C.: National Geographic Society, 1957.

Cannatella, Mary and Rita Arnold. *Plants of the Texas Shore: A Beachcomber's Guide.* College Station: Texas A&M University Press, 1985.

Castleman, Michael. *The Healing Herbs.* Emmaus, Pa.: Rodale Press, 1991.

Chesanow, Jeanne R. *Honeysuckle Sipping.* Camden, Maine: Down East Books, 1987.

Clark, Elinor. "Castilleja Growth with and without Host Species." *Journal of the National Wildflower Research Center.* (spring/summer, 1990): pp. 6–9.

Clements, Edith S. "Wildflowers of the West." *National Geographic Magazine,* May, 1927, p. 610.

Coats, Alice M. *Flowers and Their Histories.* New York: McGraw-Hill Book Company, 1956.

Coats, Peter. *Flowers in History.* New York: Viking Press, 1970.

Color Treasury of Herbs and Other Medicinal Plants. Introduction by Jerry Cowling. London: Cresent Books, 1972.

Coon, Nelson. *Using Wayside Plants.* New York: Hearthside Press, 1969.

Correll, Donovan Stewart, and Marshall Conring Johnston. *Manual of the Vascular Plants of Texas.* Renner, Tex.: Texas Research Foundation, 1970.

Culpeper, Nicholas. *Culpeper's Complete Herbal.* London: Bloomsbury Books, 1992.

Dana, Mrs. William Starr. *How to Know the Wild Flowers.* New York: Dover Publications, 1963.

DePaola, Tomie. *The Legend of the Bluebonnet.* New York: G. P. Putnam's Sons, 1983.

Dickens, Charles. *The Pickwick Papers.* London: Collins' Clear-Type Press, n.d.

Dobie, J. Frank. *Tales of Old-Time Texas.* Boston: Little Brown and Company, 1955.

Durant, Mary. *Who Named the Daisy? Who Named the Rose?.* New York: Dodd, Mead and Company, 1976.

Eichna, Ludwig W. *The Pharos* (winter, 1994), pp. 14–17.

Encyclopaedia Britannica Micropaedia I, II, VIII, 15th ed.

———. *Macropaedia* 16, 15th ed.

"Enduring Weeds are Endearing Dandelions in Diet." *Austin American-Statesman,* May9, 1992.

Enquist, Marshall. *Wildflowers of the Texas Hill Country.* Austin: Texas Monthly Press, 1987.

Flagg, Bob. "Flocks of Phlox." *Texas Highways,* Mar., 1992, pp. 42–45.

Forey, Pamela. *Wild Flowers of North America.* New York: Gallery Books, W. H. Smith Publishers, 1991.

Foster, Steven, and James A. Duke. *Eastern/Central Medicinal Plants.* Peterson Field Guide Series. Boston: Houghton Mifflin, 1990.

Friend, Rev. Hilderic. *Flowers and Flower Lore.* New York: John B. Alden, 1889.

Geiser, Samuel Wood. *Naturalists of the Frontier.* Dallas: Southern Methodist University, 1937.

Gerard, John. *Leaves from Gerard's Herball.* Edited by Marcus Woodward. New York: Dover Publications, 1969.

Gibbons, Euell. *Stalking the Healthful Herbs.* New York: David McKay, 1966.

———. "Stalking the West's Wild Foods." *National Geographic,* Aug., 1973, pp. 186–99.

———. *Stalking the Wild Asparagus.* Putney, Vt.: A. C. Hood, 1988.

Goyne, Minetta Altgelt. *A Life among the Texas Flora: Ferdinand Lindheimer's Letters to George Engelmann.* College Station: Texas A&M University Press, 1991.

Graves, George. *Medicinal Plants.* New York: Crescent Books, 1990.

Greenaway, Kate. *Language of Flowers.* New York: Crown Publishers, 1978.

Grieve, Mrs. M. *A Modern Herbal,* I and II. New York: Dover Publications, 1971.

Ham, Hal. *South Texas Wildflowers.* Kingsville, Tex.: Conner Museum, Texas A&I University, 1984.

Hamilton, Edith. *Mythology.* New York: New American Library, 1942.

Hansen, Leonard. "New Ways Offered to Good Health." *Temple Daily Telegram,* May 22, 1994.

Hardy, Thomas. *The Return of the Native.* New York: Holt, Rinehart & Winston, 1963.

Heywood, V. H. *Flowering Plants of the World*. New York: Oxford University Press, 1993.

Hollingsworth, Buckner. *Flower Chonicles*. New Brunswick, N.J.: Rutgers University Press, 1958.

Johnson, Lady Bird. "Texas in Bloom." *National Geographic*, Apr., 1988, pp. 493–511.

Johnston, Eliza Griffin. *Texas Wild Flowers*. Austin: Shoal Creek Publishers, 1972.

Kirkpatrick, Zoe Merriman. "Bear Grass and the Yucca Moth." *Native Plant Society of Texas News*, Sept./Oct., 1993, pp. 1–2.

————. *Wildflowers of the Western Plains*. Austin: University of Texas Press, 1992.

Kloss, Jethro. *Back to Eden*. New York: Beneficial Books, 1971.

Krutch, Joseph Wood. *Joseph Wood Krutch Herbal*. New York: G. P. Putnam's Sons, 1965.

Language of Flowers. Edited by Gregory C. Aaron. Philadelphia: Running Press, 1991.

Lehner, Ernst, and Johanna Lehner. *Folklore and Symbolism of Flowers, Plants and Trees*. New York: Tudor Publishing Company, 1960.

Loewer, Peter. *The Wild Gardener*. Harrisburg, Pa.: Stackpole Books, 1991.

Loughmiller, Campbell, and Lynn Loughmiller. *Texas Wildflowers: A Field Guide*. Austin: University of Texas Press, 1984.

Lust, John B. *The Herb Book*. New York: Bantam Books, 1974.

Manchee, Fred B. *Our Heritage of Flowers*. New York: Holt, Rinehart and Winston, 1970.

March, Kathryn G., and Andrew L. March. *Wild Plant Companion*. Winona, Minn.: Meridian Hill Publications, 1986.

Marden, Luis. "The Exquisite Orchids." *National Geographic*, Apr., 1971, p. 499.

Martin, Laura C. *Southern Wildflowers*. Marietta, Ga.: Longstreet Press, 1989.

————. *Wildflower Folklore*. Charlotte, N.C.: East Woods Press, 1984.

Mattiza, Dorothy Baird. *100 Texas Wildflowers*. Tucson, Ariz.: Southwest Parks and Monuments Association, 1993.

"May Brings Agarita Berries." *Texas Wildflower Newsletter*, spring, 1979, p. 3.

Moldenke, Harold N., and Alma L. Moldenke. *Plants of the Bible*. New York: Dover Publications, 1986.

Moore, Michael. *Medicinal Plants of the Desert and Canyon West*. Santa Fe: Museum of New Mexico Press, 1989.

————. *Medicinal Plants of the Mountain West*. Santa Fe: Museum of New Mexico Press, 1979.

Morris, William, and Mary Morris. *Morris Dictionary of Word and Phrase Origin*. New York: Harper and Row, 1977.

National Geographic Society. *The Book of Wildflowers*. Washington, D.C.: The National Geographic Society, 1924.

National Wildflower Research Center Staff. *Wildflower Handbook*. Austin: Texas Monthly Press, 1989.

Neal, Bill. *Gardener's Latin*. Chapel Hill, N.C.: Algonquin Books, 1992.

Newcomb, W.W., Jr. *The Indians of Texas*. Austin: University of Texas Press, 1980.

Nicholson, Geraldine. *Flower Fables*. Kansas City, Mo: Mid-America Publishing Corporation, n.d.

Niehaus, Theodore F. *A Field Guide to Southwestern and Texas Wildflowers*. Boston: Houghton Mifflin, 1984.

Nokes, Jill Senior. "Hollies of Texas." *Texas Wildflower Newsletter,* winter, 1978.
————. *How to Grow Native Plants of Texas and the Southwest.* Austin: Texas Monthly Press, 1986.
Oxford Dictionary of Quotations. 3d ed. New York: Oxford University Press, 1979.
Oxford English Dictionary. Compact Ed., vols. I and II. Oxford, England: Oxford University Press, pp. 1883, 1462.
Parvin, Bob. "The Barometer Bush." *Texas Highways,* Aug., 1981, pp. 12–13.
Peacock, Howard. "Orange Milkweed." *Texas Highways,* May, 1987, p. 48.
Peterson, Lee Allen. *Edible Wild Plants: Eastern and Central North America.* Boston: Houghton Mifflin, 1977.
Phelan, Richard. *Texas Wild: The Land, Plants, and Animals of the Lone Star State.* Excalibur Books, 1976.
Phillips Petroleum Company, *Pasture and Range Plants.* Bartlesville, Okla.: Phillips Petroleum Co., 1977.
Pickles, Sheila. *The Language of Flowers.* New York: Harmony Books, 1989.
Platt, Rutherford. *This Green World.* New York: Dodd, Mead and Company, 1988.
Poole, Jackie M., and David H. Riskind. *Endangered, Threatened or Protected Native Plants of Texas.* Austin: Texas Parks and Wildlife Department, 1989.
Prance, Ghillean T. *Wildflowers for All Seasons.* New York: Crown Publishers, 1989.
Quayle, William A. *God's Calendar.* N.p., 1907.
Ranson, Nancy Richey. "Christmas Flowers Symbolize Giving." *Dallas Morning News,* Dec. 25, 1975.
————. *Texas Wild Flower Legends.* Dallas: Kaleidograph Press, 1933.
————. *Wildflowers: Legends, Poems and Paintings.* McKinney, Tex.: Heard Natural Science Museum and Wildlife Sanctuary, 1989.
Rawlings, Marjorie Kinnan. *Cross Creek.* St. Simons Island, Ga.: Mockingbird Books, 1982.
Reader's Digest. *Magic and Medicine of Plants.* Pleasantville, N. Y.: Reader's Digest Assn., 1986.
Rechenthin, C. A. *Native Flowers of Texas.* U. S. Department of Agriculture, Temple, Tex.: Soil Conservation Service, 1972.
Reid, Mrs. Bruce. "An Indian Legend of the Blue Bonnet." *Legends of Texas.* Edited by J. Frank Dobie. Austin: Texas Folklore Society, 1924.
Richardson, P. Mick. *The Encyclopedia of Psychoactive Drugs: Flowering Plants.* New York: Chelsea House Publishers, 1986.
Rickett, Harold William. *Wild Flowers of the United States.* Vol. 3, pts. 1 and 2. New York: McGraw-Hill, 1969.
Robb, David M., and J. J. Garrison. *Art in the Western World.* New York: Harper and Brothers, 1942.
Rose, Francis L., and Russell W. Strandtmann. *Wildflowers of the Llano Estacado.* Dallas: Taylor Publishing Company, 1986.
San Antonio Botanical Center. *Native Plant Key, B-29.* San Antonio: Department of Parks and Recreation, n.d.
Sanders, Jack. *Hedgemaids and Fairy Candles.* Camden, Maine: Ragged Mountain Press, 1993.

Sanecki, Kay N. *History of the English Herb Garden.* London: Ward Lock, 1992.

Saunders, Charles Francis. *Edible and Useful Wild Plants of the United States and Canada.* New York: Dover Publications, 1976.

Schulz, Ellen D. *Texas Wild Flowers: A Popular Account of the Common Wild Flowers of Texas.* Chicago: Laidlaw Brothers, 1928.

Scully, Virginia. *A Treasury of American Indian Herbs: Their Lore and Their Use for Food, Drugs and Medicine.* New York: Crown Publishers, 1970.

Shakespeare, William. *The Complete Works of William Shakespeare.* London: Spring Books, 1964.

Shields, Helen. *Desert Plants: Recipes and Remedies.* Tularosa, N.Mex.: Okesa Publications, 1984.

Silverthorne, Elizabeth. *Christmas in Texas.* College Station: Texas A&M University Press, 1990.

————. *Fiesta! Mexico's Great Celebrations.* Brookfield, Conn.: Millbrook Press, 1992.

Simpson, Benny J., and James C. Read. "Cenizo." *Texas Parks and Wildlife,* Oct., 1976, pp. 24–27.

Squire, David, and Jane Newdick. *The Book of the Rose.* New York: Cresent Books, 1991.

Smith, Leona Woodring. *The Forgotten Art of Flower Cookery.* Gretna, La.: Pelican Publishing Company, 1990.

Spellenberg, Richard. *The Audubon Society Field Guide to North American Wildflowers: Western Region.* New York: Alfred A. Knopf, 1988.

Stahl, Carmine. *Papa Stahl's Wild Stuff Cookbook.* Houston: Grass Root Enterprises, 1974.

Texas Parks and Wildlife Department. "Threatened or Protected Native Plants of Texas." Bulletin, Apr. 12, 1991.

Thiselton-Dyer, T. F. *The Folk-Lore of Plants.* London: Chatto and Windus, 1889.

Thomas, Les. "Learning the Ways of the Desert." *Southern Living,* Apr., 1984, pp. 150–154.

Thompson, Eloise Reid. *Wildflower Portraits.* Norman: University of Oklahoma Press, 1964.

Tull, Delena. *A Practical Guide to Edible and Useful Plants.* Austin: Texas Monthly Press, 1987.

Twitchell, Paul. *Herbs: The Magic Healers.* New York: Lancer Books, 1971.

Vester, Bertha Spafford. *Flowers of the Holy Land.* Kansas, City, Mo.: Hallmark Cards, 1964.

Vines, Robert A. *Trees, Shrubs and Woody Vines of the Southwest.* Austin: University of Texas Press, 1960.

Vogel, Virgil J. *American Indian Medicine.* Norman: University of Oklahoma Press, 1970.

Ward-Harris, J. *More Than Meets the Eye: The Life and Lore of Western Wildflowers.* Toronto: Oxford University Press, 1983.

Warnock, Barton H. *Wildflowers of the Big Bend Country, Texas.* Alpine, Tex.: Sul Ross University Press, 1970.

————. *Wildflowers of the Davis Mountains and the Marathon Basin, Texas.* Alpine, Tex.: Sul Ross University Press, 1977.

————. *Wildflowers of the Guadalupe Mountains and the Sand Dune Country, Texas.* Alpine, Tex.: Sul Ross University Press, 1974.

Wasowski, Sally, and Andy Wasowski. *Native Texas Plants: Landscaping Region by Region.* Austin: Texas Monthly Press, 1989.

Weniger, Del. *Cacti of Texas and Neighboring States.* Austin: University of Texas Press, 1984.

Weslager, Clinton Alfred. *Magic Medicines of the Indians.* New York: New American Library, 1973.

Wheelwright, Edith Grey. *Medicinal Plants and Their History.* New York: Dover Publications, 1974.

White, Peter T. "The Poppy." *National Geographic,* Feb., 1985, p. 141.

Whitehead, Terrie. "Predatory Plants of Texas." *Texas Parks and Wildlife,* May, 1975, pp. 16–20.

Whitehouse, Eula. *Common Fall Flowers of the Coastal Bend of Texas.* Sinton, Tex.: Rob and Bessie Welder Wildlife Foundation, 1962.

————. *Texas Flowers in Natural Color.* Dallas: Dallas County Audubon Society, 1967.

Williams, Brian. *Orchids for Everyone.* New York: W. H. Smith Publishers, 1984.

Wills, Mary M., and Howard S. Irwin. *Roadside Flowers of Texas.* Austin: University of Texas Press, 1961.

Wirt, Elizabeth Washington Gamble, *Flora's Dictionary.* Baltimore: N.p., 1831.

Woolley, Bryan. "The Plant Hunter." *Dallas Life Magazine,* Jan. 3, 1993, pp. 8–15.

Young, Mary Sophie. Papers. Eugene C. Barker Texas History Center, University of Texas, Austin.

Index